ENTREPRENEURSHIP AND ECONOMIC DEVELOPMENT IN HONG KONG

This is the first systematic economic study of the nature, operation and contribution of entrepreneurship to the growth of Hong Kong. From a new entrepreneurial perspective of economic development, the author argues that the success of Hong Kong is attributable principally to adaptive entrepreneurship:

- product imitation
- small scale enterprise
- subcontracting

Using these entrepreneurial strategies, local manufacturers learned from foreign firms and imitated their products. By selling improved commodities at lower prices, they competed against the original suppliers from more advanced countries. Being alert to opportunities and responding rapidly to change, Hong Kong's entrepreneurs shifted their production activities from one product to another; from higher cost to lower cost regions; from traditional fishing and agriculture to manufacturing, and then to finance and other services.

These entrepreneurial activities have brought about structural transformation in Hong Kong's economy, enabling the country to compete with advanced economies. This study concludes that any policy recommendation on economic development shoud be based on analysis that incorporates entrepreneurship and provides a reappraisal of the role of government in economic development.

Tony Fu-Lai Yu is Research Associate at the School of Economics and Management, University College, University of New South Wales. His research interests include entrepreneurship, the economics of organisation and governmental economics. He is the co-author of *A Treatise on Hong Kong's Urban Problems* (1987).

ROUTLEDGE ADVANCES IN ASIA-PACIFIC BUSINESS

ENTREPRENEURSHIP AND ECONOMIC DEVELOPMENT IN HONG KONG

Tony Fu-Lai Yu

London and New York

First published 1997
by Routledge
11 New Fetter Lane, London EC4P 4EE

Simultaneously published in the USA and Canada
by Routledge
29 West 35th Street, New York, NY 10001

Typeset in Garamond by Pure Tech India Ltd, Pondicherry

Printed and bound in Great Britain by Antony Rowe Ltd., Chippenham, Wiltshire

British Library Cataloguing in Publication Data

A catalogue record for this book is available from the British Library

Library of Congress Cataloging in Publication Data

Yu, Tony Fu-Lai, 1950–
Entrepreneurship & economic development in
Hong Kong / Tony Fu-Lai Yu.
p. cm.
Includes bibliographical references and index.
1. Entrepreneurship – Hong Kong. 2. Hong Kong – Economic
conditions. 3. Industrial management – Hong Kong. I. Title.
HB615.Y823 1997 338'.04'095125–dc21 96–54273 CIP

ISBN 0–415–16240–8

To my sisters and brother

CONTENTS

FIGURES

TABLES

PREFACE AND ACKNOWLEDGEMENTS

Graduate study at Iowa State University has had significant influence on my academic development. Gerald O'Driscoll's macroeconomics course was the most difficult course that I had ever experienced. To be sure, his teaching involved little use of mathematics. Instead, he was, like other Austrian economists, very much interested in the history of economics. Apart from the works of Say, Walras, Keynes, Hicks, Patinkin, Friedman, Leijonhufvud and Clower which are widely known in Macro Theory, his lectures drew heavily on the arguments of Thornton, Menger, Bohm-Bawerk, Wicksell, Mises, Hayek and Lachmann which were absent from most of standard American undergraduate programmes.

Iowa was too cold for a student from South East Asia. I returned to my home town and taught at Hong Kong Baptist College. Around 1983, Stevens N.S. Cheung took up Chair Professorship in the Department of Economics of the University of Hong Kong. I remembered that his article on "The Structure of a Contract and the Theory of a Non-exclusive Resources" had appeared in the reading list of the Public Finance course taken at Iowa State University. Therefore, I paid much attention to his arguments, which appeared frequently in the *Hong Kong Economic Journal* (a Chinese daily newspaper). I was impressed by Cheung's attempt to link the transaction cost economics with real world phenomena. O'Driscoll is an Austrian while Cheung is a Chicago School economist. How far is Chicago from Vienna, a question that has been asked before. I regard Cheung's works as very much akin to Austrian economics. Both Cheung and the Austrian emphasise the real world, in contrast to purely abstract theory. Like Austrian economics, Cheung in recent years had not used mathematics and has even condemned its use. Though Cheung often mentions the term "equilibrium at the margin", his analysis in fact focuses on process and continuous adjustment. This can be evidenced from his best, but unfortunately neglected, article "A Theory of Price Control", published in the *Journal of Law and Economics*. In fact, Cheung's teachers, Armen A. Alchian and Ronald Coase, are already regarded by some scholars as quasi-Austrian.

Some economists may discover that certain advances in mainstream theories such as the recognition of the non-homogeneous nature of a commodity in property rights economics, imperfect information problems in price theory and industrial economics, search and adaptive expectations in macroeconomics, have long been anticipated by Austrian economists who focus on an actor's subjective evaluation, knowledge, time and ignorance, error, revision of plans, experience and expectations, market process and the evolution of social institutions. The new institutional economics led me into the world of Austrian economics, a move which was triggered by an accidental rediscovery of O'Driscoll's work, namely *Economics as a Coordination Problem: The Contributions of Friedrich A. Hayek*, in a New Zealand library, a book which I was unaware of since its publication in 1977. Since then, I have read many Austrian works, including those of Menger, Mises, Lachmann, Rothbard, Kirzner and Schutz.

I migrated to Australia in 1988. At Monash University, though I wrote some papers on electricity supply in Victoria, using transaction cost economics, I longed to undertake research in Austrian economics, especially on the role of entrepreneurship. In 1992 I moved to Canberra. At University College, the University of New South Wales, my original research plan was to examine the role of entrepreneurship in Australia's automotive industry. However, Dr. H.B. Cheah, my supervisor, suggested that I applied my ideas on entrepreneurship to the economic development of Hong Kong, an economy with which I am more familiar. Moreover, entrepreneurship plays a significant role in the East Asian development. I agreed with him and this book is the outcome. However, the book is not an Austrian work in the sense that it does not condemn government intervention as the Austrians do. Instead, it provides a reappraisal on the role of government in economic development.

I would like to take this opportunity to thank Dr H.B. Cheah, who helped me to identify this relatively unexplored research opportunity. Furthermore, he read and commented on this work at several stages of its evolution. Without him, this achievement would not have been possible.

Paul L. Robertson's article "Explaining Vertical Integration: Lessons from the American Automotive Industry" (co-authored with Richard Langlois) attracted me to Canberra. Professor Robertson has not disappointed me. Over the years, I have learned so much from him, not only intellectual knowledge, but also the characteristics of a gentleman scholar. He offered me advice even when he was extremely busy. Here I express my highest regards to him.

I am grateful for the financial support of the School of Economics and Management (University of New South Wales) in my field work and conference participations. I am also deeply indebted to Reverend Professor Paul A. McGavin, for his kind assistance and sincere care.

During the field trip in Hong Kong, I was fortunate to be affiliated to the Centre of Asian Studies at the University of Hong Kong. This helped me successfully to conduct my survey interviews. In addition, the Hong Kong Productivity Centre, Hong Kong Census and Statistics Department, Hong Kong Trade Development Council, Hong Kong Social Research Centre and Emma Fung kindly supplied me with useful information and data. I also express my gratitude to those founders/managing directors of the manufacturing firms who sacrificed their valuable time for my interviews and provided me with useful materials for my survey and case studies.

This research has also benefited greatly from discussions with and comments from Lawrence L.C. Chau, Israel M. Kirzner, Richard N. Langlois, Hafiz Mirza, Wee L. Tan, Lawrence H. White, Siu L. Wong, and participants from various conferences and school seminars. Naturally, I take full responsibility for any errors and shortcomings that remain.

Tony Fu-Lai Yu
School of Economics and Management
University College
University of New South Wales
Australian Defence Force Academy
Canberra

1

THE ECONOMIC SUCCESS OF HONG KONG

A search for an explanation

FROM A "BARREN ISLAND" TO THE MART OF EAST ASIA

When Hong Kong was ceded to the British in perpetuity by the Treaty of Nanking in 1842, Queen Victoria was most distressed to know that only a piece of useless granite was added to her Empire. The British Foreign Secretary Lord Palmerston dismissed Captain Charles Elliot for the reason that he had "obtained the cession of Hongkong, a barren island with hardly a house upon it. Now it seems obvious that Hongkong will not be a Mart of Trade" (Ho 1992, p. 1). However, entrepreneurs saw things differently. Earlier in 1836, Great Britain's most significant opium trader, James Matheson, conceived the acquisition of Hong Kong Island as a factory for British, and notably Scottish, traders.[1] He claimed in *The Canton Register* (a weekly newspaper) that "If the lion's paw is to be put down on any part of the south side of China, let it be Hong Kong; let the lion declare it to be under his guarantee a free port, and in ten years it will be the most considerable mart east of the Cape" (Chan 1991, p. 21). History has confirmed the entrepreneur's insights.

But what has puzzled economists is that Hong Kong is only a small city with approximately 6 million people living in an area of around 1,064 sq. km. It does not possess any natural resources and has relied on outside sources for its fuel and raw materials. It has also imported much of its food supplies, largely from mainland China. Before World War II, the economy depended almost entirely on entrepôt trade. The colony was described by a visiting American journalist in 1951 as a "dying city" (Ho 1992, p. 5).

This changed, however, when Hong Kong embarked on its export-led industrialisation in the early 1950s and experienced rapid industrialisation in the 1960s. Between 1961 and 1971 the average growth rate in real terms was approximately 11 per cent (Ho 1992, p. 22) and by 1971, the per capita income reached HK$6,096, placing it behind only Japan in the Asian-Pacific regions (Riedel 1974, p. 11). Since the early 1970s it has been further emerging as a major financial centre in the Asia-Pacific region. Between 1986 and 1991 the city was still growing in real terms at an average annual rate of 6.5 per cent (Chau 1993, p. 31). By 1990, the

1

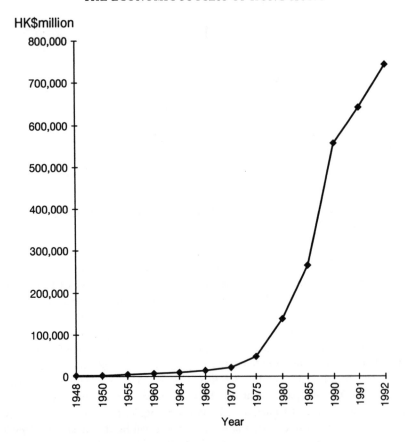

Figure 1.1 Hong Kong's economic growth, 1948–92, selective years

Source: For 1948–64, see K.R. Chou, 1966, *The Hong Kong Economy: A Miracle of Growth*, Academic Publication, p. 84. For 1966–85, see Hong Kong Census and Statistics Department, 1986, *Estimates of GDP, 1966–85*, Tables 1, 12. For 1986–92, see *Hong Kong Economic Yearbook 1992*, Part 4, p. 3.

average per capita income in Hong Kong had grown to surpass that of its colonial motherland, Great Britain, and more investment was then flowing from the colony to Great Britain than from Great Britain to the colony (Vogel 1991, p. 68). By 1992 the GDP reached HK$742,582 million (see Figures 1.1, 1.2). After more than three decades of rapid growth, it has emerged as one of the richest economies in Asia (Chau 1993, p. 1). The city economy has outgrown its historical role as an intermediary in international trade, and a centre of redistribution in its respective regional markets. It is now a major international economy in its own right (Ho 1992, p. 10). In sum, Hong Kong has been transformed from a developing economy to one of the newly industrialising economies in Asia.

2

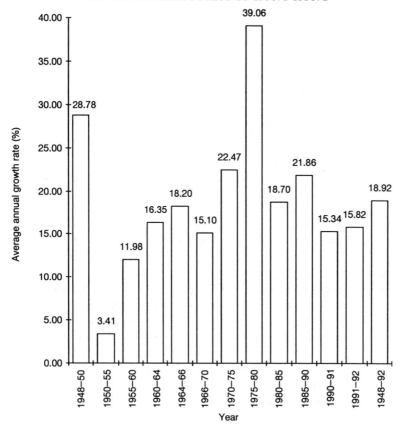

Figure 1.2   Hong Kong's average annual GDP growth rate (%)

Source: For 1948–64, see K.R. Chou, 1966, *The Hong Kong Economy: A Miracle of Growth*, Academic Publication, p. 84. For 1966–85, see Hong Kong Cenus and Statistics Department, 1986, *Estimates of GDP, 1966–85*, Tables 1, 12. For 1986–92, see *Hong Kong Economic Yearbook 1992*, Part 4, p. 3.

This miraculous performance has naturally intrigued economists interested in economic development. In particular, they asked: "Why the Emperor's new clothes are not made in Colombia but are being made in Hong Kong" (Morawetz 1981).[2]

EXPLANATIONS OF HONG KONG'S SUCCESS

A number of studies have attempted to explain the earlier economic success of Hong Kong. Szczepanik (1958) presented the first systematic study of Hong Kong's post-war growth. He argued that Hong Kong's rapid industrialisation of the 1950s was attributable to its favourable location with a good harbour, a pool of hard-working labour, the inflow of capital and entrepreneurs from China, and the system of *laissez-faire* capitalism (see also Owen 1971, pp. 146–66; Chen 1984, pp. 2–4).

3

However, the significance of natural factors, such as a deep-water port and a strategic location, to Hong Kong's economic growth has often been overemphasised (Sung 1991, p. 129). Cheung (1984, p. 94) argued that, although Victoria Harbour has provided the entrepôt facility and assisted in Hong Kong's industrialisation, the harbour is not as good as the one in Shanghai. Furthermore, in terms of Asia-Pacific trade, Shanghai is much closer to Japan and North America (Cheung 1984, p. 94). Hong Kong's products are mainly shipped to the USA and European countries but the location of Hong Kong is far from them. Similarly, in terms of trade with China, Hong Kong is less strategically situated than Shanghai but Hong Kong has surpassed Shanghai in its amount of trade with China.[3] Hence location is not a decisive factor in trade and industrialisation (Sung 1991, p. 129).

The willingness of Hong Kong's labour force to work hard has often been regarded as an unique Chinese quality which brings an advantage to its rapid industrialisation, especially in some labour intensive manufacturing industries. However, this stereotype of the Chinese workforce has not proved to be tenable in economic analysis. As observed during the Cultural Revolution, many workers in China were not willing to work.

Some scholars contended that Hong Kong's economic success has hinged on its ability to maintain a high degree of competitiveness in its export trade (Sung 1987). In their view, Hong Kong's manufacturers were able to produce goods at relatively lower costs, mainly through cheaper labour.[4] However, many other developing economies with equally low labour costs as Hong Kong in the past did not develop as successfully. In particular, Owen (1971, p. 150) noted that "the much favoured explanation of Hong Kong's success – an abundance of cheap labour – is incomplete since this explanation fails to explain why other Asian countries with abundant supplies of labour fail to achieve Hong Kong's rate of economic growth". Furthermore, while low wages existed in the early period of Hong Kong's industrialisation, in recent years this advantage has disappeared. In addition, Hong Kong today exhibits extremely high rentals in the property market, having probably the second highest rate in Asia after Tokyo. Therefore, compared to other South East Asian countries, Hong Kong at present does not possess a strong advantage.

Apart from Szczepanik (1958), other important works on Hong Kong such as Owen (1971), Riedel (1974) and Chen (1979, 1984) also noted the influences of the inflow of capital and entrepreneurship contributing to the early industrialisation of Hong Kong. In general, these economists argued that the influx of capital and Shanghainese entrepreneurs from mainland China during the period 1948–51 led to the immediate expansion of the textile industry which formed the basis of subsequent industrialisation (Owen 1971, p. 148; Chen 1984, p. 3). Unfortunately, like Szczepanik's work, most subsequent studies had not seriously examined the role of entrepreneurship in the economic development of Hong Kong.

Hong Kong has also been described as the last bastion of *laissez-faire* (Rabushka 1979). It is generally known that the tax rates in Hong Kong are low. The profit tax ranges from 15.5 per cent to 16.5 per cent and income tax is set at a standard rate of 15 per cent for the higher income group. Also, there is no foreign exchange control or a central bank. Except in land and housing, government interventions in economic affairs are minimal. This philosophy has been coined as positive non-interventionism by the former financial secretary of the Territory, Sir Philip Haddon-Cave.[5] Hong Kong's economic miracle has been cited by Milton Friedman (1976) as a classic illustration of the benefits of free market policy. But the difficulty of this argument lies with the fact that the governments of three other successful NIEs, Singapore, Taiwan and South Korea, have all introduced many interventions in and controls on their economies during industrialisation. It is said that their development has been engineered by their governments and that they are prototypes of government-led growth (Deyo 1987, p. 17; Soon 1994, pp. 144–7). If so, *laissez-faire* policy is not necessarily the only prescription for growth.[6]

In agreement with Milton Friedman and other Chicago economists, Cheung (1984, p. 97) insisted that the private property rights system is the key to Hong Kong's economic growth. He argued that the most significant contribution of the British government has been to establish a system of private property rights in Hong Kong so that people can pursue their own interests with minimal transaction costs.

A review of the literature indicates that most economists utilised orthodox theories, particularly the Cobb-Douglas production function and the theory of comparative advantage to explain the economic development of Hong Kong. For instance, Riedel (1974) presented an orthodox treatment of Hong Kong's economic growth. He maintained that an important feature of the industrialisation of Hong Kong had been the manufacture of standardised consumer goods for export. The Cobb-Douglas production function was employed to identify the contributions of labour, capital and technical change to Hong Kong's industrial growth. Riedel (1974, p. 35) concluded that "Hong Kong has been successful because she has done well what she can do best. The orthodox trade theory goes far in explaining what Hong Kong can do best, i.e., where her comparative advantage lies." As will be argued later in this study, entrepreneurs can change a given resource situation. Without exploring the role of entrepreneurship, Riedel's work is simply a tautology.

A quantitative model based on the Cobb-Douglas production function was employed by Hsueh (1976) to explain Hong Kong's economic growth. Tsiang and Wu (1985) also used a modified neoclassical growth model to illustrate the growth experience of the Asian NIEs. In their model, technological improvement and foreign trade are the most important factors for economic growth. They argued that the basic condition for take-off into self-sustained growth is that there should be enough savings to increase the capital–output ratio. They estimated that Hong Kong took off in 1965.

On the demand side, Hsia *et al.* (1975) constructed an input-output table to estimate the contribution of exports, consumption and investment to the GDP growth over the period 1962–70. Hsueh and Chow (1981) later developed a dynamic macroeconomic model to trace the growth path of the Hong Kong

5

economy from 1963 to 1979. Multipliers were derived to measure the impact of some exogenous variables such as exports, government expenditures and interest rates on GDP, private consumption, imports and capital formation. This type of analysis is essentially Keynesian and neglects the supply factors (Ho 1989, p. 2). Similarly, Peebles (1988) used the Harrod–Domar growth model to estimate the economic growth of Hong Kong for the period 1971–84. His findings strengthened the importance of capital formation in economic growth.

Using econometric analysis, Chen (1979) tried to identify the various possible sources of the economic growths of Hong Kong and other Asian economies. His work focused on the manufacturing sector during the period 1955–70. Like most of the other studies, the Cobb-Douglas production function was applied to examine the role of factor inputs, resource reallocation and total factor productivity in the growth process. His study concluded that there were other important factors contributing to the growth and remaining to be explained. In his later work, employing the concept of comparative advantage, Chen (1985) recommended that Hong Kong's manufacturers should shift their activities from low value added products towards high-skill, sophisticated technology products. In his inaugural lecture, Chen (1988) synthesised economic, cultural and political considerations into an eclectic model to explain the economic growth of Hong Kong and other Asian NIEs.

Of all the studies mentioned above, none of them considers the role of entrepreneurship seriously. Perhaps an exception is Chau (1993). In a monograph prepared for the World Bank, he took a broad-based approach to economic development. His study covered various sectors of Hong Kong's economy, such as industry and trade, banking finance and business services, the labour market and the property market. Borrowing from Chen's eclectic model (1988), he concluded that the economic success of Hong Kong, apart from other factors, is attributable to the government's non-intervention policy and to dynamic merchant entrepreneurs.

THE FAILURE OF THE ORTHODOX ECONOMIC EXPLANATIONS

Most studies employing the orthodox theories of economic development fail to give a satisfactory explanation of the economic success of Hong Kong and other Asian NIEs. Economists in the 1960s believed that use of the Harrod–Domar investment saving model in economic planning would accelerate economic growth. With this belief, they predicted that India, Pakistan and Sri Lanka, which at that time employed socialist planning techniques, would have an outstanding rate of economic growth. Specifically, Rosenstein-Rodan (1961, pp. 107–38) predicted that by 1976 Sri Lanka would have a higher per capita income than either Taiwan or South Korea where the average income would be barely 20 per cent higher than that of India. Most of the big countries in Latin America were predicted to perform well. Argentina was expected to achieve twice the per capita income of Singapore in 1976 while almost every country would be doing better than Hong Kong. Similarly, Chenery and Strout (1966, pp. 679–733) estimated that for the period 1962–76 the GNP of India and Pakistan would grow faster than that of South Korea. Hong Kong and the other Asian newly industrialising economies, namely, Singapore, South Korea and Taiwan were not expected to perform well. Even Colombia was expected to outperform Hong Kong (Hicks 1989, p. 36).

However, the outcome was surprising. Neither the Latin American nor South Asian nations, but the East Asian economies, had emerged as prosperous countries. By 1970, Hong Kong and the other Asian NIEs had grown for over a decade at average rates much higher than those of either developed or developing countries. They have created what the World Bank (1993) called East Asian "miracles".

Economists began to turn their attention to the Asian NIEs and searched for other explanations. Some of them looked into the relationship between trade and development and questioned the validity of the wisdom of import substitution. Having discovered that import substitution and inward-looking industrialisation led to high costs and balance of payment difficulties, they stressed the gains from international trade and the importance of comparative advantage. Moreover, they called for an alternative, outward looking industrialisation strategy which seems to work so well in the Asian NIEs (Hicks 1989, p. 37).

Based on the theory of comparative advantage, orthodox neoclassical economists suggested that government intervention such as tariff protection or wage policies had distorted the relative prices of factors of production, violated the law of comparative advantage, and retarded economic growth. A number of studies, for example, Chen (1987, 1989a, b), Ichimura (1988) and Dahlman (1989), analysed the economic growth of Hong Kong and other Asian NIEs by examining their changes in comparative advantages.

However, the theory of comparative advantage has certain limitations in explaining the dynamics of economic change (Lichauco 1988, pp. 136–7; Rodan 1992, p. 79). In essence, the analysis does not consider the role of entrepreneurship, the factor that can change the given resource situation of an economy. In fact, the governments of the Asian newly industrialised economies often exhibited entrepreneurship to alter the prevailing comparative advantages (White and Wade 1988, pp. 8, 53).[7]

Unaware of their shortcomings, orthodox economic theorists in the 1970s further stressed the role of shadow price in economic planning and estimated the effective rate of protection in trade. There had also been an increasing use of formal mathematical techniques for dealing with choices under uncertainty. These techniques were applied to a wide range of development issues, ranging from the effects of different forms of land tenure on risk bearing to the benefits of price stabilisation schemes (Backhouse 1985, pp. 368–9). Unfortunately, the addition of highly sophisticated quantitative techniques moves economic analysis further away from the human dimension.

Unable to explain the high growth performance of Hong Kong in particular and the Asian NIEs in general, some scholars began to examine the influences of culture on the Asian economic growth. Specifically, Kahn (1979, p. 332) first put the Asian NIEs and Japan in a single group and argued that "the success of Taiwan and Korea can be attributed to cultural factors favouring development, excellent management of the economy, the favourable international and technological climate for growth ... and quite simply, hard work and dedication". Chen (1988) integrated Confucianism into his development model.

In summary, most studies on the economic development of Hong Kong and other Asian NIEs have employed Harrod–Domar growth models, the Cobb-Douglas production function, the Ricardian theory of comparative advantage and Keynesian development planning. These works have failed to yield a satisfactory explanation of the economic success of Hong Kong because the most important prime mover in economic development, namely entrepreneurship, is missing in their analysis.

OVERLOOKED: THE ROLE OF ENTREPRENEURSHIP

To explain economic development in a country requires a dynamic theory which centres around some human agency. This means that a theory of entrepreneurship is required. In recent years, Chen (1988) admitted that entrepreneurship and labour are the most important factors of production in the first stage of export orientation. He attempted to integrate Schumpeter's theory of entrepreneurship in his model and to explain the East Asian miracle in terms of neo-Confucianism. Wu (1989) also employed Schumpeter's arguments to explain the economic activities in Hong Kong. However, the approach in both papers is inadequate. As Wong (1988b p. 166) correctly argued, Hong Kong's entrepreneurs, particularly in the cotton spinning industry, did not fit into the theoretical mould constructed by Schumpeter. Reviewing the works on overseas Chinese entrepreneurship, Mackie (1992, p. 60) concluded that scholars will need to go beyond the Schumpeterian concepts of entrepreneurship and take note of more recent thinking on the subject.[8]

As noted above, Chau (1993) is the first systematic work that used Kirzner's theory of entrepreneurship to explain the economic development of Hong Kong. He argued that the economic dynamics of Hong Kong have been attributed to what he called "merchant-entrepreneurs". A crucial point he made is that the success of merchant entrepreneurs in Hong Kong is not confined only to manufacturing, but extends to the tertiary sector as well.

In summary, very few economic works recognised the role of entrepreneurship in the economic development of Hong Kong. Specifically, "adaptive entrepreneurship" which is so significant to the economic development of Hong Kong and other Asian developing economies, has been neglected. Instead, scholars from other disciplines such as geography, sociology and management examined the role of entrepreneurship in the economic development of Hong Kong. Sit *et al.* (1979, 1988) and Tuan *et al.* (1986) presented a comprehensive analysis of the socio-economic backgrounds of Hong Kong's small business entrepreneurs. Wong

8

(1988b) examined the role of emigrant Shanghai industrialists in Hong Kong's textile industry. Redding (1988, 1990) explained the success of the East Asian economies in terms of culture, specifically the influence of post-Confucian teaching on the business management of Chinese entrepreneurs; while Siu and Martin (1992) investigated the factors that made entrepreneurs successful in Hong Kong. However, none of their works is systematically related to the theory of entrepreneurship in economics. Casson (1982, p. 9) is correct in claiming that "the subject area [of entrepreneurship] has been surrendered by economists to sociologists, psychologists and political scientists. Only the Austrian school ... still takes it seriously". This study attempts to remedy this deficiency.

THE OBJECTIVE OF THIS STUDY

This study endeavours to bring entrepreneurship back into development economics. As previously noted, a number of economic studies have attempted to explain the East Asian miracle. However, very few of them gave convincing arguments. The principal objective of this study is to examine the role of entrepreneurship in the economic development of Hong Kong and demonstrate its importance. Specifically, it attempts to examine how entrepreneurial activities have enabled Hong Kong to catch up with early industrialised nations. This research first demonstrates that the city is an entrepreneurial society. It then investigates how entrepreneurship has developed out of its unique environment. Our major task is to examine the form of entrepreneurial strategies employed by manufacturers and their relationship with firm performance. It also analyses the impact of entrepreneurial activities on structural transformation in Hong Kong and on its ability to catch up with the more advanced nations.

To achieve the objective, a theoretical framework is needed. However, a review of the literature (Chapters 1 and 2) indicates that the orthodox neoclassical theories have severe limitations and are unable to give a satisfactory explanation of East Asian dynamics. Therefore, it is necessary to put forward a new perspective on economic development. Based on Cheah's (1989a, 1992, 1994) work, Chapter 2 first identifies two distinctive modes of entrepreneurship, namely Schumpeterian and Kirznerian modes. In economic development, they are referred to as creative and adaptive responses respectively. It is argued that during the dynamic development process, Schumpeterian entrepreneurs exerted a revolutionary change in early industrialised economies and created a developing discrepancy in the world economy (creative response), while Kirznerian entrepreneurs have had an evolutionary change on late industrialising economies and attempted to resolve the discrepancy (adaptive response)(Schumpeter 1947b; Akamatsu 1961; Cheah 1992). Kirznerian entrepreneurs capitalise on the profit opportunities by employing business strategies such as small-scale enterprise, product imitation, subcontracting and spatial arbitrage. Finally, the relationship between Kirznerian entrepreneurship, structural change and catching up is discussed. The last section of Chapter 2 summarises the major propositions and the methods of analysis.

The theoretical model developed in Chapter 2 is applied to explain the economic development of Hong Kong, one of the Asian newly industrialised economies. Chapter 3 explains the influence of the Hong Kong environment on the development of Kirznerian entrepreneurship. The major empirical analysis is presented in Chapters 4, 5 and 6.

Chapter 4 examines entrepreneurial strategies in Hong Kong's manufacturing industry while Chapters 5 and 6 present empirical studies on Hong Kong's textile, garment and electronics industries respectively. Given that entrepreneurial activities will influence the performances of firms as well as the economy as a whole, our analysis therefore includes both micro and macro levels. Chapter 7 focuses on the relationship between entrepreneurship and the aggregate performance of the economy. Specifically, the impact of entrepreneurship on Hong Kong's structural change and catching up with advanced nations is discussed.

If this study sheds new light on development economics, then we would like to know what lessons can be learnt from the growth experience of Hong Kong and its applicability to other developing countries. In particular, Chapter 8 provides a new viewpoint of the controversial role of government in economic development. Finally, Chapter 9 summarises our entrepreneurial perspective of the economic development of Hong Kong.

NOTES

1 Jardine Matheson & Co., founded by James Matheson and William Jardine in 1832, remains one of the most influential "hongs" (firms) in Hong Kong.

2 It was widely known that the members of the royal family of England, especially the Duke of Kent, liked to order clothes from Hong Kong's tailors when they visited the Colony. But such purchases had been criticised by some British Members of Parliament as not being patriotic.

3 During mid-1993, the central government of China, led by the Vice Premier, Mr Zhu Rongji, the former Mayor of Shanghai, proposed an ambitious economic plan which attempts to boost Shanghai, to surpass Hong Kong, as a major financial centre in Asian Pacific region by the year 2000.

4 Morawetz (1981) rejected the idea that the Asian economic miracle is due to cheap labour. In his view, the higher productivity in East Asia is due to the differences in the management skill originating from some cultural and social factors. In particular, he noted: "US garment buyers commonly point out that you can get anything you want in Hong Kong, Korea or Taiwan – any garment, in any material (cotton, wool, synthetics, fur, leather), at competitive prices, acceptable quality and delivered on time. In Colombia, by contrast, the range of garments and fabrics is limited, prices are in general higher, and quality and delivery times are less dependable. ... Success breeds success, failure breeds failure" (Morawetz 1981, p. 199).

5 Sir Philip Haddon-Cave remarked in 1978 that the philosophy of the government policy was positive non-interventionism. It meant that the government took the view "that attempts to frustrate the operation of market forces will tend to damage the growth rate of the economy, particularly as it is so difficult to predict, let alone control, market forces that impinge on an open economy. But ... the Government must play an active role in the provision of those services and facilities essential to life in a civilised community and ... we also believe that there are certain services and facilities which it is either more

convenient and efficient for the Government to provide or which should be provided, as a matter of policy, as a charge, wholly or partly, on public funds" (Hong Kong Government Secretariat 1977–8, p. 813).

6 It will be argued in Chapter 8 that the Hong Kong government has played a significant role in the industrialisation of Hong Kong, though its interventions have been carried out in a more subtle way.

7 Rodan (1992, p. 79) contended that, "If Japan had accepted the logic of the law of comparative advantage, she would still be a farming nation today, and a poor one at that. The success of Japan and the newly industrialised states stems from, among other factors, their rejection of the neo-classical 'comparative advantage' argument." In a review article, Hicks (1989, p. 39) remarked that East Asians were less willing to listen to economists who had led other countries so badly astray.

8 Mackie referred to the works of Kirzner (1973, 1982), Casson (1982), Drucker (1985), Nafziger (1984), to name a few. This issue will be further discussed in Chapter 2.

2

ENTREPRENEURSHIP AND ECONOMIC DEVELOPMENT

An analytical framework

A major weakness of the orthodox neoclassical perspective is that it neglects the role of entrepreneurship. This chapter begins by presenting the views of Schumpeter, Nelson and Winter, Baumol, Leibenstein and Kirzner which have explicitly or implicitly criticised the conventional theories from an entrepreneurial standpoint. It is followed by a reformulation of a development model based on an entrepreneurial perspective. The last section summarises the major propositions and the methods of analysis.

CRITIQUES OF THE ORTHODOX NEOCLASSICAL PERSPECTIVE OF ECONOMIC DEVELOPMENT

Schumpeter's critique: disequilibrium dynamics and innovative entrepreneurship

Schumpeter criticised the orthodox system for its assumptions of profit maximisation, rational human conduct and the use of equilibrium and static analyses.[1] Recognising the disequilibrium dynamics of economic change, Schumpeter introduced the elements of creative response and entrepreneurial agency. The orthodox approach assumes rational human conduct, frictionless decision making and profit maximisation. But Schumpeter (1934, pp. 79, 85) remarked:

> While in the accustomed circular flow every individual can act promptly and rationally because he is sure of his ground and is supported by the conduct, as adjusted to the circular flow, of all other individuals, who in turn expect the accustomed activity from him, he cannot simply do this when he is confronted by a new task ... Carrying out a new plan and acting according to a customary one are things as different as making a road and walking along it.
>
> (Schumpeter 1934, pp. 79, 85)

Therefore, the assumption that human conduct

> is prompt and rational is in all cases a fiction. But it proves to be sufficiently near to reality, if things have time to hammer logic into men. Where this has happened, and within the limits in which it has happened, one may rest

content with this fiction and build theories upon it. ... Outside of these limits our fiction loses its closeness to reality. To cling to it there also, as the traditional theory does, is to hide an essential thing and to ignore a fact which, in contrast with other deviations of our assumptions from reality, is theoretically important and the source of the explanation of phenomena which would not exist without it.

(Schumpeter 1934, p. 80)

Schumpeter also showed dissatisfaction with the static and equilibrium analysis in the conventional system. In Schumpeter's view, economic change in the traditional sense is too slow and sluggish to bring about new phenomena. The economic evolution which lays its foundations on the fact that the economy continuously adapts itself in response to change in the data may result in certain economic changes and possible economic growth. However, such an evolution will always remain within the traditional path of economic growth. Therefore, it is incapable of producing economic revolution deriving from discontinuous change. Discontinuous change is the kind of change that arises from within the system and is the cause of many important economic phenomena. Hence, Schumpeter wrote:

In the Smith–Mill–Marshall theory, the economy grows like a tree ... [and] proceeds steadily and continuously, each situation grows out of the preceding one in a uniquely determined way, and the individuals, whose acts combine to produce each situation, count individually for no more than do the individual cells of the tree. This passivity of response to given stimuli extends in particular to accumulation of capital: in a mechanical way, households and firms save and invest what they have saved in given investment opportunities. The same passivity of response is also implied in many historical descriptions of the development of countries or industries: they are descriptions of objective opportunities created, perhaps by protective duties, victorious wars, discoveries, or inventions; and it is tacitly assumed that people react to them in a uniquely determined manner that can be taken for granted and does not offer any problems.

(Schumpeter 1947a, p. 223)

Elsewhere, Schumpeter remarked:

The difficulties we encounter will be seen to be amenable to reduction, directly or indirectly, to the one fact that economic behaviour cannot be satisfactorily expressed in terms of the values which our variables assume at any single point of time. For instance, quantity demanded or supplied at any time is not merely a function of the price that prevails at the same time, but also of past and (expected) future values of that price: we are, therefore, driven to include in our functions values of variables which belong to different points of time. Theorems which do this we call dynamic ... In order to produce new phenomena and to impair seriously the usefulness of the Walras–Marshall description, reaction to the intermediate situations

13

created by such partial adaptation would have to counteract or to reverse that tendency and to lead away from instead of toward full equilibrium.

(Schumpeter 1939, p. 48)

In summary, Schumpeter argued that the orthodox equilibrium analysis cannot deal with the fundamental phenomenon of economic change. In Schumpeter's words (1934, pp. 62–3), "it can neither explain the occurrence of ... productive revolutions nor the phenomena which accompany them. It can only investigate the new equilibrium position after the changes have occurred".

Having identified the shortcomings of the orthodox framework and recognised the disequilibrium nature of the economic change, Schumpeter introduced in economic analysis the concepts of creative response and entrepreneurial agency. The later is responsible for destroying the existing equilibrium structure. Thus, Schumpeter suggested that

> We take account of this by recognising two, instead of only one, types of responses: adaptive and creative. I further suggest that we have no choice but to admit that, from our information in the observed situation before the fact (of creative response), we cannot foresee it and that thus an element of indeterminateness inevitably enters the analysis of economic growth whenever there is creative response. We may bring this element within the range of our list of factors of growth by observing that it links up with "quality of the human material" and in particular with "quality of leading personnel". And since creative response means, in the economic sphere, simply the combination of existing productive resources in new ways or for new purposes, and since this function defines the economic type that we call the entrepreneur, we may reformulate the above suggestions by saying that we should recognise the importance of, and systematically inquire into, entrepreneurship as a factor of economic growth.

(Schumpeter 1947a, p. 243)

Schumpeter's insight, specifically his evolutionary approach to economic problems has been extended in Nelson and Winter's influential work, *The Evolutionary Theory of Economic Change*.

Nelson and Winter's critique: an evolutionary theory of economic change

Like Schumpeter, Nelson and Winter (1982, p. 24) traced the basic problems of the neoclassical system to the notions of maximising, uncertainty, competition and equilibrium. They argued that conventional production theory attempts to explain the determination of equilibrium price, inputs and outputs under various underlying product demand and factor supply conditions. The theory assumes profit maximisation and does not address the basic question of how firms make a time-consuming response to changed market conditions based on incomplete information.

14

According to Nelson and Winter, the mainstream economists "assume that there is a global, faultless, once-and-for-all optimisation over given choice sets comprising all objectively available alternatives. This clearly conflicts with ... an assumption that the firm operates at all times with a status quo policy, the profitability of which it inexactly compares, from time to time, with individual alternatives that present themselves by processes not entirely under its control" (Nelson and Winter 1982, p. 31). Therefore, optimisation techniques tend to ignore the essential features of change, including uncertainty, diversities of viewpoint, the difficulties of the decision process, the importance of search and alertness, the value of problem solving and errors in decisions (Nelson and Winter 1982, p. 31).

Neoclassical theories analyse competition in the context of equilibrium. Nelson and Winter argued that neoclassical models do not elucidate the competitive process itself, but only the structure of relations among the efficient survivors. In this way, "they cannot address such questions as the duration of the struggle or the durability of the mistakes made in the course of it" (Nelson and Winter 1982, p. 52). The theoretical neglect of the competitive process gives rise to a sort of incompleteness. In other words, disequilibrium behaviour is not fully specified.

When the neoclassical theory of production is applied to explain economic growth in general and technical change in particular, it is impossible to reconcile the maximisation principle with the fact that, in the major invention process, there are significant differences in the ability of inventors to perceive opportunities as well as differences in knowledge, capabilities and luck. Furthermore, as Nelson and Winter (1982, p. 203) pointed out, the neoclassical formulation "avoids the uncertainty related with attempts to innovate, the publicness of knowledge associated with the outcomes of these attempts and the diversity of firm behaviour and fortune that is inherent in a world in which technical innovation is important".

In summary, the neoclassical perspective fails to address uncertainty, bounded rationality, the presence of large corporations, institutional complexity or the dynamics of actual adjustment processes (Nelson and Winter 1982, p. 5).

Having explicitly rejected the notion of maximising behaviour as an explanation of decision making, Nelson and Winter proposed an evolutionary approach to understanding economic change. In their argument, firms are modelled as having, at any given time, certain capabilities and decision rules. Over time these capabilities and rules are modified as a result of both deliberate problem-solving efforts and random events. In other words, firm behavioural patterns and market outcome are jointly determined over time. Hence search and selection are simultaneous and interacting aspects of the evolutionary process. Through the joint actions of search and selection firms evolve over time, with the conditions of the industry in each period bearing the seeds of its conditions in the following period (Nelson and Winter 1982, pp. 4, 19).

Nelson and Winter focused on the concept of routines as incorporating the regular and predictable behavioural pattern of the firm. In their evolutionary model, these routines play the role that genes play in biological evolutionary theory. "They are a persistent feature of the organism and determine its possible

15

behaviour; they are inheritable in the sense that tomorrow's organisms generated from today have many of the same characteristics, and they are selectable in the sense that organisms with certain routines may do better than others" (Nelson and Winter 1982, p. 14).

Nelson and Winter put forward a dynamic theory of economic change. They focused their analysis on innovation, invention and upsetting of firms' routines. Although they claimed their intellectual debt explicitly to Schumpeter, O'Driscoll and Rizzo (1985, p. 124) contended that Nelson and Winter actually applied a Hayekian theory of rules and evolved market institutions to firm behaviour.[2] While Nelson and Winter's model is in many aspects superior to neoclassical theories and their evolutionary approach to technological change has much to be commended, they did not explicitly include entrepreneurship in their work.[3]

Nevertheless, O'Driscoll and Rizzo (1985, p. 124) did mention that an important advantage of Nelson and Winter's approach is the ease with which entrepreneurs can be integrated into the analysis. Entrepreneurs are engines for change. They disturb firms' routines by changing the environment. Conscious entrepreneurial adaptation to a changing environment is sometimes the only way in which a firm may survive when production activities are locked into a current inappropriate routine. Entrepreneurial innovation may result eventually in a new routine, an adaptation to the new environment. The market outcome reflects both the results of conscious planning and the unintended consequences of entrepreneurial inter-action in the market process. In this sense, O'Driscoll and Rizzo (1985, p. 125) concluded that Nelson and Winter's work is attractive and their contribution is a first step towards a theory of institutional change.

Baumol's critique: the significance of imitative entrepreneurship

Baumol (1968) criticised neoclassical theory explicitly from an entrepreneurial viewpoint. He argued that the neoclassical paradigm is non-entrepreneurial. Pro-duction is simply an exercise of choosing among known alternatives. Decisions are made by comparing costs and revenues with each set of values as described by the relevant functional relationships and mathematical equations. The producer then employs optimisation techniques to reach a decision. When there is a change in exogenous variables, the firm will readjust the choice accordingly (Baumol 1968, p. 52). With this optimisation technique, the entrepreneur has been removed from the model. There is no room for enterprise or initiative. The management becomes a passive calculator that reacts mechanically to change imposed on it by external developments over which it does not exert, and does not even attempt to exert, any influence. In neoclassical models, there are no clever strategies, ingenious schemes, brilliant innovations or charisma (Baumol 1968, p. 68).

Having indicated that entrepreneurship plays a significant role in economic development, Baumol (1988, p. 85) further argued that "the entrepreneur provided leadership contributing to growth in productivity and per capita income not only through innovative activity, but by means of aggressive and imaginative imitation that is a key instrument of international technology transfer". In other words, "imitative entrepreneurship deserves a place alongside innovative entrepreneurship in the front rank of those who contribute to an economy's prosperity". Moreover, in the international context, imitation demonstrably plays a significant role in the sense that each economy's welfare depends critically on ideas produced outside its borders and only imitation can bring those ideas to its own producers. Baumol (1988, pp. 86–7) hypothesised that, for any one country, on average, some 5 per cent of the technical progress can be ascribed to processes involving the participation of domestic innovative entrepreneurs while the remaining 95 per cent must have involved the agency of entrepreneurial imitators.

Thus, Baumol emphasised the importance of imitative entrepreneurs in economic development. As will be discussed, the notion of imitative entrepreneurship comes very close to Kirznerian entrepreneurship, a key contributing factor for rapid economic growth in the Asian newly industrialising economies.[4]

Leibenstein's critique: X-efficiency and routine entrepreneurship

Another challenge of the general equilibrium paradigm of neoclassical economics comes from the theory of X-efficiency devised by Harvey Leibenstein. Leibenstein (1978, p. 9) remarked that "one of the curious aspects of the relationship of neoclassical theory to economic development is that in the conventional theory, entrepreneurs as they are usually perceived play almost no role".

Like Baumol, Leibenstein (1968, p. 72) argued that the received theory of competition in neoclassical analysis gives the impression that there is no need for entrepreneurship. In particular, the conventional microtheory assumes that the basic actors are households or firms which attempt to maximise the value of some variables subject to constraints. All relevant information to make the decisions is assumed to be available. The most important phenomena explained by the model are the allocation of inputs to firms made on the basis of price signals, the choice of techniques to be used in production and the quantities of goods purchased by households (Leibenstein 1968, p. 72, 1978, p. 4). In this situation, all a potential entrepreneur has to do is to calculate possible outcomes and make his decision. The role of entrepreneurship is reduced to a trivial activity (Leibenstein 1978, p. 9).

Furthermore, in such models, how effectively the inputs are utilised in producing the goods does not enter as a variable. In particular, the distinction between the purchase of inputs by a firm and the degree of effectiveness of their use in the firm is not made. Neoclassical theorists simply assume that firms minimise costs and hence inputs will be used as effectively as possible. The degree of the effectiveness of the utilisation of inputs was ignored (Leibenstein 1978, p. 5).

In the adoption of new technology, the traditional theory assumes that profitable innovations will always be adopted because it is an obvious corollary to the usual profit maximising postulate. Leibenstein argued that if we recognise that there are some influences due to inertia or personality differences among decision-makers, then there is a possibility that the most profitable innovations will not always be adopted. Such factors are important in economic growth.

As a remedy to the neoclassical models, Leibenstein (1966) made a valuable distinction between allocative efficiency and X-efficiency. Leibenstein (1978, pp. 17–18) explained the concept of X-inefficiency as follows. Suppose that certain inputs have been allocated to a firm. These inputs can be used with various degrees of effectiveness within the firm. The more effectively they are used the greater the output. When an input is not used effectively, the difference between the actual output and the maximum output attributable to that input is the measure of X-inefficiency. The sources of X-inefficiency chiefly come from organisational entropy, human inertia, incomplete contracts between economic agents and conflicting agent–principal interests (Leibenstein 1978, pp. 36–7).

The distinction between allocative efficiency and X-efficiency has enabled us to recognise the role of entrepreneurship. Leibenstein (1966, 1978) distinguished between two broad types of entrepreneurial activity: routine entrepreneurship and Schumpeterian or "innovational" entrepreneurship. By routine entrepreneurship, he referred to "the activities involved in coordinating and carrying on a well-established, going concern in which the parts of the production function in use are well known and which operates in well-established and clearly defined markets". By "innovational" entrepreneurship, he meant "the activities necessary to create or carry on an enterprise where not all the markets are well established or clearly defined and/or in which the relevant parts of the production function are not completely known" (Leibenstein 1966, p. 73, 1978, pp. 40–1). In both the routine and innovative cases, entrepreneurs coordinate activities that involve different markets; they are inter-market operators. But in the case of innovative entrepreneurship, not all the markets exist or operate perfectly and entrepreneurs, if they are to be successful, must fill in for the market deficiencies (Leibenstein 1978, p. 41).

Hence, for Leibenstein, the roles of entrepreneurs in economic development are gap filling and input completer (Leibenstein 1978, pp. 74–5). Entrepreneurs possess "the capacities to search and discover economic opportunities, evaluate economic opportunities, marshal the financial resources necessary for the enterprise, making time-binding arrangements, take ultimate responsibility for management, be the ultimate uncertainty and/or risk bearer, provide and be responsible for the motivational system within the firm, search and discover new economic information, translate new information into new markets, techniques and goods, and provide leadership for the work group" (Leibenstein 1978, p. 74).

In conclusion, Leibenstein had correctly identified the shortcomings of the conventional system and recognised the role of entrepreneurship in economic development. However, like Baumol, his distinction between Schumpeterian entrepreneurship and the routine entrepreneur is still blurred. In particular, the function of the routine entrepreneur in economic development is not comprehensively defined. The role of two types of entrepreneurship in dynamic world development remained to be identified, leaving much room for theoretical improvement.

Kirzner's critique: the significance of entrepreneurial discovery in economic growth

The concept of entrepreneurship has always been a central part of the Austrian School of economics. Therefore, in analysing economic change, economists such as Kirzner, Hayek and Mises focused on the role of knowledge and entrepreneurship.

Kirzner (1985, p. 16) criticised the aggregate approach in the mainstream growth models where knowledge and learning are ignored. In the orthodox analysis, there is no need for mutual information among individual participants in the economy. Correct decision making means correct calculation. Decision-makers have a clear perception of the scope of their ignorance and of how this ignorance can be reduced. In a sense, they know precisely what it is that they do not know.

In Kirzner's view, the mainstream paradigm assumes that the economy is rigidly constrained by resource scarcity so that growth follows along a very definite path. In this context, nothing can be discovered regarding new ways of using given resources or regarding the existence of hitherto unnoticed resources.

While the conventional theories recognise the role of technology in economic growth, technology only appears in an impersonal manner and can be obtained without effort by all members of the society. In particular, Kirzner (1985, p. 70) remarked that

> The opportunities for growth were seen as marked out, given initial technology by a clearly defined array of inter-temporal investment possibilities that somehow existed apart from any need for them to be discovered, and whose very existence dictated the appropriate growth path. There was no suggestion that the set of opportunities likely to be in fact discovered might in some way depend on the institutional framework within which growth was sought.
>
> (Kirzner 1985, p. 70)

For Kirzner, technical knowledge can be treated as a kind of resource but the knowledge of the availability of opportunity cannot. Economic development consists not only of technical knowledge but also of the exploitation of opportunities. The development process consists of the interaction of millions of individual acts of mutual discovery. Development occurs "not because of the availability of new opportunities, but because of expanded awareness of existing opportunities" (Kirzner 1985, p. 74).

More specifically, for developing economies, two problems need to be addressed. The first is the determination of the best course of economic development available to the society. It is a matter of comparing alternative possibilities with available resources and technology. The second is to ensure that the opportunities thus computed will be fulfilled. No matter what form of economic organisation, whether central planning or market economy, the central issue is to ensure that the opportunities that exist will be discovered and seized. It is here that the entrepreneur plays a significant role (Kirzner 1979, p. 116).

According to Kirzner, the literature on growth and development consists of comprehensive discussions of what possibilities exist for raising the productivity of labour, for increasing the volume of resources, for accumulating physical and human capital, for obtaining gains through foreign trade and foreign capital. Unfortunately, entrepreneurship in this literature is treated in much the same way as economic resources in general. Although a difference is made between entrepreneurs and managers, the former still appear to be treated as an element that extends the range of possible opportunities, rather than the element needed to ensure a tendency toward the fulfilment of opportunities available in principle without them (Kirzner 1979, pp. 116–17).

Stemming from dissatisfaction with the mainstream development theories in explaining economic progress, Kirzner (1979, p. 108) urged us to re-examine the role of the entrepreneur in developing economies. In agreement with Leibenstein's distinction between allocative efficiency and X-efficiency, in 1985, he proposed two dimensions in understanding economic development. First, at a given period, output of a nation may be lower than its desired and possible level because opportunities remain unnoticed. Second, due to technical advance over time, the capacity of production increases. For this technical knowledge to be utilised, it is not enough that these opportunities exist, they must be perceived (Kirzner 1985, p. 75). In short, entrepreneurial discovery is an important ingredient in economic development.

A need for a new perspective of economic development

The orthodox theories have failed to provide us with a satisfactory explanation of the economic progress of the Asian developing economies. Their major short-coming is the neglect of entrepreneurship, the element contributing to economic dynamism. A systematic investigation of the role of entrepreneurship in economic development is of utmost importance. Moreover, using Schumpeter's concept of entrepreneurship to explain the economic development of all nations, including the late industrialising economies, is far from satisfactory. Schumpeterian mode of entrepreneurship has been a rare phenomenon in most developing countries, and even in many industrialised economies. The emergence of individuals with "heroic entrepreneurial" character was not an essential condition for the development of dynamic capitalist economies in the Third World, since rapid growth was taking place in several countries even without such entrepreneurs (Mackie 1992, p. 46). As Nafziger (1986, p. 7) argued, Schumpeter's concept of the entrepreneur is "somewhat limited in less developed countries, since the majority of indigenous Schumpeterian entrepreneurs are traders whose innovations are the opening of new markets. In light of the possibilities of technical transfer from advanced economies, no undue emphasis should be put on the development of entirely new combinations. People with technical, executive and organisational skills may be too scarce in less developed countries to use in developing new combinations in the Schumpeterian sense." Furthermore, to adapt new combinations from economically advanced countries does not involve Schumpeterian entrepreneurs. Hence, Nafziger (1986, p. 11; Kirchhoff 1994, p. 65) argued that Schumpeter's concept of the entrepreneur needs to be broadened to include those who adapt and modify already existing innovations. However, for analytical purpose, it is preferable to separate the two kinds of entrepreneurship. In other words, a different conception of entrepreneurship is required. Baumol and Leibenstein put forward the notions of imitative and routine entrepreneurship respectively. However, the most important function of entrepreneurs in the Asian NIEs, namely alertness to opportunities and adaptation to changes, were not considered in their arguments. The kind of entrepreneurship operating in late industrialising nations remained to be explored. Employing Kirzner's insight, the following section will put forward an entrepreneurial perspective of economic development.

TOWARDS AN ENTREPRENEURIAL PERSPECTIVE OF ECONOMIC DEVELOPMENT

Schumpeterian and Kirznerian modes of entrepreneurship

Cheah (1989a, 1993) identified conceptually two distinct modes of entrepreneurship, namely Schumpeterian and Austrian, and analysed their relationship in economic development. In Cheah's view (1992) the dynamic interactions between Schumpeterian entrepreneurs who are responsible for creative responses, and Austrian entrepreneurs, who are responsible for adaptive responses, constitute the entrepreneurial process. In this study, the two kinds of entrepreneurship are referred to as Schumpeterian and Kirznerian. They are discussed as follows.

Schumpeterian entrepreneurship

Schumpeter's concept of entrepreneurship introduced a new dimension into economics. According to Schumpeter (1934, pp. 81–6), entrepreneurs exert a disturbing force on an economy, which is termed "creative destruction". The entrepreneur was described by Schumpeter as the economic agent who performs the service of innovating, of introducing changes that radically change the framework of the economic system. Entrepreneurs are defined as people who innovate, and innovating is the act of combining productive factors in some new way. This includes the introduction of a new good or quality of a good, introduction of a new method of production, the opening of a new market, the utilisation of some new source of supply for a raw material or intermediate good and the carrying out of the new organisation of any industry (Schumpeter 1934, pp. 87–8, 1939, p. 66).

Furthermore, Schumpeter recognised that entrepreneurial innovation is a difficult job because it lies outside the routine framework and because the environment resists in many ways. Therefore, the entrepreneurial function does not essentially consist in either inventing or creating the conditions which the enterprise exploits. It consists in "getting [new] things done" (Schumpeter 1934, p. 93).

Schumpeter argued entrepreneurship encompasses three essential characteristics:

> First it can always be understood ex post; but it can practically never be understood ex ante; that is to say, it cannot be predicted by applying the ordinary rules of inference from the pre-existing facts ... [5] Second, it shapes the whole course of subsequent events and their long run outcome ... it changes social and economic situations for good, it creates situations from which there is no bridge to those situations that might have emerged in its absence ... Third, the frequency of its occurrence has something to do with the quality of the personnel available in the society, with relative quality of personnel and with individual decisions, actions and patterns of behaviours.
>
> (Schumpeter 1947b, p. 150)

Kirznerian entrepreneurship: alertness and arbitrageurship

Unlike Schumpeter, Kirzner, as a follower of Mises, has built his concept of entrepreneurship entirely upon the foundation of Mises' action theory (Kirzner 1973, 1979, 1982, 1985, 1992). He repeatedly stressed Mises' thesis that "each human actor is always, in significant respects, an entrepreneur" (Kirzner 1982, p. 139). It is important to note the link between action theory and entrepreneurship, more specifically, action and alertness.

> Human action, in the sense developed by Mises, involves the course of action taken by the human being to remove uneasiness and to make himself better off. Being broader than the notion of economising, the concept of human action does not restrict analysis of the decision to the allocation problem posed by the juxtaposition of scarce means and multiple ends ... but also the very perception of the ends-means framework within which allocation and economising are to take place ... Mises' homo agens ... is endowed not only with the propensity to pursue goals efficiently, once ends and means are clearly identified, but also with the drive and alertness needed to identify which ends to strive for and which means are available.
>
> (Kirzner 1973, p. 33)

Hence, we can trace an important element of Kirzner's concept of entrepreneurship, namely, alertness, from Mises. In the market, the opportunity to which human agents are alert is monetary profit. The entire role of entrepreneurs lies in their alertness to hitherto unnoticed opportunities. They proceed by their alertness to discover and exploit situations in which they are able to sell for high prices that which they can buy for low. Alertness implies that the actor possesses a superior perception of economic opportunity. It is like an "antennae that permits recognition of gaps in the market that give little outward sign" (Gilad et al. 1988, p. 483).

For Kirzner, alertness to profit opportunity implies arbitrage activities. Indeed Kirzner has not distinguished arbitrageurship from entrepreneurship (White 1976, p. 4). Regarding the arbitrage theory of profit, Kirzner (1973) argued that the existence of disequilibrium situations in the market implies profit opportunity. The entrepreneur endeavours to exploit this opportunity, eliminate errors, and move the economy toward equilibrium.[6]

The interactions between the two modes of entrepreneurship in economic development

According to Schumpeter (1947b, p. 150), there are two kinds of response in economic development, namely "creative response" and "adaptive response".

> Whenever an economy reacts to an increase in population by simply adding the new brains and hands to the working force in the existing employment, or an industry reacts to a protective duty by expansion within its existing practice, we may speak of the development as adaptive response. And whenever the economy or an industry or some firms in an industry do something else, something that is outside of the range of existing practice, we may speak of creative response.
>
> (Schumpeter 1947b, p. 150)

Moreover, adaptive response follows creative response (Schumpeter 1934, p. 228). Once the new possibility is tried, imitators arise who perceive the advantages of the new combination, and who are eager to share in those advantages. These imitators are people who did not have the will or drive to overcome the social resistance to innovation themselves, but who are ready to adopt new methods promptly as soon as the initial resistance has been overcome by the true innovator. It is in this way that an innovation achieves widespread adoption in the system. Some kinds of subsidiary innovations may be derived from the initial breakthrough (Cauthorn 1989, p. 14). Schumpeter described the relationship between the two responses:

> If one or a few have advanced with success many of the difficulties disappear. Others can then follow these pioneers, as they will clearly do under the stimulus of the success now attainable. Their success again makes it easier, through the increasingly complete removal of the obstacles ... for more people to follow suit, until finally the innovation becomes familiar and the acceptance of it a matter of free choice.[7]
>
> (Schumpeter 1934, p. 228)

Despite Schumpeter's insight, the interactions between the two modes of entrepreneurship in the development process have not been fully elaborated. As previously noted, most studies did not even appreciate the existence of two modes of entrepreneurship. They tended to neglect the existence or to dismiss the significance of Kirznerian entrepreneurship (Cheah 1994, p. 138). More importantly, most scholars (including Schumpeter) failed to see that Kirznerian entrepreneurship over time can also increase the scope for Schumpeterian opportunities. For this, Kirzner (1985, p. 162) noted, entrepreneurship consisted of "the social integration of the innumerable scraps of existing information that are present in scattered form throughout society ... Yet the same entrepreneurial spirit that stimulates the discovery in the market of the value of information now existing throughout the market also tends to stimulate the discovery or creation of entirely new information concerning ways to anticipate or to satisfy consumer preferences. The entrepreneurial process at this second level is what drives the capitalist system toward higher and higher standards of achievement." In Kirzner's view, it is important to understand the long-run entrepreneurial process (Schumpeterian) and the short run entrepreneurial process (Kirznerian) in the economic development.

Cheah (1989a) recognises the two distinctive entrepreneurial processes and formally integrates them into one framework. Schumpeterian entrepreneurs "promote change *of* an existing situation. Schumpeterian entrepreneurial activities result in major innovations and even systemic change that increase or create uncertainty and promote new development processes which serve to create and/or widen the (e.g. technological) gap between leaders and followers." In contrast, Kirznerian entrepreneurs promote "change *within* an existing situation. It stems from the discovery of profitable discrepancies, gaps, mismatches of knowledge and information which others have not yet perceived and exploited, and the entrepreneur acts to capitalise upon the opportunity for gain or advantage which that discovery presents" (Cheah 1989a, p. 11). Kirznerian entrepreneurial activities include "arbitrage, speculation, risk taking, adaptive innovation, imitation as well as planning and management efforts in response to market signals" (Cheah 1992, p. 468). They "increase knowledge about the situation, reduce the general level of uncertainty over time and promote market processes which help to reduce or to eliminate the gap between leaders and followers" (Cheah 1992, p. 466). The two kinds of entrepreneurial activities are opposites and yet complements to each other. The long-run (Schumpeterian) and the short-run (Kirznerian) entrepreneurial process are interpreted as a process of alternating hegemony (see Cheah 1989a, p. 13, 1994, pp. 134–9).

Assume initially an equilibrium situation in Schumpeter's model (1934) of the circular flow of economic life. The launching of Schumpeterian innovation produces "systemic change which destroys the existing equilibrium and re-creates uncertainties, mismatches of information, and a proliferation of new unexploited opportunities within a particular situation" (Cheah 1994, p. 137). The result is a continual series of steps that together propel the engine of long-run economic growth and development (Cheah 1994, p. 135). As the level of uncertainty rises due to the initiation of Schumpeterian activities and processes, the scope for Kirznerian entrepreneurs also grows. Kirznerian entrepreneurs discover the existence and/or the value of available knowledge, arbitrage profit opportunities, and coordinate economic activities. At the same time, Kirznerian entrepreneurial activities lead to a higher level of certainty and promote a tendency towards equilibrium (Cheah 1994, p. 135). Through the exploitation of profit opportunities, Kirznerian entrepreneurs define the full potential and approximate limits of a Schumpeterian innovation. Their activities also pave ways for subsequent Schumpeterian entrepreneurs to use that knowledge as the new foundation from which to launch the next Schumpeterian innovation (Cheah 1994, p. 137). The two modes of entrepreneurship interact in a dialectical manner. Two extremes in the entrepreneurial process, namely equilibrium (certainty) and disequilibrium (uncertainty), represent the maximum scopes for Kirznerian and Schumpeterian entrepreneurial opportunities respectively. Each force dominates the other alternately at different points in time in the entrepreneurial process (Cheah 1994, p. 137). The interactions of the two modes of entrepreneurship lay the foundation for a dynamic development process.

The two modes of entrepreneurship compared

The two modes can be further differentiated in terms of technological and marketing strategies:

Technological strategy

Schumpeterian entrepreneurs often exhibit what Freeman (1982, p. 170) called offensive technological strategies. Being a first mover, they exercise technological leadership in the market and initiate an industry life cycle. To keep their technological supremacy and maintain leadership in the industry, they emphasise fundamental research. Patents are employed to protect their benefits as long as possible (Freeman 1982, p. 172; Martin 1984, p. 53).

There is also a need for effective downstream coupling. This means that the implementation of a radical innovation requires good communication between all the departments concerned to ensure quick identification and solution of problems (Martin 1984, p. 57). To facilitate communication during innovative process, vertical integration is preferred (Langlois and Robertson, 1995).

Kirznerian entrepreneurs adopt what Freeman (1982, p. 176) called defensive technological strategies. They are in essence "follow-the-leader" policies. Such policies are attractive for two reasons. First, a radical innovation has recently been introduced in the market, but the dominant design has yet to emerge. Second, the mortality rate of launching a new product can be quite high at this stage. For these reasons, Kirznerian entrepreneurs avoid being the first to enter the market where an innovation is commercially unproved. In this way, if pioneers first launch a new innovation and prove to be commercially unsuccessful, followers have nothing to lose. If the product is successful, followers will capture much of the market by launching their own versions of the product or service (Freeman 1982, p. 178).[8]

Kirznerian entrepreneurs aim at matching or duplicating new products launched by Schumpeterian entrepreneurs. The latecomers have to ensure that their firms possess the scientific knowledge to exploit the new innovation once it appears to be successful. This implies that they have to conduct some applied research (Martin 1984, p. 60).

As an industry matures, a dominant design emerges. Opportunities can only be exploited incrementally based upon design, reliability and cost reduction rather than upon major technological breakthrough. In other words, firms will pursue an imitative or "me-too" policy. Since imitative activities mainly modify the existing designs, the costs of production are also lower. This strategy can be particularly attractive to countries that traditionally lag behind leading industrialised countries in adopting technology. Martin (1984, p. 61) argued that Japanese companies had followed this strategy very successfully since World War II, although some of them now have moved to offensive strategies.

Marketing strategy

Schumpeterian entrepreneurs employ proactive marketing strategies to introduce their new product. In other words, they seek to establish their own brand name and position their product in the target niche. Schumpeterian firms rely on highly efficient marketing and intelligence systems to generate accurate and detailed product and consumer information. Since a radical innovation brings something entirely new to market, considerable effort must be made to ensure the reliability of the product in use and to educate users in its operation (Freeman 1982, p. 175).

In contrast, Kirznerian entrepreneurs are imitative followers. They adopt reactive competitive strategies. Often they produce under the brand of other firms (customer label product) or simply sell their goods without a brand. Little effort is devoted in marketing, as the objective is to minimise cost by relying wholly on the marketing resources of the foreign buyers. They have no desire to establish their own marketing delivery systems (Ting 1985, pp. 96–7). As customers already posess some experience of using the new product, latecomers put less emphasis on education, training and advisory services. However this does not mean that education and training are not required because customers may be locked into the first version of the innovation (Martin 1984, p. 57). A comparison between two kinds of entrepreneurial strategies is summarised in Table 2.1.

Table 2.1 A comparison of the two styles of entrepreneurial strategies

	Innovative strategies	*Imitative strategies*
Technological strategies		
Product novelty	High	Low
Technology adoption	Early adopter	Late adopter
Expenditure on R&D	Large	Small
Patent for protection	Frequently employed	Seldom employed
Marketing strategies		
Brand strategy	Niche brand	No brand
Product life cycle	Initial stage	Mature stage
OEM business	Little involvement	Heavily involved
Subcontracting	Low degree	High degree
Other aspects		
Spatial arbitrage	New location	Familiar market
Size of firm (employment)	Large enterprise	Small firm
Expected payback period	Long term	Short term

Factors promoting Kirznerian entrepreneurship

In the development process, Schumpeterian innovations in developed countries have created tremendous profit opportunities for Kirznerian entrepreneurs in developing nations to capitalise upon. However, not all nations have evolved successfully into entrepreneurial economies to exploit these opportunities. Therefore, it is essential to investigate the factors that promote Kirznerian entrepreneurship in Hong Kong.

Economic factors

Paradoxically, inheritant weaknesses in an economy, such as its small size, poor natural resource endowment, and vulnerability to external shocks can sometimes become favourable conditions for economic success (Chia 1993, p. 1). Such initial unfavourable conditions, together with some non-economic factors have forced the manufacturers to embark on Kirznerian entrepreneurial strategies which enable them to catch up with more developed nations.

For manufacturers in small economies, the domestic market obviously cannot provide sufficient demand and thus exhibits the difficulties of attaining scale economies and cost competitiveness (Lee and Low 1990, p. 30). Therefore, they aim at overseas markets. As a result, they face an open world trading environment which is extremely volatile (Chia 1993, p. 1). To cope with keen global competition and constantly changing environment such as international business cycles and oil crises, producers adopt Kirznerian entrepreneurial strategies including small business operation, original equipment manufacturer (OEM) business, product imitation, spatial arbitrage and subcontracting. Such strategies provide the firms with flexibility and adaptability to cater to rapidly changing global markets.

As Bolton (1993, p. 37) remarked, the best way to tackle market uncertainty brought about by uncertain demand for a new product is to be an imitator. Lee and Low (1990, p. 30) also argued that through highly integrated international networks of marketing, exporting standardised products so as to achieve specialisation and scale economies is possible. Put differently, through subcontracting, firms specialise in a single production process and rely on other firms such as a trading company, for marketing (Sit and Wong 1988).

Government policies can also influence the choice of entrepreneurial strategies. If the state conducts policies favourable to foreign direct investment, then multinational corporations (MNCs) will have incentives to invest. Consequently, local producers will have more opportunities to learn foreign technologies and imitate their products via joint ventures, subcontracting or spin-offs. MNCs provide not only production technology but also management and marketing know-how (Yamazawa and Watanabe 1988, p. 204). Compared with Schumpeterian innovative strategy, which involves greater risk and higher cost, learning and imitating from multinationals are relatively cheaper and easier but may be equally profitable (Kingston 1977, p. 81; Bolton 1993, p. 35).

27

Obviously, for a small economy with limited natural resources, original research and development like the establishment of Silicon Valley in California cannot be afforded. Without large expense on R&D, it is difficult to conduct Schumpeterian innovation. On the other hand, technologies from overseas are abundant. It has been argued that today there is more technology than Asian producers can apply (Engardio and Gross 1992, p. 67). Provided that there is a good international communication network, local manufacturers can replicate new foreign products or processes at relatively low costs. As Ting (1985, p. 64) pointed out, "the easy accessibility and rather cheap availability of even the latest technologies ... mean that with even a minimum of technical preparation any aspiring NIC firm would have very little problem in acquiring the desired technology". In addition, loose enforcement of patents in developing economies leads to widespread technological piracy (Ting 1985, p. 63). Under this situation, manufacturers will widely adopt Kirznerian entrepreneurial strategies such as product imitation and are prone to be followers.

Compared to the more advanced nations such as the USA, Western European nations and Japan, Hong Kong is a latecomer. The advantages of being a latecomer include a lower cost of learning and imitating than original discovery and testing, an avoidance of pioneers' mistakes, the availability of a wide range of technologies to be adopted, and the production of a standardised product with the economies of scale (Woronoff 1986, p. 286; Ames and Rosenberg 1963, pp. 18–19; Perez and Soete 1988, p. 477). Those merits make manufacturers in developing nations pursue a product imitation strategy.

Moreover, in responding to rapid technological change, latecomers adopt subcontracting networks as a crucial source of flexibility. Ernst and O'Connor (1989, p. 55) argue that "subcontracting networks are an efficient structure when learning economies are significant but technology rather than firm specific".

Cultural factors

Several studies discuss the influence of culture on the development of entrepreneurship.[9] One of the arguments is that a hybrid of traditional Chinese and Western cultures is conducive to the development of entrepreneurship. Tam and Redding (1993, p. 159) noted that in the traditional Chinese culture, "entrepreneurial drive had been continually suppressed, occasionally crushed, and for centuries denied legitimacy as a basis for claiming respect and position in society". The Westernisation of the East Asian economies, for example through the British colonisation of Hong Kong and Singapore, has brought about transformations.[10] These economies have developed as multicultural, accepting Western ideology and life style within the greater framework of the ancient culture, and have slowly evolved into their own brand of management (Chau 1974, p. 155). More importantly, the pursuit of wealth in these societies has become respectable. A new merchant class has emerged. The merchants are no longer tied to traditional values and beliefs. On the contrary, they modify whenever necessary the traditional values and beliefs to achieve their ends (Siu and Martin 1992, p. 90). Similarly, Wong (1989, p. 170)

28

concluded that the entrepreneurs "have blended Western elements with their own tradition" and they have successfully combined their origins with a totally cosmopolitan world outlook.

However, as this study argues, in Hong Kong, Kirznerian entrepreneurship predominates. To explain this phenomenona, one important factor must be mentioned – Chinese family values. Wong (1980, 1988b) and Redding (1988, 1990) argue that "entrepreneurial familism" has laid the foundation for East Asian capitalism.

Entrepreneurial familism refers to the fact that the Chinese manage their enterprises like a family. This is observed in their business loans, management and marketing strategies. According to Wong (1988b, pp. 137–44, 1989, pp. 173–7), the family is the basic unit of economic competition. It provides the impetus for innovation and the support for risk taking.

Entrepreneurial familism entails three distinguishing characteristics, namely, a paternalistic managerial ideology and practice, nepotistic employment and family ownership of enterprise. First, owners of the family firms consider themselves as patriarchal business leaders who confer welfare benefits on their employees as favours, take a personal interest in their subordinates' non-job-related activities, and disapprove of trade union activities. Second, nepotism is practised in active and passive forms. Chinese firms prefer to employ close family members in key positions but take on other relatives only reluctantly or passively. Such preferential recruitment of kinsmen is a phenomenon deriving from the family mode of ownership. Third, in order to keep the ownership of the firm within the family, the founders choose to obtain capital sources through bank loans rather than through the stock market because the former will not force them to relinquish exclusive ownership.

The practice of family business has several implications for the development of Kirznerian entrepreneurship. First, when an enterprise is divided into smaller units, it provides the manufacturers with flexibility to adjust to the changing international environment (Chau 1974, p. 157).

Second, as Wong (1988a, p. 144) argued, familism can lead to the evolution of a subcontracting system, under which multiple independent small firms are linked into a network.

Third, in the family firm, it is a custom that the welfare of employees is taken care of by their patriarchal employers. This paternalistic approach weakens the labour movement, and promotes subcontracting activities.

Fourth, the reliance on family and the exclusion of outsiders for senior management positions have important effects on the shape and the size of business organisation. In particular, when an enterprise grows large, it will split into smaller parts just like the Chinese practice of dividing their family estate. Redding (1988, p. 109) argued that this practice "facilitates the initiating phase of entrepreneurship but ... places barriers to the higher levels of coordination necessary for growth of the individual firm to a large scale". The issue may be argued in terms of our perspective that familism facilitates Kirznerian entrepreneurship but is not conducive to a major creative breakthrough or Schumpeterian entrepreneurship.

29

Political factors

A siege mentality also influences the development of entrepreneurship. For example, after World War II, all the Asian NIEs were faced with problems which threatened their survival. Taiwan faced frequent threats from the communists to "liberate" it. South Korea faced the possibility of invasion from the North. Singapore, after its expulsion from the Federation of Malaysia in 1965, faced the problem of its viability as an independent nation state. For Hong Kong, its status as a British colony will end in 1997 when the Territory is returned to communist China (Tan 1992, pp. 72–3).

It is argued that in such an uncertain political environment, manufacturers will adopt Kirznerian entrepreneurial strategies. In their investment planning, they take a short-term view. They opt for the projects with quick returns and avoid large capital commitment. Hence Kirznerian business strategies such as small business operation, product imitation, subcontracting and spatial arbitrage are all consistent with these kinds of strategy. Schumpeterian strategies, requiring huge R&D spending and aiming for a technological breakthrough, are not practical because a political disturbance such as a coup or a riot may ruin the investment.

Furthermore, to secure political stability, the Asian NIEs, such as Singapore, South Korea and Taiwan, imposed anti-labour legislation banning oppositional trade union activities. The consequence of repressed labour systems was the presence of vast reserves of cheap, unorganised and disciplined labour (Appelbaum and Henderson 1992, p. 17; World Bank 1993, pp. 164–5; see also Wade 1990). If manufacturers during their business restructuring can lay off workers without paying them heavy compensation, they will have the incentive to be more alert to new opportunities. More importantly, without effective labour unions and with anti-labour legislation, piece rate wage contracts and flexible wage systems are practised. This in turn promotes subcontracting activities.

Taken as a whole, a small economy, with limited natural resources, loose enforcement of patents, government policies promoting private enterprises, reliance on family business and exporting, and under the pressure of political uncertainty will provide a most favourable environment for developing Kirznerian entrepreneurship.

Kirznerian entrepreneurial strategies in the Asian newly industrialising economies

Schumpeterian innovations in advanced industrial nations had created tremendous opportunities for Kirznerian entrepreneurs in the late industrialising economies. The conditions in the Asian NIEs allow Kirznerian entrepreneurs to capitalise upon these opportunities through imitation, small-scale enterprises, subcontracting and spatial arbitrage. These entrepreneurial strategies adopted by the manufacturing firms in late industrialising economies such as Hong Kong constitute the principal focus of this study.

Product imitation

Kirznerian entrepreneurial activities include imitation, adaptive innovation and arbitrage (Cheah 1992, p. 468). When Kirznerian entrepreneurs notice a product or a business pattern successfully launched by someone else, they will imitate it if they can produce at lower costs (and hence sell at lower prices).[11] In other words, entrepreneurs conduct arbitrages on the (factor) price discrepancies.

Imitation can be a clever competitive strategy involving investment, creativity and insight. Imitative entrepreneurs exploit the success of others. They have not invented a product or a service, but rather have perfected and positioned it. Imitation adds some product attributes so that the modified product is slightly different from the original one and fits a slightly different market. That is, imitators supply something which is still lacking. Drucker (1985, pp. 203–7) insisted that imitators do not proceed by taking away customers from the pioneers who have first introduced a new product. Instead, they serve the markets which the pioneers have created but have not yet adequately serviced. Imitators satisfy a demand that already exists rather than creating a brand new one.

To enter the market, imitators must possess some competitive edges (Hagedoorn 1989, p. 91; Freeman 1982, p. 183). Usually, firms in developing countries can produce at lower costs due to cheaper labour and rentals. In addition, unlike Schumpeterian firms which can enjoy a monopoly situation, at least for an initial period, imitators face keen competition from other similar firms in the industry. Therefore, they have to be very efficient in production. They constantly modify their product, improve the production process and exploit economies of scale.

Imitators do not aspire to leap frogging nor attempt to keep up with innovators. They are content to follow way behind the innovation leaders. In other words, imitation is strategic followership (Hagedoorn 1989, p. 91; Freeman 1982, p. 179; Bolton 1993, p. 32). Being a follower is less risky.[12] Normally, imitation occurs when the market becomes established and the original venture has been accepted. As the market segments are knowable, marketing research can easily find out the consumption patterns of customers. Bolton (1993, p. 32) showed that Matsushita's low-cost strategy in the consumer electronics business was built upon being a second mover. The company deliberately arrived late in the marketplace, waited and watched until the consumers accepted a rival's new product, then started to produce a large volume of standard improved products which it sold at lower prices.

For producers in the Asian NIEs, the following methods of imitation may be adopted:

- reverse engineering;
- spin-offs;
- becoming an original equipment manufacturer supplier.

31

Reverse engineering

Manufacturers in the Asian NIEs frequently travel abroad, participate in international trade fairs and subscribe to professional journals for the purpose of searching for imitative opportunities. After they identify a target, they may arrange to obtain a licence to duplicate the product at home. Some of them may simply buy a unit of the new product and conduct reverse engineering. Given that firms cannot afford to purchase a licence from original suppliers, which is common for small firms, then closer scrutiny of how to produce the goods is impossible.[13] Without having full knowledge of how to make the product, imitators have to fill in the remaining gaps by independent effort. This implies that the copy may constitute a substantial mutation of the original. Yet, imitators are not directly concerned with creating a good likeness, but with achieving an economic success – preferably, an economic success at least equal to that of the original.

Spin-offs

Imitation can be viewed as a strategy of copying the routines of other firms (Nelson and Winter 1982, pp. 118–20). One method is to hire the employees of the original firm in an attempt to replicate the existing one (Nelson and Winter 1982, p. 124). In other cases, managers and skilled workers leave their employers to start their own enterprises. As ambitious employees learn about the industry and technology, they seek to establish their own business (Whitley 1990, p. 60). Hence, many new firms which enter the industry and form variants of innovation are often results of spin-offs from existing firms. For example, most of the early Silicon Valley semi-conductor firms were spin-offs from Fairchild Semiconductor, one of the first firms in the industry (Rogers 1983, p. 141).

Becoming an original equipment manufacturer (OEM) supplier

For manufacturing firms in the Asian NIEs, successful imitation is often the result of initially acting as an original equipment manufacturer supplier.[14] In other words, manufacturers produce goods with design and technology specified by foreign firms. The product sold abroad will bear the brand name of the overseas companies (Ting 1985, p. 80; Hobday 1995, p. 1178).[15] There are several advantages to being an OEM supplier. First, manufacturers save on huge marketing expenses in promoting the brand which can be very high when significant cultural barriers exist. Second, they bear a lower risk of sale fluctuations. Third, they save huge R&D expenses. Fourth, as OEM suppliers, they can seek assistance or advice from overseas firms (buyers) if difficulties arise. Fifth, it allows their technological learning to be focused on products for export markets (Hobday 1995, p. 1177).

For some long-term partners, overseas buyers may only provide a general idea of product requirements and leave the specific design to the OEM suppliers. If foreign buyers are satisfied with the finished products, this indicates that the OEM suppliers can manage to produce independently. It is quite possible that the OEM suppliers may later launch similar products under their own brands and compete with the foreign firms that originally employed them.

Many firms in the Asian NIEs manufacture products that bear the labels of foreign firms (customer label products) as well as products that bear their own company labels (private label products) at the same time. The reason is obvious. Producing and promoting private label products is too risky and too costly though the business has a higher profit margin.[16] On the other hand, customer label products involve less risk but have lower profit margins. A combination of the two represents a balance of the costs and benefits of the two kinds of labels. In short, moving away from a pure OEM supplier (adaptive entrepreneurial) strategy towards the manufacture of a private label product (innovative entrepreneurial) strategy is an indication of the firms' capability to produce, and the progress of an economy.

The phenomenon in which latecomers catch up with first movers can be explained by the fact that learning and imitation can lead to innovation. Manufacturers do not just imitate others, they pick and choose from different models and combine them into a novel product. This means that imitators are not mere copycats but innovative producers using the examples of others. At first, producers may struggle to imitate the contents of a certain product. But gradually they take a portion of a design from another product, and copy a little of the styles or functions of still some others. Ultimately, this mixture becomes a single unique product scarcely recognisable as an imitation at all (Phares 1988, p. 353).[17] Explaining how the East Asian manufacturing firms learned to innovate in electronics, Hobday (1995, p. 1189) rightly noted that "latecomer innovation began with incremental improvements to manufacturing process. As competences were learned, minor innovations to product designs were made and eventually, some new products were offered to the market." The improved models manufactured in follower countries often outperform the originals. History has shown that firms can succeed by imitation. Japan's economic development is a classic example. Having begun by imitation, Japanese manufacturers went on to master Western technology in selected areas. Specifically, after the technological revolution in semiconductors occurred in the USA, Japanese manufacturers initiated a phase of adaptive response, encompassing imitation, product improvement and mass production. After a period of time, Japan eventually emerged as an important source of innovations in its own right (Kingston 1977, p. 61).

Small-scale enterprises and subcontracting

A number of economists were very concerned with demonstrating that the larger the scale of production, the bigger the internal economies of scale and the more efficient the operation. They believed that small factories would be unable to compete with large foreign corporations. In particular, a well-known work on economic development even remarked: "No longer can one build small factories and hope to compete with foreign products" (Meier and Baldwin 1957, p. 323). Other economists, such as Tibor Scitovsky and Gunnar Myrdal, also showed a bias against small firms and stated that economic development resolves around a concept of "the bigger the better" (Ho 1992, p. 109). In fact, we observed that in most industries, firms of very different sizes survived. If the position of small firms were as gloomy as they claimed, then the Asian NIEs would never have achieved their present success, for the economies of this region of the world are composed significantly of small firms (Ho 1992, p. 109).

In their study of small industries in less developed countries, Staley and Morse (1965) suggested that small-scale enterprises could contribute positively to economic development. The United Nations Industrial Development Organisation (1969) showed that the promotion of small industries was justified because they served two broad objectives, namely, the economic objectives of dispersal of industry, diversification of industrial structure and increased utilisation of resources; and the social objectives of stimulating indigenous entrepreneurship, creation of employment and transformation of traditional industry (Ho 1992, pp. 110–11). In terms of employment, the World Bank (1978) concluded that "small manufacturing firms generate more direct and probably more indirect jobs per unit of invested capital on the average". Galbraith (1968) also suggested that a large corporation is less flexible because of the need for forward planning over lengthy periods of time to meet the production imperatives of modern technology. Furthermore, inflexibility is enhanced by technological specialisation in giant concerns as well as the need to control the market for its products. Implicit in Galbraith's arguments is the assumption that small-scale enterprises do not suffer from the same penalties of technological specialisation and corporate management.

Though we have cited several references favouring small business, we do not believe that being small is necessarily the best. However, the belief that "bigger is better" must be challenged. What we concede is that the advantages for small firms may still exist even if economies of scale prevail within a given branch. Given technological heterogeneity, small firms can compete successfully by employing some intermediate and labour intensive techniques which can be operated by cheaper and lower skilled labour. Also, size specific product differentiation may allow small firms to compete directly with large-scale concerns in producing similar but somewhat differentiated products. In the case of size specific vertical specialisation, small firms may have cost advantages in producing simple parts and components, in assembling diversified products, or in providing industrial services to orders with specific requirements.

There are a number of relationships between small-scale enterprises and large-scale undertakings. First, there is a competitive relationship between small firms and large firms in producing the same kinds of good for the same markets. Second, there is a relationship of peaceful co-existence between small and large firms in producing different kinds of goods for different markets. Third, there is a relationship of mutual aid when small and large firms cooperate in making the same products, with large concerns giving work to small subcontractors. To be flexible, large-scale industries have to be based on a diverse range of small and medium-sized supporting and auxiliary industries. After all, small and large enterprises are not mutually exclusive alternatives to efficient economic development. They can be mutually supportive (Ho 1992, p. 111).[18]

Such integration is done by subcontracting and is significant for economic development of Asian economies.[19] Klein (1977, p. 179) noted that subcontracting has important advantages "not only for static efficiency, but also for dynamic efficiency. The smaller the units in which competition can take place, the easier it is to enter an industry; and with easier entry, competition is more likely to thrive."

Since subcontracting involves voluntary vertical cooperation between firms, both sides can generally expect to benefit from such cooperation. Because this type of business relationship is a form of division of labour, there must be a certain loss of independence for the enterprises involved. Our major concern is to establish why a production takes the form of subcontracting. The solution may also explain why the Asian NIEs, such as Hong Kong, are dominated by this type of organisation.

The basic issue is related to the boundaries of the firm. In production, manufacturers face the choice of either purchasing components or services from the markets or organising that portion of the production and distribution within the organisation. If they choose the former, they are using the market or more precisely piece rate contracts (Cheung 1983). Subcontracting belongs to this category. Otherwise, production activities are vertically integrated.

In recent advances in economic theory, it has been further argued that the boundary of a firm depends on two crucial factors, namely transaction cost and organisational capability (Langlois and Robertson 1995; Langlois 1988, 1991). The relative importance of the two factors hinges on whether it is a long run or a short run.

In the short run, the core of a firm consists of "those assets that are synergistic and idiosyncratically related to each other" and "the idiosyncratically synergistic core of a firm consists primarily in knowledge and patterns of behaviour such as routines that are not readily communicated to outsiders, and in the people that embody them" (Langlois and Robertson 1995, p. 42). From this perspective, the core characteristics of a firm lie in both coordination and ownership integration. In broad terms, coordination of resources is needed to achieve synergy, and the idiosyncratic nature of the core assets means that they are not contestable.

The addition of further activities to the core depends on the relative transaction costs of internalising the activities or purchasing them on the market. In many cases, the decision to internalise an activity is designed to protect firms against opportunistic behaviours. In other cases, internalisation can be a strategic decision to add new activities to its core in a way that will develop new forms of idiosyncratic synergy which yield future rents (Langlois and Robertson 1995, p. 42).

Langlois and Robertson (1995, p. 43) argued that, in the long run, "the spread of knowledge should lead to a tendency towards the generalised spread of capabilities that both breaks down idiosyncrasy and reduces transaction costs". Hence it becomes more attractive for firms to buy inputs rather than produce them internally. As a result, we may find vertical disintegration as products mature. This implies that the desirability of vertical integration may depend on the existing array of capabilities already available in the economy. As Langlois and Robertson (1995, p. 43) put it: "When the existing arrangement of decentralised capabilities is very different from that required by a major systemic innovation, vertical integration which permits a quicker and cheaper creation of new capabilities may prove superior."

Langlois and Robertson's arguments may help to explain why subcontracting is widely adopted in a developing economy. We have argued that, due to given constraints, manufacturing firms in these economies will adopt product imitation strategies and that their production involves little innovation and hence little coordination among departments. Accordingly, vertical disintegration or subcontracting is chosen.

Spatial arbitrage: alertness to cost-reducing opportunities

Another type of Kirznerian entrepreneurial strategy involves spatial arbitrage. In Kirzner's sense, entrepreneurs are alert to cost reducing opportunities. For analytical convenience, two kinds of spatial arbitrage can be classified, namely, through trade and through production.

For the spatial arbitrage through trade, entrepreneurs perform the function of a middleman. This idea has been well documented in the economic literature.[20] The mainstream price theory in general simply portrays the middleman as an intermediary. But a middleman is more than just a firm or an organisation. He or she is an entrepreneurial agency. When entrepreneurs spot an unexploited trade opportunity, they are able to use their knowledge both to realise the gain and appropriate a proportion of it for themselves. As mentioned above, this gain is a pure entrepreneurial profit. It has nothing to do with factor payment but is a reward to entrepreneurial alertness. Following this argument, not only can entrepreneurs spot existing opportunities, but they can create trade opportunities among buyers and sellers.

Spatial arbitrage can also occur through shifts in production location. In the early stage of industrialisation, developing economies can compete internationally because of cheaper wages, lower rents and factor costs. As industrialisation proceeds, rising rentals, labour costs and other factor prices lower the profit margin. To remain competitive and profitable, manufacturers have to find ways to reduce costs. By relocating their production in lower cost regions, they are able to maintain profit margins. Gains can be obtained through a joint venture, licensing, acquisition of some local businesses, direct foreign investment or in the form of subcontracting. As discussed earlier, the choice of a contractual arrangement hinges on the capability of the firm, the appropriation of the benefits and more importantly, the cost of communicating with the contractors (Langlois 1988, pp. 635–57). Above all, it requires entrepreneurs, who are alert to opportunities of various kinds of contracts, to combine the specific assets into profitable production and fulfil coordinating functions.

Kirznerian entrepreneurial activities and structural change

Economic development occurs not only "because of the availability of new opportunities, but because of expanded awareness of existing opportunities" (Kirzner 1985, p. 74). Along this line of thinking, economic development can be analysed in two dimensions.

First, at a given period, output of a nation may be lower than its desired and possible level because opportunities remain unnoticed. Second, due to technical advance over time, the capacity of production increases. For this technical knowledge to be utilised, it is not enough that these opportunities exist. They must also be perceived. In short, entrepreneurial discovery is an important ingredient in economic development. Ting (1985, p. 20) correctly remarked that "entrepreneurs anticipate and exploit the opportunities of the constantly shifting comparative advantages in the global markets". As a result, the values of resources are altered and resources are shifted from areas of low to areas of high productivity and yield (Kim 1988, p. 183). Hence, the development process can be viewed as an alteration in entrepreneurial perception of the changing local and international comparative advantages. An alteration in entrepreneurial perception of opportunity will lead to a change in arbitrage activity and consequently a structural change of an economy.

To explain our argument, we modify Ray's four phases of economic development by including the entrepôt and trading activities. This revision fits the Asian NIEs better. The four phases of economic development are thus:

- agrarian or entrepôt society:
- early industrialisation
- mature industrialisation;
- service and high-technology economy (Ray 1988, p. 6).[21]

Understandably, there is a considerable overlap between phases. Our main purpose is to examine and illustrate the role of entrepreneurship in each stage.

In the early stages of industrialisation, developing countries are characterised by a relatively large population of unskilled labour, small amounts of capital, and limited natural resources (Lin and Tuan 1988, p. 163; Ting 1985, p. 6; Woronoff 1986, p. 294). People are engaged in agricultural activities such as farming and fishery. Later, perceiving that the value of the output from the manufacturing sector is higher than that from the agricultural sector, entrepreneurs shift resources from the farm sector to the industrial sector. Facing competition, some entrepreneurs in the rural sector notice that if they want to keep resources in agricultural activities, they have to move to some high market value crops such as oyster or scallop farming.

For city states like Singapore and Hong Kong, farming activities were very limited (Nyaw 1991, p. 183). Instead, they were involved in entrepôt trade, when

British and European entrepreneurs participated in the Far East trading in the nineteenth century (Ting 1985, p. 26).

Some indigenous entrepreneurs at the early stages of industrialisation perceived that they possessed some competitive advantages in labour intensive production. Therefore they started to manufacture goods such as simple plastic products, textiles, footwear and electronics so to take the advantage of low labour costs (Ting 1985, p. 9). Constrained by a small domestic market, limited natural resources and technological skill, local producers were content to be original equipment manufacturer (OEM) suppliers and produced for overseas buyers or sold their products to export houses. This is the origin of the so-called export oriented industrialisation strategy (Ting 1985, p. 13; Nyaw 1991, p. 188; Lau 1991, p. 439; Riedel 1988, p. 7). A characteristic of the OEM strategy, as Ernst and O'Connor (1989, p. 88) argued, is that "the products involved are generally very high volume ones, with the result that even if margins are thin, total earnings from such activities may be substantial". With relatively cheaper labour and rentals, manufacturers entered into activities that were no longer economically viable in the more advanced industrial economies. For instance, many relatively simple consumer products like transistor radios and wearing apparel had reached the maturity stage of their product life cycles in the USA (Ting 1985, p. 13).

In a dynamic economy, demand and supply are constantly changing. For small open economies like the Asian NIEs, manufacturers have to be alert to external shocks as well. If demand for a certain product diminishes, they have to be the first to sense the change and move out of the "sunset" industry quickly and re-orient their production towards other new production activities, say, from wigs to plastic flowers (Woronoff 1980, pp. 254–8). So entrepreneurs bring about a change in economic activity within the manufacturing sector itself. Resources are thus shifted from production of wigs to the production of plastic flowers because the market value of plastic flowers is now higher than that of wigs.

Another function of entrepreneurs is their ability to open new overseas markets. Having perceived that a certain foreign market is saturated, they will explore others. Riedel (1988, p. 73) argued that the Asian NIEs were able to find new markets for their traditional products in the EEC, Japan and other developing countries outside the Pacific region (mainly the Middle East).

Riedel (1988, p. 6) further argued that "the process of industrialisation is ... more than just the shifting of the activities away from primary industry, it also involves shifts over time in the structure of industry, following comparative advantage, from simple technology, labour intensive activities towards progressively more capital- and technology intensive branches".

From time to time entrepreneurs assess their competitive advantages. The fact is that producers in the Asian NIEs always encounter keen competition from their rivals, especially those from low cost regions (Woronoff 1986, p. 216). On the one hand, a general rise in wage and resource costs has undermined the NIEs' previous competitive advantages in labour intensive production. On the other hand, producers from some less developed countries are able to supply goods with even lower cost. As a result, NIEs' competitiveness in the traditional labour intensive products had declined relative to the other LDCs (Ting 1985, p. 164).

Given the difficulties, there are two alternatives for entrepreneurs to maintain their profitable production: First, learning from previous experiences and now equipped with the production skills, they can move away from labour intensive industries towards technology intensive industries and/or establish their own niche brand (Woronoff 1986, p. 215). The ability to manufacture niche products, to move from simple technology industry to sophisticated technology industry, and from low value added product to high value added product reflects economic progress. Accordingly, the country's export changes from labour intensive products to technology intensive products (Chen and Li 1991, p. xi). In this way, the Asian NIEs manage to catch up with the more advanced nations in their manufacturing development (Ting 1985, p. 34); while Chen (1987, p. 358) concluded that the change from labour intensive towards capital intensive products is "the natural and expected phenomena in the process of economic development, and fully consistent with a stage approach to comparative advantage". This study contended that the changing activities are more consistent with the theory of entrepreneurial discovery.

Second, entrepreneurs can relocate their production activities to less developed countries such as Sri Lanka, the Philippines and Malaysia, where the production costs are cheaper (Ting 1985, pp. 34, 44). Again a spatial arbitrage of price differentials requires entrepreneurial alertness. When manufacturing activities are relocated out of the country, domestic resources that were previously engaged in manufacturing production are now released for some other higher value uses, notably in the tertiary sector.

In summary, as manufacturers retain the production of some high value added products domestically, and relocate those simple technology and labour intensive activities to low cost regions, through the arrangements of joint venture, subcontracting and acquisition, the economy is able to develop into a regional coordinating and sourcing centre. A sophisticated regional division of labour emerges (Lee 1981, p. 2; Chen and Li 1991, p. x).

Changing economic activities during the development process is not only confined to the manufacturing sector, i.e. not only limited to the relocation of manufacturing activities to other regions nor merely moving towards some high quality product. It also involves inter-sectoral shifts, from manufacturing to the service sector.

When entrepreneurs in the Asian NIEs perceive higher profit margins in the service sector than in the manufacturing industry, they will attempt to arbitrage (Ting 1985, p. 35; Chen and Li 1991, p. x). Resources that are previously engaged in the manufacturing sector now give way to even higher value added activities, namely, banking and finance, real estate, hotel, communications and transport.

Like the developed nations, entrepreneurs in the Asian NIEs also expand their tertiary sector overseas, using the experience they previously gained. In other words, they now act as multinationals. Though some may invest in Europe and

North America, most of them for cultural reasons remain in the Asian Pacific regions (Chen 1983, 1989b). As the internationalisation of enterprises proceeds, the economy gradually evolves into a regional financial centre, serving its neighbouring nations. A new pattern of subregional division of labour has emerged. China, Malaysia, Thailand, the Philippines and Indonesia are catching up with the Asian newly industrialising nations in the labour intensive manufacture whereas the latter are catching up with Japan in technology and knowledge intensive products, in a flying geese pattern (Akamatsu 1961; Chen 1989b, pp. 34–47; Chen and Li 1991, pp. x, xvi).

The dynamic catching up process in late industrialising economies

The entrepreneurial framework of economic development helps to explain the catching up hypothesis formulated by some development economists such as Ames and Rosenberg (1963), Berliner (1966) and Abramovitz (1988). For instance, during the postwar period, the USA was considered as the leader, with Western European countries and Japan as followers. Recent attention has been placed on the impact of the advance of Japan and of the Asian newly industrialising economies on the old leaders in North America and Western Europe (Abramovitz 1988, p. 324).

As previously noted, the interactions of Schumpeterian and Kirznerian entrepreneurship have provided a source of dynamism in the world development process. Schumpeterian entrepreneurs have brought about a breakthrough in technology, management, marketing and organisation in advanced nations. Such activities are a creative response in the sense that pioneer entrepreneurs exert an initial major discontinuity with the past, establish new production functions and change the course of development irrevocably (Kingston 1977, pp. 26–30).

The creative response brought about by Schumpeterian entrepreneurship raises the productivity and income of developed nations to an unprecedented extent. When the works of pioneers in these economies are seen to be fruitful, entrepreneurs in developing economies will start investigating the possibilities of producing something similar so as to share these insights or rewards. In Akamatsu's terms, Schumpeterian entrepreneurs create a developing discrepancy in the world economy while Kirznerian entrepreneurs tend to resolve the discrepancy by capitalising on opportunities (Akamatsu 1961, pp. 214–15).

Cornwall (1977) noted that the crucial cause of rapid growth is the ability of countries to borrow technology from the industrial leaders. But the ability to borrow technology is a function not just of the distance from the world innovation frontier – the technology gap – but also and primarily of the existence of an "entrepreneurial class" keen and eager to exploit the available "world stock" of technology (Pavitt and Soete 1982, p. 122).

During the second half of the twentieth century, a large pool of knowledge was available to developing countries. Entrepreneurs in late industrialising economies simply examined what had been done before and imitated them. The imitators could adopt forms of technology which were not available to the pioneers when they were at the imitators' present position (Berliner 1966, p. 164; Dore 1973, p. 68).

As mentioned earlier, manufacturers in late industrialising nations initially do not intend to overtake advanced nations. They are content to follow the pioneers (Bolton 1993, p. 32). On many occasions, they even purposely delay adopting a new product or practice. There are several advantages in this strategy. The later the start, the more sophisticated the technology available for manufacturing. For example, latecomers do not have to invent the wheel all over again, nor have to repeat the whole process of trial and error which leads from Indian corn to the hybrid maize of Iowa (Dore 1973, p. 68). They can study the past performances of developed nations (Woronoff 1986, p. 290). They have a wide range of choices. It is generally agreed that learning and imitating are typically cheaper and faster than original discovery and testing. Followers can peek over the shoulders of pioneers to see what they are doing, then they can project into the future what will be possible when they reach the same point as their predecessors (Woronoff 1986, p. 286). Avoiding the mistakes made by pioneers, they can then decide whether to do things in the same way or in new improved ways (Ames and Rosenberg 1963, p. 18).

Latecomers can also avoid another cost incurred by pioneers. Early adopters may develop a wide range of standards and specifications which may in turn hamper the achievement of economies of scale in production (Ames and Rosenberg 1963, p. 18). In contrast, latecomers do not have to create the market for a new product. They can sell standard products in the existing market and therefore, quickly follow established standards. While the pioneers may consider switching to newer standards, due to the interrelated nature of technologies in production, they can do so only at a very high (transaction) cost (Ames and Rosenberg 1963, p. 19).[22] Perez and Soete (1988, p. 477) remarked that firms that have enjoyed great advantages in the now superseded technology systems face increasing costs in getting rid of the experience and the externalities of the "wrong" sort and in acquiring the new ones. The argument can be viewed from the dimension of capital structure. Abramovitz (1988, p. 337) argued that "the capital stock of a country consists of an intricate web of interlocking elements. They are built to fit together, and one cannot replace one part with more modern and efficient equipment without a costly rebuilding of other components ... the adaptation of old capital structures to new technologies may be a difficult and halting process."[23]

Following this argument, earlier commitments to certain forms of production also mean that the firms are using specific kinds of routine (Nelson and Winter 1982). Thus, institutional commitments induced by past development may stand as obstacles to further development (Abramovitz 1988, p. 337). As Dore (1973, p. 66) argued, the constraints operating in a country at one point of time will lead to an unique development path and such "differences in the process persist in differences in the structure of society well on into very advanced stages of industrialisation". As production costs in developed nations rise, producers are forced to invest in other regions with lower costs. While more and more of the manufacturing is done abroad, they are losing those industries at home. When firms in late industrialising economies become proficient enough to export, they can capture the markets previously engaged by firms from developed nations (Woronoff 1986, p. 336).

It is true that producers in late industrialising nations initially rely on cheaper labour for their competitive edge. However, it is not easy to identify potential industries because profit can only be realised in the future. Thus, it requires entrepreneurs' imagination to discover and create them. With profit as their guiding principle, they proceed by trial and error. As Woronoff put it: "they had one eye on the plan, the other on the balance sheet" (Woronoff 1986, p. 213). Economic calculation via market signals guides their choices (Mises 1949).

Kirznerian entrepreneurs do not limit themselves to those sectors where cheaper labour has an obvious advantage. They also explore profit opportunities through the utilisation of more sophisticated technology from overseas. Kirznerian entrepreneurs adapt new techniques by trial and error. Mistakes may be painful and costly, but if foreign technologies are successfully adopted, benefits from the new opportunities will be exploited. Increased specialisation and the accumulation of know-how enable production to move along the learning. Some of them might increase their efforts in R&D and move away from pure copying (Woronoff 1986, pp. 231–2). On the other hand, to gain overseas customers, it is necessary for them to be alert to foreign conditions, to know more about the trends and fashions in advanced countries. Furthermore, they have to be familiar with other related products, new machinery and techniques, and different ways of combining production factors. Also they need to learn how modern corporations are run and adopt these lessons for themselves. In general, they have to find out what is going on in advanced economies and to identify new products or innovations so that they can imitate or modify them later. More importantly, they have to choose suitable combinations of quality and price carefully as they move up the high value added product market (Woronoff 1986, pp. 233–5). Hence, catching up means that they eventually sell more sophisticated goods with better design, greater reliability and longer durability, but at a cheaper price (Woronoff 1986, p. 216).

In summary, Kirznerian entrepreneurs in late industrialising economies first "duplicate" foreign products at lower costs made possible through cheaper labour. Once established in the market, they then enhance productivity and quality by introducing better machinery and managerial techniques. Having begun by imitating, they later innovate (Ting 1985, p. 96). Often they are able to outsell multinational firms in the Third World and even penetrate Western markets so aggressively that some of their competitors collapse (Woronoff 1986, p. 360). These entrepreneurial efforts have enabled the Asian NIEs to catch up with more advanced nations.

PROPOSITIONS AND METHODOLOGY

The principal propositions

With the entrepreneurial perspective of economic development developed in the last section, five major propositions with respect to Hong Kong can now be put forward. They are listed as follows:

- **Proposition 1:** Hong Kong is an entrepreneurial economy.
- **Proposition 2:** The Hong Kong environment favours the development of Kirznerian entrepreneurship over Schumpeterian entrepreneurship.
- **Proposition 3:** Kirznerian entrepreneurship is manifested in the forms of small scale enterprise, subcontracting, product imitation and spatial arbitrage.
- **Proposition 4:** Over time, Kirznerian entrepreneurial activities lead to the structural transformation of the economy.
- **Proposition 5:** The outstanding performance of Kirznerian entrepreneurs has enabled Hong Kong to catch up with economically more advanced nations

Methodology: the integration of micro and macro analysis

The empirical study will include both micro and macro levels. C. Wright Mills (1963) argued that there are two styles of economic analysis, namely the molecular and the macroscopic styles. For Mills, research which focuses either purely on the molecular level or purely on the macroscopic level is inadequate. If the economic problem is molecular but the explanation is macroscopic, the analysis suffers from the error of falsely concretising a concept. When the problem is macroscopic but the solution is molecular, the analysis is over-generalised. Therefore, Mills (1963, p. 563) maintains that if we want to present a clear and convincing exposition, we must "shuttle between macroscopic and molecular levels in instituting the problem and in explaining it". Porter (1991a, p. 109) also holds the similar view that economic analysis must deal simultaneously with the firm itself as well as the industry and broader environment in which it operates.

Following Mills and Porter, this study undertakes both micro and macro analyses. It examines manufacturing firms in the textile, garment and electronics industries (Chapters 5 and 6), the manufacturing sector (Chapter 4) and the aggregate economy (Chapters 3 and 7).

The electronics, textile and garment industries were chosen for our investigation because, first, they are two leading manufacturing industries in Hong Kong (Redding 1994, pp. 71–89). They can best illustrate the industrial development of Hong Kong. By examining these industries, we can gain some insights into the industrialisation and catching up process of the economy. Second, the products of these industries are mainly exported and are therefore exposed to severe international competition. Hence, the kind of entrepreneurial strategies adopted by manufacturers is of utmost importance to their survival. Furthermore, these industries can be used to demonstrate the global division of labour, the transfer

43

of technology and the international coordination of economic activities. Third, the rapid technological change in electronics products and the fashion changes in garments have significant implications for product strategies, management, marketing and organisational forms.

Questionnaire survey and case studies

The data required for the empirical analysis were collected in three separate ways, namely a questionnaire survey, case studies and other primary and secondary documentary sources. The field study absorbed more than eight months in Hong Kong, from 16 December 1993 to 31 August 1994. The survey and the interviews were facilitated by affiliation with the Centre of Asian Studies, University of Hong Kong.

The questionnaire

The aim of the questionnaire survey was to obtain opinions on a few issues from a large group of entrepreneurs. Specifically it was used to collect data regarding:

- the number of the firms that employ a particular kind of technology strategy;
- the performances of the firms as a result of using a particular strategy;
- the reasons for adopting it.

The target respondents of this survey were the owners of the manufacturing firms. The survey was conducted over a period of five months. The Hong Kong Government Census and Statistics Department supplied a list of the names and addresses of a 20 per cent sample of firms from each of two industries: electronics, and textile and garment. From this list, the researcher drew a sample of 50 companies from each industry. The sample comprised firms located in the major industrial areas of Hong Kong, namely, Shum Shui Po, Kwun Tong/Kowloon Bay, Hungham/Tokwawan and Tsuen Wan. All firms in the sample were owned by local Chinese entrepreneurs, though many of them had cooperated with foreign multinational corporations in the form of subcontracting, and original equipment manufacturer (OEM). There is no foreign firm in the sample.[24] In terms of firm size, 72 per cent of the textile and garment firms in the sample are small, i.e. employing less than 50 people; while in the electronics industry, 63 per cent of the sampled firms are small. For the total manufacturing industry in Hong Kong in 1992, nearly 95 per cent of the firms were small (i.e. employing less than 50 people). Because of the resource constraints in the field work, the sample does not constitute a random sample, and the small size of the sample (50 firms in each of two industries) does not justify the use of more sophisticated statistical techniques in the analysis of the collected information.

One week before the visits, letters of introduction explaining the purpose of the survey were sent to all establishments in the sample. This was followed up by an attempt to contact the owners of the companies by telephone, and a request for an interview was made. When the request was accepted, interviews were conducted, guided by a questionnaire. This process was repeated until 50 firms from each industry were interviewed successfully. The interviews were conducted in Cantonese. There were three cases in which the questionnaire was returned by post, as requested by the owners of the firms.

The questionnaire was composed mainly of structured responses, though several questions were open ended, permitting the entrepreneurs to express their views. The questionnaire, which was originally developed by Sit *et al.* (1979, 1989), was modified to meet the requirements of this study. It was also revised to reduce ambiguities (Goode and Hatt 1952, pp. 138–45; Babbie 1973, pp. 140–51; Kane 1985, pp. 72–89). A total of 31 questions was asked (see Appendix 1). A pre-test was conducted in ten factories from two industries and the questionnaire was subsequently modified before a formal survey was performed (Goode and Hatt 1952, pp. 145–7). Each survey interview took an average of 20 minutes, though several cases took around 30 minutes.

The case studies

While the questionnaire survey was intended to obtain opinions from a large sample, the case studies allowed a deeper understanding of the issues over time. Yin (1994, p. 9) argued that case studies are the preferred strategy "when a 'how' and 'why' question is being asked about a contemporary set of events over which the investigator has little control or no control".[25]

The materials for case studies in the electronics and textile/garment industries were obtained from two sources, namely published documents, for example, a company handbook or a commercial directory (see below), and direct in-depth interviews. The latter allow researchers to probe an issue over a period of time.[26] Hence, the choice of entrepreneurial strategies over time can be analysed (Goode and Hatt 1952, p. 334).

For each of the industries, five case studies were undertaken. The selection of the firms was guided by a prior understanding of the companies' backgrounds. This information was obtained from published sources such as company directories and handbooks. The choice was unavoidably influenced by the willingness of the owners to cooperate. The selected firms are all local Chinese firms and have been established for at least five years.

The length for the first meeting in each case study ranges from 1 hour to 1 hour and 30 minutes. It involved an interview with the founder, (sometimes together with his/her assistants), and visits to the workshops (in most cases). The interviews were recorded on a tape recorder.[27] Annual reports and other publications of the companies were always asked for, though these were not always available. Subsequent communications with the owners, their assistants or marketing managers were made to clarify some points relating to the company strategies or to request more information.

The major difficulty in this fieldwork was to obtain the owners' approval. Some companies rejected the requests, giving excuses. Others simply did not reply. In addition, though some firms agreed to an interview, it was not easy to arrange an appointment. The interview was often postponed because the owners were engaged in other matters. Owners' overseas trips could delay the interview for several months, particularly as many owners now spent most of their time on their business in mainland China. Nevertheless, most owners were willing to express their views during the interview, though one showed more caution in releasing his company's documents because it planned to become a listed company. The results of the case studies are reported in Appendix 2.

The documentary sources

The materials collected from the survey and the case studies are "subject to the common problems of bias, poor recall, and poor or inaccurate articulation" (Yin 1994, p. 85), so their reliability was checked against published sources including:

- company profiles and annual reports;
- directories, handbooks and manuals in manufacturing, commerce and industry such as *The Directory of Hong Kong Industries*,[28] *Hong Kong Economic Yearbook, Members' Directory of the Federation of Hong Kong Industries*, and *Hong Kong Smaller Companies Review;*
- books on biographies of entrepreneurs such as *Hong Kong New Rich*, and *Hong Kong Entrepreneurs;*
- newspapers and magazines such as *Hongkong Industrialist, Capital, Asiaweek; Far Eastern Economic Review, Hong Kong Economic Journal Monthly, Economic Reporter;* and *Economic Digest , International Business Week*, and *Fortune;*
- professional trade journals and periodicals such as *Electronics Business Asia* and *The Textile and Garment Journal.*

Most of the above published documents were obtained from the University of Hong Kong Library. The Hong Kong section of the library holds a very comprehensive collection of materials relating to Hong Kong. Despite the resource constraints of this field work, useful data were collected. Equipped with information on the operations of local enterprises, we can then apply the concept of Kirznerian entrepreneurship to explain Hong Kong's growth experience. The empirical findings will be presented in the following chapters.

NOTES

1 Though Schumpeter was an admirer of Leon Walras, his dissatisfaction with Walrasian theories, in particular, and the neoclassical framework in general are well documented in his works.
2 The Hayekian theory of rules and institutions is discussed in Hayek (1967, 1978a, b).
3 The term "entrepreneur" was not indexed in their seminal work: *An Evolutionary Theory of Economic Change*. See Nelson and Winter (1982).

4 Baumol and Kirzner are both associated with New York University where the Centre for Entrepreneurial Studies is located.

5 De Bono (1992, p. 15) argued that every valuable creative idea must always be logical in hindsight.

6 Such an argument has raised a number of criticisms both from within and outside the Austrian camps. Specifically, White (1976) commented that Kirzner failed to recognise the highly important part played by entrepreneurial imagination. Defending his position, Kirzner subsequently differentiated two kinds of markets, namely single-period and multi-period markets (Kirzner 1982). For the multi-period market, with the passage of time and uncertainty, Kirzner accepted the elements of creativeness and imagination into his model. Hence, "incentive for the market entrepreneurship along the intertemporal dimension is provided not by arbitrage profits generated by imperfectly coordinated present markets but more generally, by the speculative profits generated by the as yet imperfectly coordinated market situations in the sequence of time" (Kirzner 1982, p. 154). In a multi-period situation, the entrepreneur "must introduce ... his own creative actions, in fact construct the future as he wishes it to be" (Kirzner 1982, p. 63). Accordingly, his position comes closer to Schumpeter's vision. However, in a personal correspondence to the author (13 January 1994), Kirzner remarked that he preferred to consider Kirznerian entrepreneurship as a subset of entrepreneurship, confined to those activities which take advantage of existing scattered knowledge.

7 Nelson and Winter (1982, p. 275), drawing the argument from Schumpeter, described the interaction of the innovative and imitative firms in the market process as follows: "a central aspect of dynamic competition is that some firms deliberately strive to be leaders in technological innovations, while others attempt to keep up by imitating the success of the leaders".

8 For a detailed discussion of the advantages of being a latecomer, see the later section of this chapter.

9 For example, see Redding (1988, 1990); Wong (1989); Siu and Martin (1992).

10 For a detail account of the impact of colonialism on the formation of an entrepreneurial society in Hong Kong in terms of the power, economic, social and knowledge structures, see Tam and Redding (1993, pp. 158–76).

11 Vesper (1990, p. 6) called these people "pattern multipliers".

12 This idea will be fully elaborated later in this chapter.

13 According to Nelson and Winter (1982, p. 123), there are two cases of copying, namely cooperative and non-cooperative. Cooperative copying can be either a joint venture, subcontracting or licensing. Non-cooperative copying means that the imitator cannot directly observe what goes on in the production. When a problem arises in copying, it is not possible to resolve it by closer scrutiny of the original.

14 The term OEM originated in the 1950s among computer makers that used subcontractors (called the OEM) to assemble equipment for them. It was later adopted by US chip companies in the 1960s who used OEMs to assemble and test semi-conductors (Hobday 1995, p. 1190).

15 For a discussion of the economic functions of brandname, see Alchian and Allen (1983, pp. 238–9).

16 If firms sell products without promoting their brands, this means that they attempt to gain customers through very low prices. However, the profit margin is slim. On the other hand, if they promote their own brands, then consumers" confidence in the product is the major concern. To gain customers' confidence, imitators in developing countries follow closely the design style and the packaging of other successful branded products from overseas and try to avoid the locally made image. For instance, they may use a German name for their brand name. They strive to promote a high quality and a high class image for their products similar to those manufactured from the technologically advanced nations.

17 Broehl (1982, p. 267) argued that the ability to link together individual pieces of information distinguishes Kirznerian entrepreneurship.

18 We can take an excellent example from Japan. Japan had successfully integrated small firms into the large-scale industrial network by maintaining a mutually beneficial dualistic structure long after its industrial take-off (Ho 1992, p. 111).

19 Subcontracting is defined by the United Nations as "an arrangement between two manufacturing units, under which one of the units (the subcontractor) provides the other (the principal), on agreed terms and conditions, with products (components or final goods) that are used or marketed by the principal under his sole responsibility. Subcontracting orders may include the processing, transformation or finishing of materials or parts by the subcontractor at the request of the contractor. Subcontracting can be domestic, when both units work in the same country. Otherwise it is international" (UNCTAD 1985, p. 2).

20 For an exposition of the role of the middleman in Kirznerian entrepreneurial context, see Ricketts (1987, pp. 51–63).

21 Ray's original stages of economic development consists of (1) agrarian or resource society; (2) early industrialisation; (3) mature industrialisation; (4) service and high-technology economy. See Ray (1988, p. 6). Hill classified a three-stage transformation process in Asian manufacturing. In the early stage of industrialisation, the manufacturing sector consists predominantly of simple processing and resource-based activities. As capital accumulation proceeds, a range of non-resource-based activities emerges, initially unskilled labour intensive but subsequently of products which are more capital and technology intensive. See Ariff and Hill (1985, p. 156).

22 Rosenberg (1976) and Nelson and Winter (1977) have made some pertinent comments on the problems of inter-relatedness of innovations and natural trajectories of technology.

23 The issue of capital structure in production has been neglected by Keynesian economists in their aggregate analysis but has long been recognised by Austrian economists. The latter approach the issues from the subjectivism, uncertainty, errors, knowledge and expectation. In particular, Lachmann (1956, p. 12) summarised his argument as follows: "Heterogeneity of capital means heterogeneity in use; heterogeneity in use implies multiple specificity; multiple specificity implies complementary; complementary implies capital combinations; capital combinations form the elements of the capital structure." Therefore, specificity and complementary nature of capital structure pose a "switching problem" during the market process, a key concept in the Cambridge Controversies.

24 Foreign manufacturing firms in Hong Kong represented only 1 per cent of manufacturing industry in terms of the number of establishments (Ho 1992, p. 139). In 1992, there were more than 472 foreign manufacturing establishments in Hong Kong, of which 82 firms (17.4 per cent of the total) were electronics firms and 96 firms (20.3 per cent of the total) were textile or garment firms (Hong Kong Government Industry Department 1993, p. 18). This does not mean that foreign multinational firms have played an insignificant role in Hong Kong's manufacturing industry. On the contrary, they have exerted quite a substantial influence on local entrepreneurship.

25 Similarly, Siu and Martin (1992, p. 56) argued that while questionnaire surveys may be useful for broad interpretation, they are not entirely effective in understanding the actions, meanings and intentions of the entrepreneurs. Long and McMullan (1984, pp. 575–9) argued that while survey research design may be appropriate for identifying factors which influence people's perception of new venture ideas, it does not permit the in-depth exploration required to determine whether entrepreneurs have experienced a sense of alertness when first envisaging a new venture opportunity.

26 For a discussion of interviewing techniques, see Goode and Hatt (1952, pp. 184–208) and Kane (1985, pp. 68–71).

27 For an account of the problems associated with the use of tape recorder during a interview, see Yin (1994, p. 86).

28 *The Directory of Hong Kong's Industries* provides comprehensive and up-to-date information on manufacturing industries in Hong Kong. It has been compiled on the basis of the latest list of local manufacturing establishments provided by the Census and Statistics Department and other lists of member firms, maintained by the Hong Kong government and industrial organisations. The directory provides a detailed reference to about 6,000 major manufacturing companies in Hong Kong. It contains an alphabetical list of manufacturing companies providing readers with the page number of the manufacturing companies about which he or she wishes to obtain company information. The basic information for every manufacturing company listed includes: full names of companies in English and Chinese, registered address, telephone number, name of proprietors/ directors, employment size of the companies in Hong Kong and outside Hong Kong, floor space, products manufactured/subcontracted works rendered, paid up capital, annual turnovers and brand names, nature of ownership, major markets, year of establishment, local of branch offices and trademarks.

3

THE HONG KONG
ENVIRONMENT AND
ENTREPRENEURSHIP

HONG KONG: AN ENTREPRENEURIAL SOCIETY

The first proposition of this study is that Hong Kong is an entrepreneurial society. It was argued in Chapter 2 that an entrepreneurial economy encourages certain traits, such as a profit-seeking mentality and a tendency towards venture initiation.

The profit-seeking mentality

Hong Kong has a long tradition of approving profit-seeking (King 1987, p. 59). Rafferty (1991, p. 167) once noted that "Hong Kong, more than any other place in the world, is dedicated to the pursuit of making money, more money." Thus, a profit-seeking mentality can be observed in everyday life. Most Hong Kong households worship the God of Fortune (King 1987, p. 59; Siu and Martin 1992, p. 90). They also greet each other with "Kung He Fat Choy" [wish you rich] in Chinese New Year celebrations (Hughes 1968, p. 51; Chau 1993, p. 26). Wealthy people bid for the car licence number eight because it means rich in Cantonese. Some name their companies or even their children with words meaning rich and wealthy. Affluent families and their business empires are highly regarded. Successful entrepreneurs, such as Li Ka-Shing, are modelled as business heroes (Ho 1992, p. 123).[1] In the surveys conducted by Sit *et al.* (1979, 1989), Hong Kong small manufacturers were asked about the motivations for starting a business. The findings indicated that profit was their most important reason (see Table 3.1). Similarly, in a survey conducted by Lau (1982), when Hong Kong people were asked about their criteria for choosing a job, approximately 60 per cent of them stated that a high salary was their major concern. Such an attitude was described as pragmatic or utilitarian oriented by political scientists, M. Topley, A. King and S.K. Lau (King 1987, pp. 61–2).

Venture initiation and spin-off

Hong Kong people are very enthusiastic to establish their own businesses (Ho 1992, p. 123). According to Wong (1988a, p. 143), a common ideal of the majority of residents is to become one's own boss. Especially in the Shanghainese tradition,

Table 3.1 Distribution of entrepreneurs' motivation for starting their businesses (%)

Motivations	1978	1987
Profit	37.0	28.1
Chance	29.5	24.8
Survival	17.0	17.2
Inheritance	6.5	3.6
Autonomy	5.5	8.8
Prospect	0.0	15.7
Others	4.5	1.8
Total	100.0	100.0
No. of entrepreneurs	[413]	[274]

Source: Sit and Wong 1989, p. 113.

it is said that "a Shanghainese at forty who has not yet made himself the owner of a firm is a failure, a good-for-nothing". Wong's study in the cotton spinning industry revealed that two-thirds of the entrepreneurs chose the option of becoming the owner-manager of a smaller firm rather than the senior executive of a large corporation if both alternatives were available to them early in their career.

Spin-offs are very common in Hong Kong's manufacturing industry (Woronoff 1980, p. 125; Lam and Lee 1992, p. 112). The managing director of a software company in Hong Kong who frequently lost experienced programmers once complained that "Hong Kong people are too keen to be a boss" (*Economic Reporter* 1991a, p. 20). It is not unusual for employees, after working in a company for several months or half a year and being familiar with the products and customers, to open another similar company and compete with their former employers. Geiger and Geiger (1975, p. 75) once claimed that "typically, the new Hong Kong entrepreneurs are former employees of existing manufacturing establishments, usually technicians, foremen and skilled workmen or junior managers, salesmen and other office personnel". Sit *et al.* (1979, p. 294) found that over 60 per cent of the small entrepreneurs in both the electronics and garment industries acknowledged that

Table 3.2 Types of industry of the first job of entrepreneurs and their present enterprises

Types of industry of the first job of entrepreneurs	Present industry, % of total					
	Wearing apparel	Textiles	Plastics	Electronics	Machinery	All
Garment/textiles	63.5	34.2	5.3	9.1	0.0	37.3
Plastics	0.5	2.6	43.0	9.1	0.0	13.6
Electronics	2.0	5.2	4.4	63.6	25.0	7.7
Metal	0.0	0.0	4.4	4.5	0.0	1.5
Others	34.0	57.9	43.0	13.6	75.0	39.9
Total	100.0	100.0	100.0	100.0	100.0	100.0
No. of entrepreneurs	[197]	[38]	[114]	[22]	[20]	[391]

Source: Sit *et al.* 1979, p. 295.

Table 3.3 Reasons for leaving first job

Reasons	Distribution %
To open a factory	65.0
For a change of environment	7.4
Low wages/no prospects	6.0
They had the chance	4.6
Factory closed	3.7
Others	13.4
Total	100.0
No. of entrepreneurs	[217]

Source: Sit and Wong 1989, p. 107.

their first job had a direct bearing on their present enterprises (Table 3.2). In 1989, when the manufacturers were asked why they left their first job, 65 per cent of them replied that they had opened a factory (Sit and Wong 1987, p. 107; Table 3.3).

Establishment and employment

The above arguments can be further substantiated by examining the establishment–employment ratios. The greater the number of entrepreneurs in an economy, the higher the number of businesses (Lee and Low 1990, p. 10). On this point, Woronoff commented as follows:

> It should not be surprising to find a proliferation of business establishments. By 1979, there are well over 220,000 or one for every twenty people or so. This is quite high even when compared to a bastion of capitalism like the United States, where the ratio was about half of that. There are still about 35,000 new firms founded every year and another 25,000 disappeared. Since the end of the War, over half a million firms had been founded, of which only about a third survived. Yet the number of new attempts has consistently outweighed the failures and the total keeps on rising while, in other places, it has long since begun to decline ... If your definition [of capitalists] implies that the person is his own boss, as opposed to someone else's employee, then mention can be made of the fact that self-employed hawkers represent some 2.2 per cent of the working population. Self-employed in other categories, such as doctors, lawyers, and so on, amounted to as much as 4.1 per cent. But much more impressive is the large number of employers, 4.1 per cent of the working population, as compared to the number of employees, namely 85.4 per cent. There are not many countries where the ratio of employers to employees is as high as 1:21 and that employers plus self-employed to employees is as good as 1:8.
>
> (Woronoff 1980, p. 115)

Table 3.4 A comparison of the establishment–population ratios among Hong Kong, Singapore and Taiwan, 1986

Activities	Hong Kong	Singapore	Taiwan
Manufacturing	15,636	3,456	44,413
Commerce	105,110	36,621	355,335
Transport and communications	3,691	5,611	34,906
Financial, insurance, real estate and business services	16,959	11,335	21,564
Social and other services	19,642	13,600	75,207
Total of above	161,038	70,623	531,425
Population (000s)	5,533	2,586	19,455
Establishments per 1,000 people	29.1	27.3	27.3

Source: Lee and Low 1990, p. 32.

In this regard, Hong Kong is also compared favourably to other Asian NIEs. According to Lee and Low (1990, p. 10) in 1986 the number of manufacturing establishments (with at least ten workers) per thousand people in Hong Kong (29.1) was slightly higher than in Taiwan (27.3) and in Singapore (27.3) (see Table 3.4). It was noted by Lee and Low (1990) that their data excluded those establishments with employment of less than ten workers. If these were included, the comparison would be even more favourable to Hong Kong.[2]

The company formation rate

Table 3.5 yields further insights by comparing the number of companies registered, the number of new businesses incorporated, and the business failure rates between Hong Kong and the USA. The USA has been regarded as an entrepreneurial economy (Drucker 1984, pp. 58–64; Casson 1990, p. 145). However, in terms of the number of firms per 10,000 people, in 1992, Hong Kong (618) had a higher ratio than the USA (344). In terms of new firms registered per 10,000 people, in 1992, Hong Kong (10.11) also had a higher start-up rate than the USA (3.9), indicating that Hong Kong was even more "entrepreneurial" than the USA.

The failure rate can also help to reinforce our arguments. Table 3.5 also shows that in 1992 Hong Kong (118) had a slightly higher failure rate than the USA (109). Hong Kong has been well known for its flexibility in production (Sung 1987). If business people perceive little prospect for their enterprises, they will move rapidly to other businesses. Particularly, for the small and medium-sized firms, they have little sense of belonging to any one industry. The owners behave like grasshoppers to exploit profit opportunities (Lam and Lee 1992, pp. 107–24). Hence both the high start-up rate and the high failure rate reflect the dynamics of Hong Kong's entrepreneurs.

Table 3.5 A comparison of the numbers of firms, new incorporation rates and failure rates in Hong Kong and the USA, 1981–92

Year	Population (1,000)	No. of firms registered	New firms	No. of failures	No. of firms per 10,000 people	New firms per 1,000 people	No. of failures per 10,000 firms
Hong Kong							
1981	5,183	97,808	14,850	887	188.7	2.87	90
1982	5,345	109,601	12,679	966	208.2	2.41	92
1983	5,345	120,552	11,986	1,372	225.5	2.24	103
1984	5,398	132,727	14,080	1,241	245.9	2.61	111
1985	5,456	149,728	17,990	1,757	274.4	3.30	113
1986	5,533	16,422	418,722	2,466	296.8	3.38	154
1987	5,613	188,351	2,702	42,897	335.6	4.85	155
1988	5,681	220,469	34,548	2,430	388.0	6.08	110
1989	5,782	245,030	27,371	2,810	423.8	4.73	115
1990	5,801	270,292	28,862	3,600	466.0	4.98	133
1991	5,912	313,502	48,163	4,953	530.0	8.25	158
1992	6,100	370,811	61,685	4,376	618.0	10.11	118
USA							
1981	229,966	2,745	581,000	16,794	119.4	2.53	611
1982	232,188	2,806	566,000	24,908	120.9	2.45	88
1983	234,307	2,851	602,000	31,334	121.7	2.57	110
1984	2,363	484,885	635,000	52,078	206.7	2.68	107
1985	238,466	4,990	663,000	57,078	209.3	2.78	115
1986	240,651	5,119	702,000	61,616	212.7	2.92	120
1987	242,804	6,004	685,000	61,111	247.3	2.82	102
1988	245,021	5,804	685,000	57,098	236.9	2.80	98
1989	247,342	7,694	677,000	50,361	311.1	2.74	65
1990	249,908	8,038	647,000	60,747	322.6	2.59	74
1991	252,648	8,218	629,000	881,40	325.3	3.49	107
1992	255,458	8,805	667,000	97,069	344.0	3.90	109

Source: Hong Kong Government, *Registrar General Annual Departmental Report*, various issues; *Statistical Abstract of the United States 1994*, Austin, Texas: The Reference Press, pp. 8, 547.

Scholars' views

The argument that Hong Kong is one of the most dynamic entrepreneurial societies in the world can also be evidenced from the following commentaries. Owen (1971, p. 133) stated that Hong Kong was overendowed with entrepreneurship. Geiger and Geiger (1975, p. 13) argued that the dynamism of Hong Kong entrepreneurs was reflected in the city-state's steadily improving standard of living and popular welfare. Chen (1979, p. 183) argued that the supply of entrepreneurs was exceptionally plentiful in Hong Kong. Woronoff stated that:

> Hong Kong's entrepreneurs seem to have done quite well. This applies to all of them, the Chinese, expatriates and Indians. They certainly compare favourably to businessmen in other parts of the world and also to others of their own race or nationality back home. They are much more dynamic and ... are willing to launch into new ventures and take necessary risk.
>
> (Woronoff 1980, p. 165)

In explaining why Hong Kong's industry had been able to expand rapidly, Cheng (1982, p. 140) maintained that the Colony "has a group of highly sophisticated entrepreneurs". Comparing the role of government of the four Asian NIEs (Hong Kong, Korea, Taiwan and Singapore), Clarke and Cable (1982, p. 29) stated that "the extent of government involvement will vary considerably from the more 'organised' and 'dirigiste' approach of South Korea to the more entrepreneurial style of Hong Kong, with the other two countries [Singapore and Taiwan] somewhere between these extremes". Similarly, Pang (1988, p. 230) noted that Hong Kong's development pattern, which is characterised by a high dependence on small and adaptable entrepreneurs to find new business opportunities and a minimal involvement of the government in production, may be described as the result of entrepreneurial capitalism. King (1990, p. 116) dramatically remarked that "[Hong Kong] people were entrepreneurial magicians; they had created a great industrial city on a bare rock in the South China Sea; show them another rock – in Scotland, in Australia – and they could do it again". Ho (1992, p. 27) also argued that Hong Kong has been developed into a highly adaptive, entrepreneurial and competitive economy. Accepting the view that Hong Kong is an entrepreneurial society, Tam and Redding (1993, pp. 158–76) further showed how Hong Kong had been transformed into an entrepreneurially friendly society. Chau recently remarked that:

> Hong Kong was founded 150 years ago by traders. For the next hundred years, it remained a city of merchants. ... Industrialisation was initiated by migrant industrialists ... But the spread of industrialisation, the initiation of a self-sustaining process of industrial development, was the work of local businessmen. ... They have maintained a merchant's mentality, and have operated much ... as "merchant entrepreneurs".
>
> (Chau 1993, p. 23)

55

Apart from the scholarly works, outstanding Hong Kong entrepreneurs have been frequently highlighted in major international magazines and newspapers. For instance, *Fortune* (1987) listed the two Hong Kong Chinese entrepreneurs, Li Ka Shing and Y. K. Pao, as two of the 100 wealthiest people in the world. In 1993, Li, with personal wealth of US$5.8 billion, was ranked number 16 by the journal. It must be stressed that, unlike other billionaires in the list who are either a royal family member (e.g. Queen Elizabeth II of England), head of state or owner of a petroleum empire (e.g. Sultan Hassanal Bolkiah of Brunei or King Fahd of Saudi Arabia), the two Hong Kong businessmen accumulated their wealth solely through their entrepreneurship.

Likewise, in the 1993 Global 1000 Largest Corporations List prepared by *International Business Week* (1993, pp. 76–80), 21 companies came from Hong Kong. Their ranks in the list range from 91, with market value US$16,462 million to 928 with market value US$928 million. Of these 21 firms, more than half were owned by Chinese entrepreneurs. Again when the mass media discuss how entrepreneurs shape the world economy, they often cite Hong Kong as an illustration. For instance, recently a special report on entrepreneurship (Byrne 1993, p. 53) wrote "the spirit of enterprise is increasingly celebrated around the globe, whether in Hong Kong, where free-wheeling entrepreneurship is moving across the border into China's Guangdong and Fujian provinces, or in Germany, where that country's midsize companies – the so-called 'Mittelstand' – are a dynamic engine of growth".

Likewise, in 1994, Hong Kong topped *Fortune*'s List of Best Cities in the world for businesses. The journal described how Hong Kong residents – both ethnic Chinese and Westerners – "are well equipped to seize the many opportunities unfolding before them ... they possess more of the entrepreneurial energy and speed ... than managers and dealmakers in the west" (*Fortune* 1994, p. 69). All this evidence indicates that Hong Kong is an entrepreneurial society.

Finally, it must be emphasised that, though most studies agreed that Hong Kong is an entrepreneurial city, only a few scholars in economics have taken a serious look into the role of entrepreneurship in the economic development of Hong Kong. This research fills such a gap.

THE HONG KONG ENVIRONMENT AND KIRZNERIAN ENTREPRENEURSHIP

Why is Hong Kong able to produce so many entrepreneurs? The answer is related to the Hong Kong environment. Lau and Kuan (1988) argued that the cultural, ethnic, sociological and political factors in Hong Kong were found to be favourable to the supply of entrepreneurship in the course of its economic development. Ho (1992, p. 27) argued that an influx of management expertise, hardworking migrants from China, heritage in the entrepôt trade in the form of a well-developed physical, commercial and financial infrastructure, a very stable yet flexible institutional framework in the form of an efficient and well-disciplined bureaucracy, an efficient and relatively non-arbitrary legal system, free trade and free enterprise, a strategic geographical location and an excellent port situated in a good time zone are all important factors that have enabled Hong Kong to develop into a highly adaptive and entrepreneurial economy. This study will analyse how Hong Kong's political, economic and cultural factors influence the supply of entrepreneurship in general and Kirznerian entrepreneurship in particular.

Political factors

Hong Kong has been a British colony for more than 150 years. Under the colonial administration, the top positions in the civil service had been dominated by British government expatriates. There was little chance for the Hong Kong Chinese to move up to the top decision-making posts.[3] Lau (1982, pp. 68–72) argued that the blocking of upward mobility through political channels in a colonial society had made the Chinese use economic mobility, such as starting a business, as the most viable alternative.

Moreover, Hong Kong's unique political environment is conducive to Kirznerian entrepreneurship. The colony was regarded as a "borrowed place and borrowed time" (Hughes 1968). Although the Beijing government from time to time has reassured Hong Kong's residents that, under the arrangement of "one country, two systems", the city will be allowed to operate under a capitalist system for 50 years after 1997, many businessmen are still in doubt about Hong Kong's future, especially for those who have painful experiences of their properties and businesses in mainland China being confiscated by the communists in 1949. To deal with the political uncertainty, business people in Hong Kong have engaged in industrial activities with a short gestation period and a high labour content.

Ho (1985, p. 23) remarks that the short-term outlook of Hong Kong's manufacturers is a direct consequence of its unique situation and "the tendency to look for the maximum gain in the shortest period of time means that people are actively watching out for business opportunities and quick to respond to clues from the external environment". The short-term perspective limits the scope of planning. Ho (1992, p. 122) claims that the "get rich quick" mentality is always close to the surface in Hong Kong. In sum, the unique political environment in Hong Kong has forced its residents to pursue a Kirznerian style of entrepreneurship.

Economic factors

Small open economy

A significant fact about industry in Hong Kong is its volatility. Its growth history demonstrates the sensitivity of a small economy in which home demand is almost irrelevant and external factors have great effects (Redding 1994, p. 73). Given this situation, business people are compelled to be alert to any change in world markets.

More importantly, the export-oriented character of Hong Kong's industry means that local production relies on orders from overseas and hence the prediction of future demand is more difficult. Ho (1985, p. 23) comments that "responsivity is necessary for the economic well being of Hong Kong because of the export oriented character of its economy". In this situation, the best business strategy is to keep business small and avoid being involved in advanced technology. Furthermore, it is preferable to invest in machines with a very short pay-off period, so that firms can better adjust to the changing market demand (Poon 1992, p. 216). Subcontracting, another form of Kirznerian entrepreneurial strategy, is widely practised by Hong Kong manufacturers to tackle such fluctuations (Ho 1992, p. 121).

Economic policy

Hong Kong is often described as a capitalist paradise and generally regarded as the last bastion of *laissez-faire* by free market economists (Rabushka 1979; Woronoff 1980). The traditional philosophy of Hong Kong government's public finance can be evidenced from the famous statement made by the former Financial Secretary of the Colony, Sir John Cowperthwaite: "Let money fructify in the pockets of taxpayers. Government should not presume to tell any businessman and industrialist what he should or should not do; attempts to frustrate the operation of market forces will tend to damage the growth rate of the economy" (Hong Kong Government Secretariat 1963, p. 51).

Hence economic transactions in Hong Kong have relied primarily on voluntary exchange through the market mechanism. It has a small public sector. The government has spent around 17 per cent of its GDP on public expenditure which is relatively low compared to other countries. In particular, in terms of general government consumption as a percentage of GDP, Hong Kong was the lowest in the world, with a record of only 7 per cent and 8 per cent in 1965 and 1990 respectively (Table 3.6). This low level of government involvement has given Hong Kong one of the lowest tax rates in the world (Siu and Martin 1992). In 1990, profits of unincorporated businesses were taxed at a flat rate of 15 per cent, those of corporate business at a flat rate of 16.5 per cent. There was no payroll tax nor social security contribution (Ho 1992, p. 121). The government refused to make taxes more progressive on the grounds that they would erode the incentive to invest (Riedel 1974, pp. 142–3; Chau 1993, p. 28). In short, Hong Kong has the most pro-business government in the world (*Fortune*, 1994, p. 69).

The effect of this liberal economic policy on Hong Kong's business affairs can be further illustrated from the following two facts.

First, Hong Kong's business world is open to any newcomer. If people have an idea and want to start a business, all they need to do is to pay a small registration fee to the Company Registry and they can then promote their businesses with minimum intervention from the government. This is very important because it means that everyone is given a chance to work their way up (Woronoff 1980, p. 149).

Table 3.6 General government consumption as a percentage of GDP, 1965 and 1990

Countries	General government consumption as a % of GDP	
	1965	*1990*
Hong Kong	7	8
USA	17	18
Japan	8	9
Singapore	10	11
Malaysia	15	13
India	9	12
Brazil	11	16
Low-income economies	9	11
Middle-income economies	11	14
East Asia and Pacific	8	10
South Asia	9	12
European Community	15	18
Latin America and Caribbean	9	13

Source: World Bank 1993, *Sustaining Rapid Development in East Asia and the Pacific,* Washington DC, pp. 78–9.

Ho (1992, p. 121) claimed that "no economy in the world has a simpler or easier way to set up a business than Hong Kong". A limited company can be established in a matter of days. There are also few costs to start a business. In 1990, the first registration fee was only HK$1,000, no more than a week's pay for an unskilled worker (Ho 1992, p. 121).

Second, the Territory allowed Chinese refugees to find freedom and opportunities and use their talents and technical expertise when they first migrated to Hong Kong in the 1940s. Most of the Chinese refugees were intellectuals, technicians and industrialists and were able to succeed in realising their wishes through hard work and ingenuity in the last 30 years (Siu and Martin 1992, pp. 87–92). In general, Hong Kong had provided settlers with an opportunity to pursue their goals and allowed them to exploit their potential, regardless of their cultural or religious backgrounds.

Though economic policy in Hong Kong is more liberal than in many other countries, this does not mean that the Hong Kong government has played no role in economic development. Underneath the government's policy is a strong pro-growth stance (Peeble 1988, p. 30; Chau 1993, p. 28). The government has deliberately provided a great incentive for entrepreneurs to exploit their potential to the maximum extent.

In terms of industrial policy, the government has given little technological assistance to manufacturing industry, apart from establishing some organisations such as the Hong Kong Productivity Centre, Hong Kong Trade Development Council and Export Insurance Corporation. Since a large expenditure on R&D can only be afforded by giant multinational corporations and the government has provided very little support for R&D in the manufacturing sector, small local entrepreneurs have opted for adaptive imitation strategies.

The wage and price structures

As noted in Chapter 2, a free and flexible wage and price mechanism will develop a subcontracting system because it enables entrepreneurs to exploit freely very small profit margins to the limit.[4] In contrast, a wage and price system which is heavily influenced by labour unions or government regulatory agencies will discourage subcontracting activities.

We have already mentioned that Hong Kong is essentially a free economy. There is no regulatory agency like the Trade Practice Commission or Price Surveillance Authority (Australia); Federal Trade Commission or Antitrust Authority (USA) to restrict price adjustment. Furthermore, the Hong Kong labour movement has never been influential. As Chau (1993, p. 27) wrote, "the extremely weak unionism in this economy greatly surprises many visiting economists". It was reported that during the decade 1978 to 1987, there was an average annual loss through disputes of only 6.4 working days per 1,000 employees, one of the lowest averages among industrialised countries (Poon 1992, p. 215; see also Table 3.7).

While it is beyond our scope to examine in detail the reasons for a slow development of the labour movement in Hong Kong, some of them are noteworthy: First, Hong Kong has had a businessman's government (Riedel 1974, p. 77) and is described as a capitalist paradise (Woronoff 1980). Any labour legislation or labour movement that reduced the profits of industrialists would not be encouraged (Woronoff 1980, p. 96). Second, Hong Kong's employees believed that they should be loyal to their employers. They also expected their employers to be paternalistic and in absolute authority. Third, the fragmentation of trade unions resulting from ideological differences between the pro-Communist China left-wing and the pro-Nationalist Taiwan right-wing unions also retarded the growth of the labour movement in Hong Kong (Poon 1992, p. 215; Riedel 1974, pp. 77–8; Woronoff 1980, pp. 95–9). In short, with a flexible wage and price system, Hong Kong entrepreneurs can practise subcontracting and exploit very narrow profit margins.[5]

Table 3.7   Number of work stoppages, 1969–87

Year	No. of work stoppages	Total working days lost (man days/annum)
1969	27	40,726
1971	42	25,600
1973	54	56,691
1975	17	17,600
1977	38	10,814
1979	46	39,743
1981	49	15,319
1983	11	2,530
1985	3	1,160
1987	14	2,774

Source: Hong Kong Census and Statistics Department, *Hong Kong Annual Digest of Statistics*, various issues.

Cultural factors

Perhaps the most significant element which facilitates the development of entrepreneurship in Hong Kong is its culture. Although Hong Kong is a Chinese community and 98 per cent of the population is Chinese, it is wrong to conclude that the culture is homogeneous. The Colony is virtually an open society, exhibiting various religious beliefs, life styles, languages and political ideologies. First of all, the economy was characterised by a large number of immigrants from mainland China. Most of them were refugees as a result of several political movements such as the Great Leap Forward in the 1950s and the Cultural Revolution from 1967 to 1977. Coming from various provinces of China, the people spoke different dialects and exhibited different life styles. There was also a large number of Vietnamese and Cambodian refugees flowing to Hong Kong periodically. Apart from British expatriates, people from the USA, Japan, Germany and Pakistan, to name a few, have come to the Colony to do business. Due to an extreme shortage of labour, the Hong Kong government in recent years also allows women from the Philippines and Thailand to work in Hong Kong as amahs. More significantly, a long period of British control of the Territory has created a community with a hybrid of Chinese and Western cultures (Tam and Redding 1993, pp. 158–77). It has been argued that a society with a diverse culture will stimulate creativeness and entrepreneurship (Gilad 1986, p. 204).

We have to examine to what extent Hong Kong's society is influenced by Western culture and the traditional Chinese values. The Chinese culture can be classified into the "great tradition" and the "small tradition". The great tradition, an attempt to achieve a wealthy and strong nation, was pursued by scholars, philosophers and men of letters, while the small tradition, an attempt to keep a good life and good earnings, was pursued by the unlettered peasants. The culture of Hong Kong belongs to the small tradition. The great tradition of Confucianism has never found its root in Hong Kong. The society, under British control, has been heavily influenced by Western culture, particularly in pursuing material life and social status. As a result, profit seeking is generally regarded as acceptable. Therefore, it is not surprising to learn that the most popular God in Hong Kong is Choi Shen, the God of Fortune (King, 1987, p. 59; Siu and Martin 1992, p. 90).[6] Lau's survey (1982) confirmed that Hong Kong's people have placed great emphasis on materialistic need and satisfaction (see also Redding and Wong 1986, pp. 34–5; Siu and Martin 1992, p. 91).

Hong Kong's culture also influences the development of entrepreneurship through family values. This can be illustrated from several phenomena. First, as reported earlier, Shanghainese males were expected to be owners of their own businesses. If not, they were considered to be failures. In Hong Kong, like the Shanghainese, most Chinese males from a business family also looked forward to the day when they would have their own portion of the family estate and become heads of their own family businesses (Wong 1988a, p. 143, 1989, pp. 174–9).

Table 3.8 Distribution of birth order of entrepreneurs in Hong Kong (%)

Birth order	1978	1987
First	42.1	31.4
Second	23.2	20.1
Third	16.5	18.6
Fourth and below	18.2	29.8
Total	100.0	100.0
No. of entrepreneurs	[413]	[264]

Sources: Sit *et al.* 1979, p. 250; Sit and Wong 1989, p. 88.

Second, the new entrepreneurs were often the children of the old entrepreneurs. This is more likely in a world of family-based firms. It was argued that in Hong Kong many firms or factories were established under a family business with family members involved in the production. Hence, "the children grew up in the factory or company. They learn about the business practices when they are young and are thus infected by the founder's enthusiasm. This training grants them specific business exposure and product knowledge" (Siu and Martin 1992, p. 91). Furthermore, in the Chinese tradition parents expected their sons to continue their businesses. The eldest son had the obligation to continue his father's enterprises.[7] According to Sit *et al.* (1979, p. 250), 42 per cent of the entrepreneurs in the 1978 survey were first-borns. A similar survey conducted ten years later by Sit and Wong (1989, p. 88) indicated that 31.4 per cent of the entrepreneurs were first-borns (Table 3.8). Therefore, it is no surprise that some of the successors have had university training in science and engineering but have become industrialists and run the businesses successfully.

Chinese culture, notably familism, is the most significant concept in explaining why and how the Hong Kong environment has facilitated the development of

Table 3.9 The participation of entrepreneur's spouses/relatives in medium/small firms, 1987

Spouse/relative	% of total no. of establishments
Spouse	21.1
Son/daughter	8.5
Brother/sister	10.2
Father/mother	4.4
Wife's family member	1.4
Father's family member	0.7
Not close relatives	5.1
Unknown	1.4
None	47.3
Total	100.0
No. of establishments	[294]

Source: Sit and Wong 1989, p. 164.

Table 3.10 Employing relatives in the manufacturing industries

Industry	% of establishments in industry	% employing family members
Wearing apparel	50.0	44.7
Plastics	50.0	39.2
Textiles	36.2	29.8
Electronics	22.7	13.6
Machinery	50.0	25.0
Total	46.9	38.8

Source: Sit *et al.* 1979, p. 353.

Kirznerian entrepreneurship. Wong (1988b) used the term "entrepreneurial familism" to denote the dynamic economy of Hong Kong. Scholars noted that overseas Chinese in South East Asian nations in general and in Hong Kong in particular manage their businesses like a family (Chau 1974; Wong 1980, 1988b; Redding 1988, 1990; King and Man 1979; King 1987). Chau (1974) argued that manufacturing enterprises in Hong Kong were principally family affairs. Employment of relatives, especially of family members, was a characteristic of Chinese small business. Sit *et al.* (1979, p. 354, 1989, p. 164) reported that nearly half of the establishments in the surveys employed relatives in their businesses, of which the majority were members of the owners' families (Tables 3.9, 3.10). In the spinning mills, Wong (1988b, p. 138) reported that approximately 60 per cent of the manufacturing firms employed relatives (Table 3.11). The application of familism extended to financial loans, management techniques and marketing strategies.[8]

Entrepreneurial familism involves "the JIA (family) as the basic unit of economic competition" (Wong 1988a, pp. 142–3). The family provides the impetus for innovation and the support for risk taking. This is not only confined to rich families, but permeates the whole society. Specifically, when poor families have little physical capital to be deployed, they still manage to cultivate human capital for collective advancement. Hence, "each family thus aspired to improve its position in life by means of combining the income of wage-earning members" (Wong 1988a, p. 143).

Wong (1988a, p. 144) argued that the Chinese entrepreneurial familism "has led to the evolution of a system of subcontracting, under which the production

Table 3.11 Employing relatives in Hong Kong spinning mills

Relatives employed	No. of firms	% of total
Yes	20	59
No	14	41
No response	6	–
Total	40	100

Source: Wong 1988b, p. 138.

process is broken up into multiple independent parts. This enhanced Hong Kong's industry flexibility and responsiveness to external market fluctuations." The reliance on family and the exclusion of outsiders for senior management positions have important effects on the shape and size of business organisation. Such reliance makes it relatively difficult for Chinese enterprises to grow large as such firms usually split eventually into smaller firms so as to follow the Chinese practice of divisible inheritance. Redding (1988, p. 109) concludes that this kind of Chinese culture, namely familism, facilitates business initiation but impedes the higher level of coordination necessary for the growth of the individual firm on a large scale (see also Nishida 1992, p. 191). This argument may make more sense if we put it into our interpretative framework. Familism initiates incremental innovation (i.e. Kirznerian entrepreneurship, a typical feature of Hong Kong's industrialisation) but is not conducive to a major creative breakthrough, or Schumpeterian entrepreneurship.

As a result of the influence of familism, Hong Kong's manufacturing industry works under a network of subcontracting and small businesses. With a high degree of flexibility and adaptability and being extremely versatile and dynamic, the manufacturing firms are able to react to the rapidly changing conditions of international markets (Chau 1974, p. 157).

In summary, this chapter has argued that Hong Kong is an entrepreneurial society. Moreover, Hong Kong's unique political, cultural and economic environment facilitates the development of Kirznerian entrepreneurship which has laid the foundation for Hong Kong's economic dynamics. Chapters 4, 5 and 6 will illustrate the operations of Kirznerian entrepreneurship in the manufacturing industry.

NOTES

1 Li Ka-Shing was initially a small plastics factory owner and later became an internationally known businessman. He was born in Chiu Chau (Guangdong, China) in 1928. In 1950 he started a plastics factory. In the 1950s he shifted his production between plastic toys, plastic flowers and other related products. During the 1960s he saw a growth potential in the property market and invested heavily in real estate. By 1976 he had become the Colony's most important Chinese real estate developer. During the late 1970s he acquired shares of several major British firms such as Jardine's and Hutchison and diversified his investment in land, transport, retailing/wholesaling, hotel, construction and softdrinks, etc. (Guo 1990, pp. 1–11; Rafferty 1991, pp. 307–23). According to *Fortune* (1989), he was the wealthiest Chinese in the world. *International Business Asia* (1993, p. 18) concluded that "He's what Hong Kong is all about, an inimitable part of the Hong Kong success story."

2 Lee and Low (1990, p. 228) pointed out that in 1986 the ratio of number of establishments with five to nine workers with respect to the number of establishments with ten or more workers was 0.81 for Hong Kong and 0.59 for Singapore.

3 As 1997 approaches, the system is changing. The Hong Kong government is forced to pursue localisation in the civil service and has promoted the Hong Kong Chinese (with British nationality) to some top administrative jobs. For example, Mrs Anson Chen, a typical Hong Kong resident, had been promoted to the position of the Colonial Secret-

ariat, the number two position in the Hong Kong civil service system. This arrangement would have been inconceivable ten years ago.

4 The extent of subcontracting (i.e. using piece rate methods instead of vertical integration) depends a great deal on transaction cost. For an excellent exposition of the role of transaction cost on various contractual arrangements, see Cheung (1984).

5 The British Labour Party often condemned Hong Kong for allowing "the exploitation of workers" to exist. It is not difficult to understand why they condemned it. By allowing the subcontracting system to work, manufacturers in Hong Kong can export their products at competitive prices. This has harmed the UK economy so much that Britain is the first Western country to call for restrictions on the import of Hong Kong's textile products, so as to protect Manchester's mills. Certainly it is ironic that Britain, as a sovereign state, does not allow the Colony's products to enter. Moreover, many imports are actually supplied or manufactured by British businessmen, such as Jardine Matheson, an East India company in a modern form.

6 The God of Fortune manages and controls the financial matters of all people on earth. There is no comparable kind of god in Western culture. When Chinese make a wish to the God of Fortune they present a gift by burning some paper money (legal tender in heaven or in hell). In the Chinese culture, this is "legitimate" bribery. Indeed, bribery was once common business practice in Hong Kong before the government set up the Independent Commission Against Corruption (ICAC).

7 If parents have only daughters, then they let their daughters manage their businesses, although in the traditional Chinese culture a married daughter belongs to her husband's family and hence becomes an outsider. However, this attitude has changed.

8 For a detailed discussion of the practices of familism in Hong Kong, including employment, business organisation, decision-making and capital financing, see Chau (1974, p. 157).

4

ENTREPRENEURSHIP IN THE MANUFACTURING SECTOR

This chapter examines the role of entrepreneurship in Hong Kong's manufacturing industry. In particular, it attempts to demonstrate that in exploiting profit opportunities Hong Kong manufacturers have adopted Kirznerian entrepreneurial strategies in the form of small-scale enterprise, product imitation, subcontracting and spatial arbitrage.

HONG KONG'S INDUSTRIAL STRUCTURE

Hong Kong's industrialisation began in the early 1950s. After the communists took over mainland China in 1949, a large number of immigrants and refugees moved into the Colony. Many of them were entrepreneurs from Shanghai. They brought capital and skill with them and built Hong Kong's first spinning mill. The new textile industry expanded. In the early 1950s there were only 26,300 workers in the textile industry employing about 35 per cent of the total labour force in the manufacturing sector. By 1960 employment had risen to 61,800 (Youngson 1982, p. 11).

Apart from textile manufacturing, other industries such as metals, plastics, artificial flowers and wigs had also developed. During the period from 1948 to 1965, two-fifths of the Hong Kong labour force was engaged in manufacturing activities. By 1967 there were more than 11,000 factories reported at the Labour Department. It was estimated that between 1950 and 1964 industrial output rose at an average of at least 3 per cent per year (Brown 1971, p. 8).

The development of Hong Kong's manufacturing industry can be seen in Table 4.1. The manufacturing industries exhibited an impressive annual growth of approximately 45 per cent in the decade 1973–83. However, the annual growth rate slowed down to only 10 per cent for the period 1983–91. Textiles, clothing and electronics are still the leading industries. In 1991 they accounted for more than half of the economy's gross manufacturing output. The share of the textile output has declined over the last twenty years but the electrical and electronic industry in 1991 maintained a share of approximately 25 per cent of the economy's gross manufacturing output (Table 4.1).

Table 4.1 Hong Kong's manufacturing gross output, 1973–91, selected years

Industries	Distribution by sector (%)					1973–83		1983–91	
	1973	1978	1983	1988	1991	Absolute change (HK$mil)	Annual growth (%)	Absolute change (HK$mil)	Annual growth (%)
Wearing apparel (except knitwear and footwear)	22.0	24.0	21.1	18.9	26.2	29,623	46.4	49,089	17.0
Textile (including knitting)	29.0	19.0	16.7	15.0	9.9	19,984	23.5	3,651	1.6
Plastic products	8.0	7.0	7.0	7.9	5.0	9,482	39.0	4,403	4.6
Paper products, printing and publishing	4.0	4.0	4.5	6.2	5.3	64,409	49.7	9,393	15.2
Metal products, machinery and equipment	12.0	17.0	18.4	19.0	9.1	27,884	79.2	−5,024	−2.0
Leather, wood and cork	3.0	3.0	2.6	2.0	*	3,566	40.7		
Food and beverage	5.0	4.0	4.4	3.9	4.2	6,107	45.8	6,160	10.4
Electrical and electronic products	11.0	14.0	18.3	19.0	24.9	27,934	86.4	41,317	16.6
Chemical, rubber and non-metallic mineral products	3.0	4.0	3.6	3.4	*	5,246	62.6		
Others	3.0	4.0	3.5	4.6	5.8	4,992	50.2	10,827	22.6
Total	100.0	100.0	100.0	100.0	100.0				
Total output (HK$ million)	[29,400]	[68,100]	[160,500]	[315,900]	[289,900]	[133,100]		[129,400]	

Source: Hong Kong Government Census and Statistics Department, *Survey of Industrial Production*, various issues.
Note: * they are grouped into the 'others' category.

The development of Hong Kong's manufacturing industries can also be observed in terms of the number of persons employed (Table 4.2). Total employment in the manufacturing industry increased from 51,000 in 1950 to 655,000 in 1991. Most impressive growth occurred in the 1960s and 1970s, particularly for electronics, clocks and watches and home appliances. However, in the 1980s employment in most of the manufacturing industries declined. There were two reasons for this phenomenon. First, these industries used more capital intensive inputs which substituted labour as a result of rising labour cost. Second, part of the manufacturing activities had been relocated to China so that the offices in Hong Kong were used mainly as sourcing and coordinating centres.

The development of Hong Kong's manufacturing industries can also be viewed in terms of their export contribution. In 1950 Hong Kong's export trade was composed mainly of textiles, clothing and metal products (Table 4.3). In the early 1960s other industries such as toys, plastics and electronics began to export. By 1992, the major manufacturing industries, textiles, clothing, electronics, watches and clocks and plastics, contributed to more than 75 per cent of the economy's export. High growth rates are observed in the electronics industry in the 1970s, the watch and clock industries in the 1960s and 1970s and the jewellery industry in the 1980s (Table 4.3).

Multinational corporations in Hong Kong

Investment from overseas in Hong Kong's manufacturing industries has a long history. It gained significance in the 1970s when there was growing recognition of Hong Kong as an excellent offshore base for the production of light consumer goods (Ho 1992, p. 134; Hong Kong Government Industry Department 1993, p. 11). The value of overseas investment in Hong Kong's manufacturing industries has steadily increased over the last decade. The 1993 survey by the Industry Department identified 472 companies with investment from overseas (Hong Kong Government Industry Department 1993, pp. 11–21). The total value of overseas investment in Hong Kong's manufacturing industry at the end of 1992 was HK$37,279 million. Japan and the USA were the leading source countries of overseas investment, contributing 33 per cent and 27 per cent respectively to the total value of investment. More than 53 per cent of total overseas investment was concentrated in three industries: electronics (31 per cent), electrical products (11 per cent), textiles and clothing (11 per cent).

In terms of the number of establishments, the relative significance of multinationals in Hong Kong's manufacturing sector does not appear to be impressive. In 1992 firms with overseas interests represented only just over 1 per cent of the economy's manufacturing establishments (Ho 1992, p. 139). However, they are much larger than the local firms. In 1992 the multinational companies in the manufacturing industry employed 72,148 persons, or about 13 per cent of Hong Kong's manufacturing employment. The average number of employees of these companies was about 150, compared with an overall average of 14 for the

Table 4.2 Number of persons in the manufacturing sector, 1950–91, selected years

	1950	1960	1965	1970	1975	1980	1985	1990	1991	Absolute change ($)			Average annual growth (%)		
										1960–70	1970–80	1980–91	1960–70	1970–80	1980–91
Wearing apparel	2.4	23.8	25.6	28.8	37.9	30.9	34.5	34.5	34.4	106,107	117,793	−50,893	20.40	7.45	−1.68
Electronics		0.1	1.5	7.0	7.9	10.4	10.1	11.7	10.9	38,271	54,551	−21,539	2,091.31	14.19	−0.23
Textile	30.6	24.4	19.1	14.0	12.5	10.0	7.8	9.4	9.5	22,298	11,755	−26,808	4.07	1.53	−3.02
Printing/publishing	7.1	4.0	4.4	3.3	2.9	3.0	3.6	5.1	6.0	9,613	8,052	11,669	10.94	9.38	4.42
Plastic products	0.3	8.3	12.8	12.9	9.4	9.7	10.0	7.3	6.3	52,827	15,356	−44,792	29.14	2.16	−5.19
Metal products	17.6	8.5	6.5	6.5	6.7	7.0	5.6	5.7	6.0	17,050	27,186	−23,756	9.21	7.64	−3.79
Machinery				1.2	1.3	1.4	2.4	3.7	4.1	–	5,596	14,111	–	8.21	11.38
Clock and watches	4.2	1.1	1.3	1.8	2.3	5.5	4.3	3.7	3.7	7,340	39,681	−25,518	30.17	40.6	−5.16
Food processing		3.9	3.5	2.5	2.5	2.5	2.5	3.2	3.4	5,301	8,670	133	6.29	6.31	0.06
Toys		3.3	5.9	7.2	5.5	6.2	6.0	3.4	2.9	32,043	16,171	−36,929	43.13	4.1	−6.64
Jewellery		0.4	0.6	0.5	1.2	1.2	1.6	12.5	2.5	1,720	8,316	5,315	20.17	32.32	4.88
Home appliances		0.4	2.2	0.5	0.9	1.8	2.3	1.6	1.3	2,112	13,359	−7,937	27.46	46.37	−4.89
Photographic and optical goods		0.3	0.7	0.6	0.5	0.9	1.3	1.0	1.1	2,473	4,652	−334	41.56	15.16	−0.43
Others	37.8	21.5	15.9	13.2	8.5	9.5	8.0	7.2	7.8	35,488	12,272	−33,650	9.60	1.69	−3.97
Total	100.0	100.0	100.0	100.0	100.0	100.0	100.0	100.0	100.0						
Total employment (000s)	[51]	[172]	[287]	[549]	[679]	[892]	[849]	[730]	[655]	377	343	−237			

Source: Hong Kong Government Census and Statistics Department, *Hong Kong Annual Digest of Statistics*, various issues.

Table 4.3 The export contribution of Hong Kong's manufacturing industries, 1950–92

Industries	Distribution of export contribution of the manufacturing industries (%)								1950–60		1960–70		1970–80		1980–90	
	1950	1960	1965	1970	1975	1980	1985	1992	Absolute change (HK$mil)	Annual growth %	Absolute change (HK$mil)	Annual growth %	Absolute change (HK$mil)	Annual growth %	Absolute change (HK$mil)	Annual growth %
Clothing	4.4	35.2	35.5	35.1	44.6	34.1	34.6	33.0	847	52.0	3,327	32.9	40,575	93.6	48,907	21.0
Electronics			4.2	8.7	12.0	19.7	20.8	25.8	–	–	–	–	12,343	114.9	45,149	33.7
Textiles	17.6	19.3	16.6	10.3	9.4	6.7	6.0	7.4	–98	15.0	723	13.1	3,258	25.5	12,371	27.3
Watches, clocks		0.6	0.6	1.7	3.5	9.6	7.4	6.6	–	–	191	112.4	6,368	306.2	12,557	19.1
Plastic products		9.1	13.1	12.3	8.6	9.0	8.2	3.1	–	–	397	15.2	4,605	30.3	2,065	3.4
Jewellery		0.7	0.6	0.9	1.5	1.1	2.0	2.2	–	–	92	48.4	661	60.0	5,290	68.1
Metal products	2.4	4.1	3.1	2.8	2.6	3.0	2.3	2.0	29	3.3	227	19.2	1,692	49.0	2,486	12.2
Printing		1.1	0.9	0.7	1.0	1.1	1.3	2.0	–	–	58	18.1	2,828	70.7	2,828	39.0
Others	75.6	29.9	25.4	27.5	16.8	15.7	17.4	17.9	–	–	–	–	–	–	–	–
Total	100.0	100.0	100.0	100.0	100.0	100.0	100.0	100.0	[778]	–2.3	[5,015]	33.1	[70,138]	42.3	[131,653]	21.2
Total export (HK$million)	[3,705]	[2,869]	[5,023]	[12,356]	[22,648]	[64,714]	[138,125]	[229,500]								

Source: Hong Kong Government, Hong Kong Trade Statistics, various issues.

Table 4.4   Number of establishments and persons employed in the manufacturing sector

Year	Number of establishments	Persons employed	Average no. of persons per establishment
1950	1,478	81,718	55
1955	2,437	110,574	45
1960	5,346	218,405	42
1965	8,646	341,094	39
1970	16,507	549,178	33
1975	31,034	678,857	22
1980	45,409	892,140	20
1985	48,065	848,900	18
1990	49,087	730,217	15
1992	41,937	571,181	14

Source: Hong Kong Government Industry Department 1993, p. 17.

economy's manufacturing industry (Hong Kong Government Industry Department 1993, p. 13; Table 4.4).

The value of sales of the multinationals in 1992 was HK$90,414 million, and 60 per cent of the sales belonged to export. These export sales accounted for 23 per cent of Hong Kong's domestic exports (Hong Kong Government Industry Department 1993, p. 14). In terms of value added, in 1987 these firms contributed about 27 per cent of the economy's gross manufacturing output (Ho 1992, p. 146).

Foreign technology can be transferred to Hong Kong through foreign direct investments. Of the 472 multinational firms mentioned above, nearly 40 per cent were joint ventures with a local partner, a form of cooperation which provides opportunity for technology transfer. Furthermore, in 1992 almost 50 per cent subcontracted part of their production to other manufacturers. They established 379 subcontracting arrangements which were most common in the electronics, electrical products, textiles and clothing industries (Ho 1992, p. 150). In most of these multinational firms, local technologists and technicians participate actively in various areas of manufacturing. In 1988 over 80 per cent of the firms had local technologists involved in R&D. Moreover, of the 72,148 persons employed by all multinational firms, 97 per cent were local staff, a large proportion of which worked as operatives and craftsmen (Ho 1992, p. 139).

In summary, although the number of multinational firms in the manufacturing sector is relatively small, these firms make a contribution out of all proportion to their number. Moreover, they have brought with them technology, modern management skills and secure access to overseas markets. As will be argued, local firms can take opportunities to learn and imitate from these firms though joint ventures, subcontracting, spin-offs or OEM business, thus catching up with advanced firms.

SMALL FIRMS, OPPORTUNITY EXPLOITATION AND FLEXIBILITY

Cheng (1982, p. 50) remarked that Hong Kong's manufacturing firms are "capable of accepting orders subject to widely differing requirements as to amount, date of delivery and special specifications and that there is a constant attempt to develop new lines of products in response to change in the world market". The small-scale enterprises have played an indispensable part in this regard.

A major characteristic of Hong Kong's industrial structure is that each industry includes only a few large undertakings and a large number of small concerns whose activities are largely responsive to buyers' orders, especially to those from original equipment manufacturers or to subcontracting orders from either their larger counterparts or their peers (Ho 1992, p. 111).[1] In 1950 there were 1,478 manufacturing establishments, employing more than 81,000 people. The average size of a firm was approximately 55 persons per establishment. In 1992 the total number of establishments increased to 41,937, but the number of persons employed had declined to 571,181. The average size was 14 persons per establishments (Table 4.4).

Table 4.5 and Figure 4.1 compare the size of manufacturing firms for the years 1977, 1983 and 1992. It can be observed that the number of establishments of all sizes had decreased except for firms employing 1–9 persons. In other words, over time, the portion of small firms had exhibited a clear tendency to increase at the expense of larger businesses. For this, Ho commented:

> The average size of Hong Kong's industrial undertakings, which was small already by international standards, had actually become smaller over a period of rising prosperity. The data clearly shows that Hong Kong's manufacturing sector has been dominated by small and medium establishments. The argument that the dominance of small and medium enterprises is only a characteristic of an early stage of industrialisation, and that they are deemed to decrease gradually as an economy industrialises does not seem to apply in Hong Kong.
>
> (Ho 1992, p. 112)

The contributions of small and medium manufacturing firms to Hong Kong's economy are summarised in Table 4.6. In 1987 small and medium firms

Table 4.5 Distribution of the number of establishments in the manufacturing industry by number of persons employed, 1977, 1983, 1992 (%)

Number of persons employed	1977	1983	1992
1–9 persons	66.1	67.0	74.5
10–19 persons	14.9	14.6	12.2
20–49	11.1	10.9	8.4
50–99	4.4	4.3	2.9
100–199	2.1	2.0	1.3
200–499	1.0	0.9	0.6
500–999	0.3	0.2	0.1
1,000 and over	0.1	0.1	0.0
Total	100.0	100.0	100.0
No. of establishments	[37,568]	[46,817]	[41,938]

Source: Hong Kong Government Census and Statistics Department, *Hong Kong Annual Digest of Statistics*, various issues.

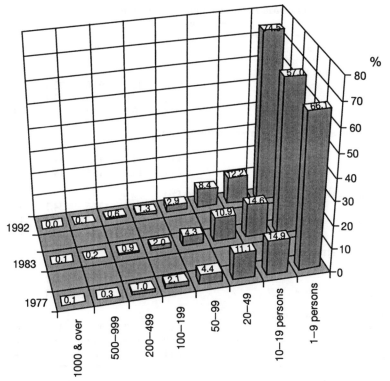

Figure 4.1 Distribution of the number of establishments in the manufacturing industry by number of persons employed

Source: Hong Kong Census and Statistics Department, *Hong Kong Annual Digest of Statistics,* various issues.

contributed nearly 85 per cent to manufacturing employment, 80 per cent to value added in the manufacturing industry and 18 per cent to the economy's GDP.

Chen and Li (1991, p. 10) observed that Hong Kong had a low degree of industrial concentration and weak barriers to entry and that product differentation applies mostly to local consumables, with few established brand names in exportable products. They concluded that the industrial structure was relatively efficient. Otherwise firms in Hong Kong would not be able to survive. Therefore, "as long as opportunity for new products and new industries are plentiful, small firms in Hong Kong can survive" (Chen and Li 1991, p. 5). Small firms in Hong Kong survived by being flexible, alert to economic change and responding rapidly to market needs (Youngson 1982, p. 23; Sung 1987, pp. 47–8; Chau 1993, p. 25). For small firms, with small overheads, machinery and personnel, the opportunity cost of shifting to other sectors was small. Kwok (1978, p. 72) reported that the cessation rate of small firms was seven times higher than that of large ones. This implies that small firms were more ready to close down or switch to new kinds of production. Davies *et al.* (1993, p. 12) recognised that speed was essential in

Table 4.6 Contributions of small and medium manufacturing firms to Hong Kong by size, selected years

Contributions of firms by size	1977	1981	1983	1985	1987
Distribution of firms (%)					
Small firms	91.0	91.6	92.0	92.4	92.6
Medium firms	8.5	8.0	7.7	7.3	7.1
Large firms	0.5	0.3	0.3	0.3	0.3
Contribution to employment in manufacturing (%)					
Small firms	36.7	40.5	40.5	41.1	42.2
Medium firms	43.2	43.3	43.6	44.4	42.5
Large firms	20.1	16.3	15.9	14.4	15.3
Contribution to value added in manufacturing (%)					
Small firms	30.3	32.7	31.7	34.3	35.1
Medium firms	45.0	44.8	45.8	46.8	45.7
Large firms	24.7	22.5	22.4	18.9	19.1
Contribution to GDP (%)					
Small firms	8.3	7.5	7.2	7.1	7.7
Medium firms	12.4	10.2	10.4	9.7	10.0
Large firms	6.8	5.1	5.1	3.9	4.2
Value added per employee ($'000)					
Small firms	18.9	29.2	37	46.1	66.8
Medium firms	23.9	37.5	49.5	58.3	86.3
Large firms	28.1	50.1	66.5	72.5	100.6

Source: Ho 1992, p. 117.
Notes: Small firms refer to all establishments employing fewer than 50 persons; medium firms, 50–499; and large firms, over 500 persons.

product development in Hong Kong. Normally, small firms were the first groups to get out of a declining sector and move into new markets.

A study of Hong Kong's manufacturing industry in 1989 by the Faculty of Business Administration, Chinese University of Hong Kong, revealed that 24 per cent of the establishments in the survey changed their product designs once a year. About 53 per cent of the firms altered their product designs once a quarter while 15 per cent of them changed their product designs once a month (*Economic Reporter* 1989, pp. 18–19).

Ho (1992, p. 119) concluded that "the economy in Hong Kong is extremely vulnerable to fluctuations in the world market. To survive, Hong Kong firms, large or small alike must be ready to move into new lines, to vary their production plans and even to switch technologies at short notice. There is no room for inertia." Only by grasping new opportunities and making decisions quickly can small firms in Hong Kong continue to survive. In this respect, they can be regarded as vehicles for flexible adjustment.[2]

Apart from lower management and coordination costs, small firms in Hong Kong are able to handle small orders. Woronoff (1980) observed that some factories even managed a multiplicity of small jobs at the same time. The jobs were so small that big companies could not handle them profitably. Especially during the recession, orders came only in small quantities and only small firms could manage this type of order within a very narrow profit margin. For example, the only three semi-conductor firms in Hong Kong could take advantage of their small size to produce shorter, more customised chips. The firms in Japan such as Toshiba would not consider small orders but Hong Kong producers may readily accept an order as small as 20,000 chips (Wilson 1991b, p. 71). Sometimes, they received orders with a value as small as US$1,000 (Engardio and Gross 1992, p. 64).

In order to be flexible and adaptable, small firms in Hong Kong prefer not to specialise in one product, so that they can switch quickly to other activities. Furthermore, manufacturers tend not to expand their production capacity. A survey of Hong Kong manufacturing firms in 1978 by Kwok (1978, p. 83) revealed that 30.4 per cent of firms in the sample did not want to expand in the next three years because they were afraid of problems which might come with expansion. Another 11.4 per cent of firms were afraid of losing the advantage of being small and 25.3 per cent were satisfied with their present size (Table 4.7). Hence, over-loading is a normal phenomenon among small firms in Hong Kong. Overloading results in rush orders, overtime work, and late delivery. Empirical evidence supported this. Sit *et al.* (1979) revealed that rush orders were prevalent among small enterprises in Hong Kong. About 28 per cent of small and medium firms in the survey frequently could not meet orders on time. Furthermore, in order to meet the delivery date, 60 per cent of establishments in 1978 occasionally worked overtime while 13 per cent of them frequently worked overtime (Table 4.8). In addition, nearly 62 per cent of the establishments did not have a quality control department. They relied heavily on foremen or owners for quality control. Only 30 per cent of the firms had a quality control department. In this way, most firms could shorten production time (Sit *et al.* 1979, pp. 366–8).

Sit and Wong (1989, p. 27) summarised that "flexibility and diversity of products through minute changes in design, creating new variable products within the same industries and filling existing market niches are more significant elements behind the dynamism of Hong Kong manufacturing". Referring to this feature as guerrilla capitalism, Lam and Lee (1992, p. 109) remarked that Chinese small and medium

Table 4.7   Reasons for small firms not expanding in next three years

	Textile	*Plastic*	*Machine*	*Others*
It would bring more problems	33.33	42.86	22.22	25.81
Satisfied with present size	23.81	14.29	22.22	32.29
No reliable employee	14.29	14.29	11.11	12.90
Expansion will cause firm to lose present advantages	9.52	14.29	11.11	12.90
Satisfied with subcontracting	19.05	14.29	33.33	16.13

Source: Kwok 1978, p. 143.

Table 4.8 Overtime work and problems in delivery in small manufacturing enterprises

		% of response
Overtime work	a. Frequently	13.1
	b. Occasionally	37.8
Reasons for overtime work	a. Rush order	57.7
	b. Shortage of labour	38.1
Problems in delivery	a. Frequently	27.9
	b. Occasionally	16.9

Source: Sit *et al.* 1979, p. 368.

family-owned firms succeed by exploiting market opportunities using the strategy of a guerrilla force: seek out an opportunity for high profit margins in a particular good, develop a formula, exploit it by rapidly flooding the market before the established firms can respond, make profits over the short term, and then leave the market for another before competition forces the prices down to the point where they are no longer profitable without large-scale investments in technology or infrastructure. In short, Kirznerian entrepreneurial strategies were employed.

SUBCONTRACTING

During the early stage of Hong Kong's industrialisation, many trading firms dispatched production contracts to small local factories. Ho (1992, p. 117) remarked that a large number of small firms in Hong Kong acted as subcontractors for large manufacturing concerns and export houses, producing parts or complete products. Others occupied a supportive role and provided intermediate goods and services for the export sector and the economy as a whole.

A survey by King and Man (1979, pp. 58–9) revealed that small factories in Kwun Tong and in Hong Kong as a whole depended on a significant degree of subcontracting with larger firms or upon marketing their products through wholesalers, merchants or export houses. Similarly, Woronoff (1980, pp. 142–5) observed that many small firms belonged to original equipment manufacturer (OEM) suppliers, producing for overseas companies or multinationals. Moreover, it was found that if firms could not produce in any given area or the orders exceeded their own capacities, they would subcontract to other factories.

Table 4.9 shows the sources of orders for small enterprises. Sit and Wong (1989, p. 153) found that in 1988 a significant proportion (40.8 per cent) of small firms obtained their orders solely from import–export houses. Another 8.9 per cent obtained their orders from import–export houses and other sources. Approximately 29 per cent of small firms in their survey received orders solely from local factories and 8.9 per cent of them claimed local factories as one of the sources. So roughly one-third of the establishments were linked up with other local factories in the form of subcontracting.

Table 4.9 Sources of orders for small business enterprises, 1978, 1988 (%)

	1978	*1988*
Import–export houses	44.8	40.3
Local factories	23.9	29.2
Direct overseas orders	11.1	8.9
Wholesalers and retailers	4.3	9.6
Direct sales to consumers	3.4	4.1
Above combinations	12.2	8.9
Total	100.0	100.0
No. of firms	[413]	[213]

Sources: Sit *et al.* 1979, p. 340; Sit and Wong 1989, p. 153.

Import–export houses had provided technical advice and assistance in the designing and marketing of small factories' products and had helped small manufacturers to secure loans. Unlike the subcontracting system in Japan which was one of a steady relationship, subcontracting in Hong Kong was seldom a long-lasting one. Hong Kong manufacturers regarded their relationships as a short-term convenient business deal (Sit *et al.* 1979, p. 345).

Furthermore, under the subcontracting network, many small firms in Hong Kong undertake one production process or participate in the production of finished goods for large firms. Hence large firms can gain flexibility. It was revealed that, in 1978, nearly 26 per cent of the manufacturing firms had the whole product contracted out. Approximately 27 per cent of the firms had parts or components contracted out and 47 per cent subcontracted one production process to other firms (Sit *et al.* 1979, p. 345).[3] In some extreme cases, firms might have no production site at all. They simply had an office for administrative purposes and subcontracted all jobs to others from the orders they received. They exploited profit margins by providing their managerial and marketing knowledge to foreign buyers and sellers. Their efforts have made Hong Kong an important international coordination centre.

Ho (1992, p. 117) concluded that, like Japan's early industrial development, small-scale enterprises in Hong Kong were well integrated into the economy through subcontracting, which contributed to the efficiency of the manufacturing sector and maintenance of Hong Kong's competitive edge in export markets by reducing production costs. In short, subcontracting is an essential Kirznerian entrepreneurial strategy for Hong Kong manufacturers to deal with rapid change and fluctuation in export markets. It contributes significantly to the economic success of Hong Kong.

PRODUCT STRATEGY

Hong Kong's manufacturers traditionally have relied upon trading firms in the Colony to market their products and most of them have produced as original equipment manufacturer (OEM) suppliers. They are more production oriented and many of them have no marketing department. Kwok's finding (1978, pp. 103–5) showed that for those firms having no separate marketing department, nearly 88 per cent replied that owner-managers were responsible for marketing activities. They received technical know-how from foreign agents operating in Hong Kong and learnt through imitation. It was contended that "Hong Kong's manufacturing industries traditionally are oriented towards incremental, rather than radical change, technological followership rather than leadership and cost reduction rather than product differentiation" (Davies *et al.* 1993, p. 12). They have competed in world markets on their capacity to manufacture at low cost and their flexibility to meet changing patterns of demand at very short notice (Redding 1994, pp. 81, 85).

The smallness of the firms and their low capitalisation mean that R&D is avoided (Redding 1994, p. 81). A survey by the Hong Kong Government Industry Department and Census and Statistics Department (1991, pp. 84–8) revealed that 88 per cent of manufacturing establishments in Hong Kong did not carry out R&D. Of these, 79 per cent said that they did not plan to do so in the future. Only 12 per cent of the firms in the survey carried out R&D regularly. These firms were largely involved in the electronics, garment, watch and clock, food and beverage industries. Most of them were larger firms. In terms of R&D expenses, only 36 per cent of the establishments spent 5 per cent or more of their total annual revenue. About 42 per cent of the establishments spent less than 5 per cent of their annual revenue on R&D, and 22 per cent of the establishments had no fixed R&D budget.

Furthermore, Kwok's study (1978) showed that 13 per cent of the manufacturers felt that their equipment at the time of the survey was obsolete. Woronoff (1980) reported that owners and their families of small firms in Hong Kong could only afford to buy cheap and secondhand machines. Likewise, Davies *et al.* (1993, p. 1) observed that manufacturers in Hong Kong used mature or even obsolete production equipment and technologies to combine relatively cheap inputs to produce goods designed by overseas customers.

Kwok's survey (1978, p. 143) of small manufacturing firms in textile, plastic and metal industries revealed that new product development was not a main factor for their success. Similarly, in a study of the failure of Hong Kong's manufacturing firms, Lung (1986, pp. 130–1) found that firms failed often because they pursued radical entrepreneurial strategies such as developing entirely new products or markets.

In a comprehensive study of Hong Kong's manufacturing industry, Espy (1970, p. 50) revealed that manufacturers in Hong Kong adopted product strategies that were labour intensive and employed a low level of technology, that did not require any design skills, and that aimed at mature products. In other words, they adopted Kirznerian entrepreneurial strategies. In terms of design skills, about 50 per cent of the firms (13 out of 27) in Espy's survey mentioned that their production required little design skills. One third (9 out of 27) of them required the design skill. Approximately 88 per cent of them (24 out of 27) said that their production was labour intensive and focused on mature products. All of them used simple technology (Table 4.10).

Table 4.10   Product strategies in the manufacturing industry, 1970

Industry	No. of firms	Design skill	Labour intensive	Low technology	Mature product
Cotton yarns	4	No	Yes	Yes	Yes
Fashion dress	1	Yes	Yes	Yes	Yes
Simple garment	3	Some	Yes	Yes	Yes
Plastic toy	1	Some	Yes	Yes	Yes
Plastic housewares	2	Some	Yes	Yes	Yes
Plastic toothbrush	1	Some	Yes	Yes	Yes
Transistor radio	3	Yes	Yes	Yes	Yes
Box camera	1	Yes	Yes	Yes	Yes
Alarm clocks	1	Yes	Yes	Yes	Yes
Lady wigs	1	Yes	Yes	Yes	Yes
Metal torch	1	Yes	Yes	Yes	Yes
Simple machine tool	1	Yes	Yes	Yes	Yes

Source: Espy 1970, p. 50.

Table 4.11   Product strategy and growth rates of Chinese firms

	High growth rate	Low growth rate	Total
Firms use all three product strategies	13	9	22
Firms did not use any one of these three product strategies	1	4	5
Total	14	13	17

Source: Espy 1970, p. 51.

Furthermore, Espy's survey (1970) revealed that such strategies contributed to the firms' success. About 14 firms (out of 27) achieved high growth rates and 13 (out of 27) achieved low growth rates. Among 14 firms that achieved high growth rates, 13 of them used all three product strategies, i.e., labour intensive, low technology and mature product. Only one firm in his sample did not use any one of these three strategies, showing that these kinds of Kirznerian entrepreneurial strategies were useful for Hong Kong manufacturing firms to survive (see Table 4.11).

SPATIAL ARBITRAGE

A major problem encountered by Hong Kong's manufacturers during industrialisation has been the rising cost of production. Sit *et al.* (1979, p. 386) revealed that 55 per cent of the small firms in Hong Kong regarded labour as the major problem (Table 4.12). Chen's survey (1983, p. 112) on the motivation of Hong Kong's firms for foreign direct investment also confirmed that labour was a major problem in production. The shortage of labour supply in Hong Kong ranked foremost in the motivation for the relocation of production plants. The high labour costs and

Table 4.12   Major problems envisaged by small entrepreneurs (%)

	1978	1987
Labour	55.0	60.4
Finance	18.9	6.2
Market	18.9	15.9
Factory premises	4.3	–
Technical	2.5	4.5
Bureaucracy	0.3	2.3
Raw material cost	–	6.6
Total	100.0	100.0
No. of small entrepreneurs	[413]	[213]

Sources: Sit and Wong 1979, p. 386; 1989, p. 203.
Note: Market problems refer to quota and market limitation.
Labour problems refer to rising wage, labour shortage and labour turnover.
Bureaucracy refers to government regulation.

rentals in Hong Kong also ranked relatively high. Altogether, labour problems occupied the top three positions (see Table 4.13).

Encountering these difficulties, Hong Kong's producers have searched for cost reduction opportunities. In fact, they already possessed substantial experience in exploiting the advantages of lower production costs in regions such as Indonesia, Malaysia, Thailand and the Philippines (Chen 1983, pp. 89–126).

Table 4.13   Motivations for Hong Kong's firms to invest overseas

Motivations	Score
Shortage of labour in Hong Kong	5.6
High labour costs in Hong Kong	5.2
To facilitate the export to other regions	5.0
High land cost and rent in Hong Kong	4.9
To open up new markets by directly investing there	4.3
Lack of technical and skilled labour force in Hong Kong	3.8
To circumvent tariffs and quota	3.6
Expanding existing markets	3.3
To avoid the pressure of competition from other firms	2.8
To exploit further the advantage of the managerial and marketing skills of the Hong Kong parent firm	2.6
Diversification of product	2.5
High capital costs in Hong Kong	2.0
To exploit further the advantage of the technical and production know-how of the Hong Kong parent firm	1.6
As a means of managing the financial assets of the Hong Kong firm	1.4
Lack of high levels of technology in Hong Kong	1.1
To make use of the outdated machines	0.9
Lack of management manpower in Hong Kong	0.4

Source: Chen 1983, p. 106.

Table 4.14 A comparison of wage rates in manufacturing industry between Hong Kong and China

	Average monthly wages (US$)		
	1985	*1991*	*Increase (%)*
Hong Kong	400	810	109
China:			
A Guangdong Province	39	55	42
B Shenzhen Special Economic Zone	65	79	22
C Fujian Province	29	39	33
D China, National	32	38	20

Source: Abegglen 1994, p. 92.

Table 4.15 A comparison of the purchase prices and monthly rentals of flatted factories in Hong Kong and Shekou, 1986

	Sale price (HK$) per sq. ft		*Monthly rental (HK$) per sq. ft*	
	Ground floor	*Upper floor*	*Ground floor*	*Upper floor*
Hong Kong	278–465	139–232	2.8–3.7	1.85–2.78
Shekou	180–250	120–40	1.4–1.6	1.20–1.30

Source: Wong, Y. 1989, p. 28.

After China began its economic reform in the early 1980s, Hong Kong's producers noticed much lower factor prices on the mainland. There were significant wage and rental differentials between Hong Kong and China (Tables 4.14 and 4.15). In 1985 Hong Kong's average monthly wages in the manufacturing industry were 12.5 times higher than in China (US$400 versus US$32), while in 1991 the difference increased to 21.3 times. For the period 1985–91, Hong Kong's average monthly wages in the manufacturing industry increased 109 per cent but those in China increased only 20 per cent (see also Redding 1994, p. 74). Industrialists in Hong Kong rapidly took advantage of the much lower costs across the border and shifted part of their production processes over there. They moved their labour intensive activities to China, while keeping the final stages of production in Hong Kong.

In this manner, they have created a large volume of transactions known as outward processing trade (OPT) between Hong Kong and China, resulting in a substantial increase in Hong Kong's trade figures. In 1989 the outward processing trade was reported at around 76 per cent of Hong Kong's domestic exports to China (Mok 1990, p. 251).

The scenario of Hong Kong's investment in China for the period 1979 to 1984 is summarised in Table 4.16. In 1979 Hong Kong entrepreneurs invested US$2.1 million in China to set up nine joint ventures, accounting for 84 per cent of the foreign investment and 90 per cent of the agreements in the Mainland

Table 4.16   Hong Kong's investment in China by types, 1979–84

Types of investment	1979	1980	1981	1982	1983	1984	Total	Annual growth 1979–84 (%)
Joint venture								
Number	9	15	17	14	78	534	667	220.82
Value (US$Mil)	12	29	12	8.4	62.5	705	879.2	345.01
Cooperative enterprise								
Number	10	22	25	–	23	32	112	32.95
Value (US$Mil)	190.2	363	374	–	200	242	1,370	13.62
Sole-capital enterprise								
Number	–	4	14	12	17	21	68	767
Value (US$Mil)		13.63	261.6	54.9	42.3	52.6	425	435

Source: Wang 1991, pp. 452–54.

that year. In 1984, the number of joint ventures rose to 534 with a value of US$705 million. The Sino-Hong Kong cooperative enterprises were set up in 1979 and Hong Kong business people invested US$19 million in them. From 1979 to 1983, the total value amounted to nearly US$1370 million. Hong Kong's industrialists established four sole capital enterprises in 1980, with a value of approximately US$14 million. By 1984, the number of sole enterprises rose to 21, with total value estimated at US$52.6 million (Wang 1991, pp. 452–5). Altogether, from 1979 to 1987, Hong Kong's business people invested US$12,800 million in China, about 86.7 per cent of the total foreign investment in China, and signed 7,431 business agreements, about 75 per cent of the total foreign investment in China. Both ranked number one in foreign investment in China (Wang 1991, p. 451).

A survey by the Federation of Industries (1992, p. 14) revealed that 41 per cent of the Hong Kong companies invested in the Pearl River Delta (Southern China),

Table 4.17   Forms of investment chosen by Hong Kong investors in the Pearl River Delta, China, 1992

Forms of investment	Establishments (%)
Wholly foreign owned enterprise	43.2
Equity joint venture	22.6
Processing of imported raw materials	17.2
Cooperative joint venture	9.1
Mixed forms of investment	5.7
Compensation trade	1.0
Others	1.0
No answer	0.3
Total	100.0
No. of establishments	[616]

Source: Federation of Industries 1992, p. 41.

which accounted for approximately 50 per cent of the total investment and 74.9 per cent of the product finished or processed there. About 43 per cent of the investment made in the Pearl River Delta by Hong Kong manufacturers was in the form of wholly foreign owned enterprise, while 23 per cent of the investment belonged to equity joint ventures and 17 per cent of them were processors of imported raw materials (Table 4.17).

Table 4.18 shows the total value of the outward processing trade with China. Approximately 50 per cent of the trade between Hong Kong and China belonged to this type. Of all imports from China, 58 per cent were processed goods made from raw materials and semi-manufactured items previously exported to China for that purpose. Furthermore, of all exports to China, 53 per cent were raw materials and semi-manufactured items for processing. Hong Kong's domestic exports to China for further processing were as high as 76 per cent of total exports to China (Mok 1990, p. 251).

Table 4.19 shows in detail the contents of Hong Kong's outward processing trade. The percentage of OPT to total imports was generally very high except in textiles. This was because textile materials exported for processing would most probably be reimported as apparel. All the percentages of OPT in Hong Kong's domestic exports were high as they reflected the corresponding high percentages of imports (Mok 1990, p. 252).

Table 4.18   Outward processing trade (OPT) with China, 1992

	Total (HK$million)	Estimated OPT (HK$million)	% of OPT to total
Imports from China	352,136	254,013	72.1
All exports to China	270,503	141,639	52.4
Domestic exports to China	59,557	44,271	74.3
Re-exports to china	210,946	97,368	46.2

Source: Hong Kong Government Industry Department 1993, p. 23.

Table 4.19   Outward processing trade (OPT) by commodity, 1989

Commodity	% of OPT to total		
	Imports	Domestic exports	Re-exports
Textiles	12.8	84.8	71.5
Apparel	84.5	85.0	87.3
Plastics	73.4	83.9	58.0
Machine and electrical equipment	77.8	56.7	24.9
Sound and recording	85.2	94.6	43.0
Clocks and watches	94.6	98.5	93.5
Toys, games and sports	94.0	96.4	60.0
Metals	30.2	64.2	37.8
Others	44.7	59.0	28.2

Source: Mok 1990, p. 252.

In terms of employment, it was reported that Hong Kong's producers in 1991 hired three times as many industrial workers in China than in the Colony. The figure for China was estimated to be more than 2 million people (McCormick 1991, p. 39). It was estimated that in 1990 Hong Kong companies employed about 1.5 million people in Guangdong province, or about twice the 850,000 employees in manufacturing within Hong Kong itself (Chee 1991, p. 423). The Federation of Industries (1992, p. 28) reported that each Hong Kong firm on average employed 787 workers in the Pearl River Delta (Table 4.20). Their favourable locations were Shenzhen, Dongguan and Guangzhou (Table 4.21).

Regarding the performance of Hong Kong's investment in China, more than half of Hong Kong's manufacturers reported that the performance of their investments in the Pearl River Delta region was good (Table 4.22). Approximately 40 per cent of the manufacturers indicated that their business performance was fair. Only 0.6 per cent considered their business performance poor (Federation of

Table 4.20 Investment of Hong Kong manufacturing firms in the Pearl River Delta, China, 1992

Percentage of companies having investment in China	40.7
Percentage of companies planning to invest in China	5.5
Average percentage of China investment in total investment	49.0
Average no. of workers employed in China	787
Average percentage of workers employed in China	97.5
Average percentage of product finished/processed in China	74.9
Percentage of China made products which are sold in China	6.9
Total no. of employees recruited in China	393,646

Source: Federation of Industries 1992, p. 41.

Table 4.21 Distribution of Hong Kong's industrial establishments in the Pearl River Delta, China

	% of response
Shenzhen	47.7
Dongguan	20.3
Guangzhou	8.6
Huizhou	7.1
Foshan	3.6
Jiangmen	2.9
Zhuhai	2.3
Shantou	1.1
Zhaoxing	0.5
Others	1.5
No answer	1.3
Total	100
No. of establishments	[616]

Source: Federation of Industries 1992, p. 28.

Table 4.22   Performance of the investments in the Pearl River Delta, China, 1992

Response	*Distribution (%)*
Excellent	4.5
Good	51.1
Fair	39.7
Poor	0.6
No answer	4.1
Total	100.0
No. of manufacturers	[511]

Source: Federation of Industries 1992, p. 33.

Industry 1992, p. 28). Hence, by integrating China's R&D and Hong Kong's marketing expertise, Hong Kong has developed into a regional trade centre. Entrepreneurs in the Colony earn their rewards in banking, trading and testing activities.

CHANGING ECONOMIC ACTIVITIES WITHIN THE MANUFACTURING SECTOR

The changing economic activities within the manufacturing industry have been enhanced by Kirznerian entrepreneurs. Woronoff (1980, p. 143) once mentioned that "any sector, no matter how good it looks at a given time, goes through periods of greater or lesser popularity, higher or lower demand, better or worse profits. No one ever knows when a sector that has performed well for years will slip or become overcrowded." When an industry begins to decline, entrepreneurs who are on constant alert will rapidly react to such change and explore other new opportunities. Therefore, flexibility is important for them to survive. Ho (1992, p. 28) correctly pointed out that Hong Kong's success has been attributed to the economy's ability to shift resources into sectors of growing world demand for light manufactures and traded services. This is shown dramatically in the wigs and hair products industry. In 1964 there were only three establishments in wigs and hair products, with a total of 484 persons, about 1.6 per cent of the total manufacturing employment. The industry peaked in the late 1960s and declined rapidly in the 1970s. By 1986, it accounted for only 0.02 per cent of the economy's manufacturing output (Nyaw 1991, p. 193).

In the electronics industry, manufacturers in recent years moved away from transistor radios, sound reproducing and recording equipment towards computing machinery and equipment and electronic industrial apparatus (Table 4.23). This picture can be reinforced in the export sector. Before 1965 Hong Kong virtually had no electronics production. Between 1965 and 1980 manufacturers were mainly involved in the production of parts and components, LCD radios and cassette recorders. However, in the 1980s they shifted to telephones, computers and peripherals (Table 4.24).

Table 4.23   Change in the number of establishments by types of electronics products, 1982 and 1992

Items	1982	1990	Annual growth rate %
Transistor radio	240	27	−11.18
Television	100	94	−0.75
Sound reproducing and recording equipment	151	27	−10.26
Electronics toys	54	73	4.39
Electronic industrial apparatus	16	52	28.13
Computing machinery and equipment	21	213	114.28
Electronic parts and components	394	372	0.69
Electronic watch and clock	722	480	4.19

Source: Hong Kong Government, *Survey of Industrial Production*, 1982, 1992.

In the textile and garment industry adjustment also took place. During 1982–92 there was growth in activities such as spinning synthetic fibre, bleaching and dyeing, textile stencilling and printing, but activities such as wool spinning, silk weaving and the knitting of wool fabrics disappeared (Table 4.25).

Producers may move into related industries: for example, a textile manufacturer may move from weaving to dyeing and then to clothing; printers may move into typesetting; electronics firms into digital watches; and plastic makers into toys. Yet it is quite common that some firms may move into other fields that have almost no relation to their present activities (Woronoff 1980, p. 143).

As will be further argued in Chapter 7, being alert to opportunities, entrepreneurs in Hong Kong shifted their business from one type to another, from one region to another, hence constituting the dynamics of Hong Kong's economy.

In summary, in a small open economy and with a unique political structure like Hong Kong's, manufacturers have encountered an extremely volatile economic condition. They have tackled these problems by being alert to business opportunities, making quick decisions, acting promptly, and maintaining a high degree of flexibility and adaptability. They have preferred family businesses and made informal or oral agreements based on trust. They have taken shortcuts to produce some non-capital-intensive and not too sophisticated commodities, with short gestation periods (Chau 1993, p. 25). In sum, their survival has relied on Kirznerian entrepreneurial strategies, namely small-scale enterprise, subcontracting, product imitation and spatial arbitrage. This line of argument will be elaborated in Chapters 5 and 6 where in-depth case studies in the textile/garment and electronics industries will be provided.

Table 4.24 Export of Hong Kong's electronics products, 1965–92, selected years

Items	Distribution (%)								1980–92	
	1965	1970	1975	1980	1985	1990	1991	1992	Absolute change, HK$million	Annual growth, %
Parts and components	39.6	46.6	35.2	27.2	38.8	45.7	52.8	60.3	32,683	74.66
Watch, clock and movement				29.9	23.9	23.7	20.4	17.1	6,296	13.08
Computer and peripherals				0.0	3.1	6.2	6.5	5.6	3,367	93.52
LCD radio and cassette recorder	60.4	51.1	46.6	31.8	14.1	2.6	2.0	1.9	−3,111	−6.07
Telephone		0.1	0.1	0.3	6.7	5.3	2.8	1.7	975	192.80
Electronic games and TV games				1.1	1.7	0.7	0.5	0.3	39	7.74
Computing machinery and equipment										
Others		2.2	5.8	6.2	9.8	15.4	14.7	13.0	6,987	69.48
Total	100.0	100.0	100.0	100.0	100.0	100.0	100.0	100.0		
Total export (HK$million)	[128]	[1,074]	[2,741]	[13,412]	[26,995]	[58,542]	[58,640]	[60,250]	[46,838]	29.10

Source: Hong Kong Industry Department 1993, p. 58.

Table 4.25 Change in the number of establishments in the textile and garment industry, 1982–92

	1982	1990	*Annuaal growth rate* (%)
Outer garment including infants wear	6,590	7,237	1.23
Under garment or night garment	800	775	−0.39
Wearing apparel (except fabrics)	9,446	8,938	−0.68
Spinning cotton	25	24	−0.50
Spinning wool	20	3	−10.63
Spinning synthetic fibre	20	31	6.88
Weaving cotton	370	212	−5.34
Weaving silk	36	3	−11.45
Wearing synthetic fibre	42	24	−5.35
Knitting of fabrics cotton	241	248	0.36
Knitting of fabrics wool	32	3	−11.33
Knit outerwear	1,535	1,442	−0.76
Bleaching and dyeing	274	437	7.44
Textile stencilling and printing	402	626	6.96

Source: Hong Kong Government, *Survey of Industrial Production*, 1982, 1990.

NOTES

1 It was estimated that in 1951, there were 1,434 small establishments (i.e. less than 50 workers). By 1961, the number increased to 4,710. The 1971 census reported 23,140. By 1977, the number further increased to 34,632 (Sit *et al.* 1979, p. 25). In terms of the number of establishments, the share of small manufacturing enterprises steadily increased from 79.7 per cent in 1961 to 86.5 per cent in 1971, and then to 92.1 per cent in 1977 (Sit *et al.* 1979, p. 25).
2 Using examples in developing countries, Jacobson (1992) argued that flexibility is a critical strategic factor in the entrepreneurial discovery process.
3 As will be shown in Chapters 5 and 6, subcontracting still plays an important role in Hong Kong's manufacturing industry.

5

ADAPTIVE RESPONSE IN THE TEXTILE AND GARMENT INDUSTRY

HONG KONG'S TEXTILE AND GARMENT INDUSTRY

The textile and garment industry has been a major manufacturing industry in Hong Kong. In 1991, its gross output amounted to HK$117,248 million, approximately 36 per cent of Hong Kong's manufacturing output. In 1992, it contributed to more than 40 per cent of the economy's exports (Hong Kong Government Industry Department 1993, p. 26; Table 5.1).

Textiles

The spinning and weaving activities are the oldest textile industries in Hong Kong. In the late 1940s a group of Shanghainese entrepreneurs migrated to Hong Kong and started the first spinning mill in the Colony. In the early 1950s the industry witnessed dramatic growth. It accounted for some 30 per cent of both the total manufacturing establishments and employment in Hong Kong (Ho 1992, p. 165). Subsequently, the industry expanded steadily. The number of spindles increased from 490,000 in 1960 to 833,100 in 1979, while the number of looms grew from 17,000 to 31,876 over the same period (Cheng 1982, p. 146).

Table 5.1 Hong Kong's textile and garment industry

Industry	Share in the total manufacturing output (% by gross output value)					
	1973	1978	1983	1988	1991	
Textile	29.0	19.0	16.7	15.0	9.9	
Garment	22.0	24.0	21.0	19.0	26.2	

Industry	Share in the total export (% by export value)					
	1950	1960	1970	1980	1990	1992
Textile	4.4	35.2	35.1	34.1	31.9	33.0
Garment	17.6	19.3	10.3	6.7	7.5	7.4

Source: From Tables 4.1 and 4.3.

However, the industry in the last decade was significantly smaller in relative terms than it was in the 1950s. In 1988 it accounted for only 7 per cent of the total number of manufacturing establishments and less than 9 per cent of the total manufacturing employment (Ho 1992, p. 166). Its share in Hong Kong's domestic exports declined considerably from a peak of over 19 per cent in 1960 to about 7 per cent in 1992. By 1991 it accounted for less than 10 per cent of the total gross manufacturing output (Figures 5.1 and 5.2).

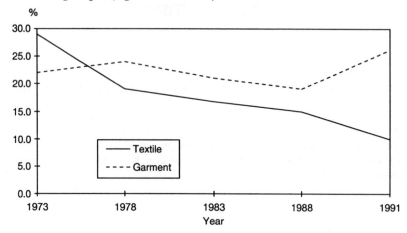

Figure 5.1 Share of the textile and garment industry in Hong Kong's total manufacturing gross output (per cent by gross output value)
Source: Table 5.1.

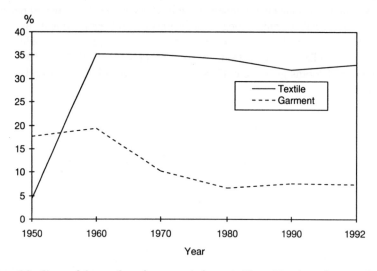

Figure 5.2 Share of the textile and garment industry in Hong Kong's total export (per cent by export value)
Source: Table 5.1.

Garments

Since the early 1960s the garment industry had overtaken the textile industry to become the largest foreign exchange earner and employer in the manufacturing sector. It grew in relative terms from 2.8 per cent of the total number of manufacturing establishments and 2.4 per cent of the total manufacturing employment in 1950 to 20 per cent and 34 per cent respectively in 1988. By 1991, it accounted for nearly 26 per cent of the economy's manufacturing output (Figure 5.1). To meet ever-changing overseas demands, its rapid expansion during the 1960s and the 1970s was accompanied by a steady move towards product diversification and sophistication. In 1975, Hong Kong replaced Italy as the world's leading exporter of garments in terms of both quantity and value (Cheng 1982, p. 147; Ho 1992, p. 170). By 1992, it contributed to 33 per cent of the total export value of Hong Kong (Figure 5.2).

Hong Kong's garment firms are largely export oriented. My survey revealed that, in 1994, 48 per cent of the firms in the sample sold their products only in overseas markets, while 44 per cent of the respondents sold mainly in overseas markets (Table 5.2). This was not the result of the government development policy or subsidy. Instead it resulted from a process of organisational learning. For instance, Tsui Hang Hing Garment Factory Ltd at first accepted any order, whether from local or overseas customers (see Case 1, Appendix 2). The owner soon found that the local market was very limited. What he contacted were generally import/export companies, or foreign trading agents in Hong Kong. Consequently, the firm received orders largely from foreign buyers and the business became export oriented. In 1994, 96 per cent of the company's products were exported, of which 54 per cent were shipped to Holland, UK, Germany, France, Belgium and Austria, 21 per cent to the USA and 18 per cent to China.

Table 5.2 Market locations of the textile and clothing products

Market locations	Distribution (%)
Wholly overseas	48
Mainly overseas	44
Equally in both local and overseas markets	2
Mainly local	6
Wholly local	0
Total	100
No. of firms	[50]

Source: 1994 Field Survey of Hong Kong's Textile and Garment Industry.

SMALL-SCALE ENTERPRISE AND SHORT-TERM PLANNING HORIZON

Hong Kong's textile and garment industry has been dominated by small- and medium-scale enterprises. My survey shows that, in 1994, 72 per cent of the firms

Table 5.3 Distribution of the textile and garment firms by number of workers employed (%)

No. of workers	Distribution (%) of firms for plant located in	
	Hong Kong	Hong Kong + China
1–9 persons	12	4
10–19 persons	18	4
20–49	42	18
50–99	14	12
100–99	10	20
200 and over	4	42
Total	100	100
No. of firms	[50]	[50]

Source: 1994 Field Survey of Hong Kong's Textile and Garment Industry.

in the sample employed less than 50 people for their plants in Hong Kong, though their factories in China hired more workers (Table 5.3). Sit and Wong (1989, p. 29) reported that, in 1985, 88 per cent of the textile factories and 84 per cent of the garment firms were small (less than 50 workers) or medium (less than 500 workers). They had contributed to the strength of the industry as providers of a variety of fashion products, and responded quickly to constant shifts in market demands (Hong Kong Government Industry Department 1991, p. 40).

Certain production such as woven garments involves a series of processes that are labour intensive. The small garment firms in Hong Kong, which did not possess any automation equipment, fitted into this kind of production and were able to provide a wide range of styles at lower costs (*Economic Reporter* 1988a, p. 5).

For small firms, efficient communication and quick response to external change can be possible. It is generally agreed that the industry had been able to produce small quantities of high quality garments at short notice (Hong Kong Government Industry Department 1991, p. 39).[1]

Table 5.4 shows that in 1994 nearly 86 per cent of the textile and garment firms had changed product designs in the previous 12 months while 3 per cent of the firms had also changed product lines. Only 8 per cent of the respondents remained

Table 5.4 Change in products or designs in the last 12 months

Product or design strategy	Distribution (%)
Maintain same product and same design	8
Change in products and designs/models	6
Change in designs/models only	86
Total	100
No. of firms	[50]

Source: 1994 Field Survey of Hong Kong's Textile and Garment Industry.

Table 5.5 Expected payback period among textile and garment firms

Expected payback period	Distribution (%)
5 years or below	62
5–10 years	6
>10 years	4
Do not know or no answer	28
Total	100
No. of firms	[50]

Source: 1994 Field Survey of Hong Kong's Textile and Garment Industry.
Note: $X^2 = 43.6$; df $= 3$; p > 0.001; Contingency coeff. $= 0.6825$

with the same product lines and designs. This indicates that firms were ready to adjust their production according to changing requirements of international markets.

To maintain such competitive edges, manufacturers in the industry tended not to expand their production capacities.[2] Furthermore, manufacturers in the industry avoided long-term commitments. When asked what payback period they expected at the time of planning their investments, 62 per cent of the textile and garment firms in the survey expected a payback period of less than five years. Only 4 per cent made commitments longer than ten years (Table 5.5).

PRODUCT IMITATION, TECHNOLOGY ADOPTION AND R&D

Product imitation

Most textile and garment firms in Hong Kong do not aim at creating new fashions. Instead, they focus on garments which consumers demand most. In my survey, 88 per cent of the manufacturers replied that similar garments were sold both in Hong Kong and in overseas markets by other firms while only 8 per cent of them regarded their products as unique both in Hong Kong and overseas markets (Table 5.6A).

In supplying those garments, most manufacturers imitate others. My survey indicates that 42 per cent of the respondents simply copied exactly from other manufacturers, while 44 per cent of them copied from others but with some modifications (Table 5.6B). Furthermore, 88 per cent of the respondents did not use patent protection (Table 5.6C).

Imitation has been a short cut to their success. The case of Goldlion (Far East) Co. Ltd supports this. Founded by Tsang Hin-Chi, an immigrant from China, Goldlion Company had been principally engaged in the production and marketing of men's apparel such as ties and shirts. Since its establishment in 1968, the company had developed into one of the largest manufacturers of menswear. In 1994 Goldlion supplied the markets with 20,000 different colour designed ties.

Tsang attributed the success of his company to the strategy of "borrowing ideas from overseas", which is widely adopted by Hong Kong's manufacturers.

Table 5.6 Product strategies employed by textile and garment firms

	Distribution (%)
A On product novelty	
The product is the first, or one of the few, of its kind both in Hong Kong and in overseas markets	8
The product is the first or one of very few of its kind in Hong Kong, but one of the many in overseas markets	4
The product is one of many both in Hong Kong and in overseas markets	88
Total	100
No. of firms	[50]
$X^2 = 68.55$; df = 2; p > 0.02; Contingency coeff. = 0.7604	
B Product imitation	
Copy exactly from other manufacturers	42
Copy from others but with some modifications	44
Completely new product design	14
Total	100
No. of firms	[50]
$X^2 = 8.42$; df = 2; p > 0.02; Contingency coeff. = 0.3796	
C Trademark protection	
Use trademark protection	12
Do not use trademark protection	88
Total	100
No. of firms	[50]
$X^2 = 28.88$; df = 1; p > 0.001; Contingency coeff. = 0.6051	

Source: 1994 Field Survey of Hong Kong's Textile and Garment Industry.

He implemented this imitative strategy through his four quick principles, namely "quick design, quick sampling, quick production and quick marketing".

Specifically in the tie market, France and Italy possess many first-class designers and supply world markets with ties of new designs and styles. Goldlion simply sent its staff overseas and adopted these new designs by paying licence fees. In the Hong Kong factory, the new designs were rapidly modified into Goldlion's products and then put into mass production. In this way, Goldlion could guarantee a quick supply of new styles. Hence Tsang's "four quick operations" enabled his company to catch up with world fashions.

Apart from manufacturing, Goldlion also replicated selling and marketing methods. Tsang adopted the idea of counter sales from some famous foreign brands operating in Hong Kong and established the Goldlion counters, which sold Goldlion products within department stores. They had a standard design and layout in accordance with the company's specification. All the counters were managed by the company's uniformed sales staff. The company was responsible for the decoration, fitting out and management of the counters while the department stores provided the floor area, which ranged from 200 sq. ft to 600 sq. ft for each counter. The revenue derived from such counters was shared between the company and the department stores on a predetermined basis but the department stores were guaranteed a minimum payment by the company. The company also established an extensive regional distribution network in China, Taiwan, Indonesia, Singapore, Malaysia and Thailand.

Technology adoption

In garment production, Hong Kong manufacturers are late adopters of technology. Sit and Wong (1989, p. 171) reported that 20 per cent of the small or medium textile firms in the survey admitted that they did not have enough equipment. But when asked whether more equipment was purchased, about 35 per cent of these firms replied that they did not take any action, indicating that they did not want to commit to larger investment.

A survey in 1989 revealed that most textile and garment firms, large or small, still used outdated equipment and procedures. Many techniques depended on manual labour. The level of Hong Kong firms' technology has historically been lower than that of parent firms or overseas competitors (Hong Kong Economic Survey Ltd 1989, p. 215). Similarly, a manpower survey conducted by Hong Kong Training Council revealed that the textile and garment industry largely employed low-skilled workers (Lin and Tuan 1988, p. 174; Table 5.7). In 1967, the textile industry employed more than 85,000 persons, approximately 84 per cent of the workers employed were operatives or unskilled. None of them was in the category of technologist. This situation persisted in the 1970s and the 1980s, although, over time, it showed a slight improvement in the skill level of the workforce. In the garment industry, an even higher proportion of employees was unskilled. Of the

Table 5.7 Skill levels of textile and garment employees, selected years

Year	Technologist (%)	Technician (%)	Craftsman (%)	Unskilled (%)	Total (%)	Number employed
Textiles						
1967	0.0	5.3	10.8	83.9	100.0	[85,045]
1975	1.1	4.9	13.3	80.7	100.0	[68,040]
1979	2.1	7.0	15.4	75.5	100.0	[70,341]
1985	1.6	7.7	16.9	73.8	100.0	[49,927]
Garments						
1969	0.0	4.0	3.0	93.0	100.0	[114,189]
1975	0.7	4.4	1.2	93.7	100.0	[184,128]
1981	1.4	5.4	3.7	89.5	100.0	[239,558]
1985	1.4	6.5	4.6	87.5	100.0	[262,904]

Source: Lin and Tuan 1988, p. 174.
Note: According to Hong Kong Training Council, a technologist is a person who applies his professional skills to a wide range of engineering activities. A technician is a person who performs technical duty normally under the supervision of a technologist.

114,189 workers engaged in garment production in 1969, none of them was in the category of technologist. Only 7 per cent of the workers were technicians and craftsmen. The rest (93 per cent) were unskilled workers. In 1985 the situation slightly improved. However, 87 per cent of the workers in the industry were still unskilled.

It was also found that the textile and garment firms were aware of new manufacturing advances such as etching for printing, colour control systems for mixing dyes, optical/pressure sensors for inspection of material, but they neither developed nor used them. Most often, new technology was rejected because of the perceived high costs. The industry did not have experience in innovation at the design, processing, or production stages of manufacturing (Hong Kong Economic Survey Ltd 1989, p. 215).

The firms depended on industry trade shows, parent companies and trading partners for technology transfer. The users of the most current technology were usually subsidiaries of foreign companies or joint ventures that received modest transfer of skills and technology from parent companies. For example, software for pattern development was used by larger companies. Small and medium-size companies were not prepared to buy these state-of-the-art products (Hong Kong Economic Survey Ltd 1989, p. 217).

Research and development

Hong Kong's textile and garment firms in general did not invest in R&D, though some large firms had a design department to undertake fashion development (Hong Kong Economic Survey Ltd 1989, p. 217). My survey in 1994 revealed that 84 per cent of the textile and garment firms did not have any formal R&D department. For those without an R&D department, 32 per cent of them replied that they could not afford one while 12 per cent of them could afford to but remarked that it was not an effective strategy. About 16 per cent of the firms in the survey replied that they had a design department to handle sampling activities (Table 5.8). A survey by the Hong Kong Industry Department and the Census and Statistics Department (1991, p. 86) revealed that only 12 per cent of the textile firms and 14 per cent of the garment firms carried out R&D more regularly. Moreover, the larger firms did not necessarily carry out R&D more regularly than the smaller firms. In particular, only 9 per cent of the garment firms with more than 100 workers carried out R&D regularly, compared with 13 per cent for the firms employing between 1 and 19 workers (Table 5.9).

In summary, innovations in textile and garment production through R&D were seldom undertaken in Hong Kong and the manufacturers were rarely interested in them. Hong Kong has been viewed by its partners as a low-cost producer, not an innovator (Hong Kong Economic Survey Ltd 1989, pp. 215–17). Despite this, small innovations, such as improvements in the quality of silk garments, were observed (Sit and Wong 1989, p. 33). The case of Tsui Hang Hing Garment Factory Ltd will further illustrate the above arguments.

Table 5.8   R&D activities among textile and garment firms

R&D activities	Distribution (%)
No, the company cannot afford	32
No, the company can afford but not an effective strategy	12
No, no need	40
Yes, but is not a priority	6
Yes, the company always emphasises on R&D	10
Total	100
No. of firms	[50]

Source: 1994 Field Survey of Hong Kong's Textile and Garment Industry.

Table 5.9   Distribution of establishments which carried out R&D regularly by size of firms (%)

Industry	Size of establishments (employment)			
	1–9 persons	20–49	50–99	100+
Textile	14	0	13	26
Garment	13	31	5	9

Sources: Hong Kong Government Industry Department & Census and Statistics Department 1991, p. 86.

Tsui Hang Hing Garment Factory had adopted imitative strategies. The company competed with many other manufacturers that produced similar products. It obtained its competitive edge by building up a professional image to gain confidence among foreign buyers. The company did not have a formal R&D department, but it had a fashion design team with ten specialists working on new design/style of garments. The aim of this team was to catch up with world fashions. Each year the design team supplied a new list of sportswear and casual wear. Each line of product took approximately six months to complete. The design team worked closely with the marketing department to make sure that their garments were in line with world fashions. The design and marketing team frequently visited Europe and the USA to observe market trends and communicate with potential buyers (see Case 1, Appendix 2).

SUBCONTRACTING AND CUSTOMER LABEL GARMENT BUSINESS

Subcontracting activities are common in Hong Kong's textile and garment industry. After receiving orders from local trading firms, or directly from overseas buyers, many manufacturers subcontract a part of production processes to other factories. My survey indicated that, in 1994, 72 per cent of the textile and garment firms subcontracted some production processes to other firms. A survey of small and medium enterprises by Sit and Wong (1989, p. 181) revealed that

Table 5.10   Reasons for subcontracting (%)

Reasons	Clothing	Textile
Lack of capacity	36.8	34.3
Labour shortage	34.2	16.4
Reducing cost	5.8	13.4
Reducing seasonal impact	12.5	13.4
Lack of specific equipment	6.6	14.9
Total	100.0	100.0
No. of firms	[75]	[60]

Source: Sit and Wong 1989, p. 187.

approximately 28 per cent of the garment firms and 21 per cent of the textile firms subcontracted certain production processes to local factories. Labour shortage, insufficient capacity and rush orders were three major reasons for the manufacturers to use subcontracting. In Sit and Wong's survey (1989, p. 183) 36.8 per cent of the garment firms and 34.3 per cent of the textile firms subcontracted because of lack of capacity. Labour shortage was another major reason to use subcontracting (Table 5.10).

The situation of subcontracting in Hong Kong can be further observed from the share of the contract value in the total business value. Sit and Wong (1989, p. 186) found that 56.3 per cent of the textile firms and 60.7 per cent of the garment firms in their survey claimed that 90-100 per cent of the total sales were covered by subcontracts (Table 5.11). Furthermore, the firms obtained contracts from not just one but several firms. The same survey revealed that only 7.7 per cent of the textile firms and 4.3 per cent of the garment firms had only one contractor.

Regarding the method of contracting, Sit and Wong (1989, p. 188) revealed that 36.4 per cent of the small and medium manufacturing firms in the survey replied that the contractors decided the price. The contract had to be completed in a very short time and the manufacturers could not afford to spend time in negotiations. Many business contracts were only oral agreements. Only 35 per cent of the firms in the survey replied that their business contracts were made in the form of written documents. However, a breach of contract was rare. Quick delivery was the major concern for both parties.

Table 5.11   Value of subcontract as a percentage of total sales

Subcontract value as % of total sales	Clothing	Textile
<50%	25.1	37.6
50–80%	14.3	6.3
90–100%	60.7	56.3
Total	100	100
No. of firms	[75]	[60]

Source: Sit and Wong 1989, p. 186.

Subcontracting is one of the strategies which contributed to the success of the textile and garment firms. About 35 per cent of the textile and garment firms in my survey indicated that subcontracting contributed to their business success. The extent of subcontracting is further illustrated in the cases of Goldlion (Far East) Ltd and Tak Sun Alliance Co. Ltd

Goldlion (Far East) Ltd

Except in tie production, the manufacturing of all garments sold by Goldlion (Far East) Company was subcontracted to outside manufacturers. In order to ensure quality and to control costs, the company sourced its own raw materials and accessories for shirts and T-shirts which were then provided to subcontractors for processing. In 1992 the company worked with 17 subcontractors for its garment products based mainly in Hong Kong. A major problem for subcontracting was quality control. For Goldlion, commercial production of the company's garments by subcontractors would only commence after production run samples had been checked by the company for quality, design and colour. For all garments manu-factured by subcontractors in Hong Kong and Macau, the company's merchandis-ing staff undertook online inspection. Finished products delivered to the company would also be checked again to ensure that all specifications and quality require-ments had been met (see Case 5, Appendix 2).

Tak Sun Alliance Company Ltd

To enhance the company's competitiveness, increase its production capacity and circumvent quota restrictions, Tak Sun Alliance Company Ltd in the 1980s sub-contracted the production of certain ranges of garments to other independent manufacturers. Own label garments were manufactured by the company as well as by 28 independent manufacturers overseas to the company's specifications for sale in the USA and Europe. Own label garments manufactured for the company by independent manufacturers represented approximately 76 per cent of the total value of own label garments sold. No single one of these manufacturers accounted for more than 11 per cent of such external contracting. According to Mr Ma Kai-Tak, the owner of Tak Sun Alliance Ltd, the policy of subcontracting with independent manufacturers allowed for greater flexibility in pricing and delivery times, reduced fixed overheads, lessened the impact of seasonal sales fluctuations and helped to alleviate stringent quota restrictions on goods produced in Hong Kong for import to the USA.

Through its subsidiaries in the USA, the company subcontracted with independ-ent manufacturers in Latin America, the Caribbean, Asia and the USA for the supply of own label garments for sale in the USA market. On the other hand, through its subsidiaries in Europe, the company subcontracted with independent manufacturers in Europe and Asia for the supply of own label garments to the European markets.

For own label garments sold in Hong Kong and other parts of Asia, the company subcontracted with independent manufacturers in Hong Kong and Thailand. In addition, all knitwear for sale as own label garments was subcontracted to independent manufacturers as the company did not have knitwear manufacturing facilities. In 1991, approximately 36 per cent and 97 per cent in terms of value of own label garments distributed in the US and Europe respectively were sourced from independent manufacturers.

For certain production processes requiring facilities which the company did not own, such as label making, embroidery, washing and orders, or beyond the capacity of the company's own facilities, which might occur during peak seasons, they were subcontracted out to independent manufacturers. In general, urgent orders, garments which were subject to strict customer requirements and fancy fashion wear were subcontracted in Hong Kong, while large volume orders for garments with simpler designs were subcontracted overseas. All the orders processed by the subcontractors were monitored by the company's senior staff (see Case 4, Appendix 2).

Subcontracting and customer label garment supplier

Many firms receive orders from foreign manufacturing or trading firms. In this international subcontracting, local manufacturers produce garments which bear the labels of the foreign firms. In other words, local firms produce customer label garments (CLG). My survey in 1994 shows that 78 per cent of the respondents had been and would have continued to be involved in the customer label garment business. Only 6 per cent of the firms in the sample answered that they ceased to be customer label garment suppliers (Table 5.12A).

As customer label garment suppliers, manufacturers produce whatever their customers demand. In this arrangement, product designs are therefore largely specified by foreign buyers. My survey revealed that, in 1994, 64 per cent of the textile and garment firms had their product designs specified by buyers. Only 1 per cent of the firms in the sample supplied their own designs (Table 5.12B). About 26 per cent of the firms replied that their product designs were specified by both buyers and the companies. This response has two possible interpretations. One is that both buyers and manufacturers participated in product design. Another is that manufacturers produced customer label garments as well as their own label garments. Hence, in the first case, the designs were specified by buyers while, in the second case, the designs were specified by local firms themselves. In both cases, local manufacturers could learn and imitate from foreign firms. Some of them later competed with original suppliers.

Being customer label garment suppliers, local firms do not need to establish their own labels, nor do they need to take care of marketing and promotion activities. Though some firms may have their own labels, they do not promote them because rapid exploitation of profit margins was their concern. My 1994 survey revealed that 68 per cent of the textile and garment firms had never

Table 5.12 Customer label garment, design specification and brand policy

Items	Distribution (%)
A On customer label garment (CLG) business	
It has been and continues to be an CLG supplier	78
It was previously but now no longer is an CLG supplier	6
It has never been an CLG supplier	16
Total	100
No. of firms	[50]
$X^2 = 46.604$; df = 2; p. > 0.001; Contingency coeff. = 0.6947	
B Design specification	
Mainly the company	1
Mainly buyers	64
Both the company and buyers	26
Total	100
No. of firms	[50]
$X^2 = 23.815$; df = 2; p > 0.001; Contingency coeff. = 0.568	
C Own label garment	
The company has never established its own label	68
The company has established its own label in recent years	16
The company has long established its own label	16
Total	100
No. of firms	[50]
$X^2 = 27.818$; df = 2; p > 0.001; Contingency coeff. = 0.5979	
D Contribution to the success of the company	
Produce as a customer label garment supplier	76
Promote the company's own label	16
Use both of the above	6
Total	100
No. of firms	[49]
$X^2 = 41.95$; df = 2; p > 0.001; Contingency coeff. = 0.6755	

Source: 1994 Field Survey of Hong Kong's Textile and Garment Industry.

established their own labels. Only 16 per cent of the firms in the sample had promoted their own labels in recent years (Table 5.12C). This indicates that some manufacturers were moving towards high value added products. Furthermore, approximately 76 per cent of the firms in the survey indicated that customer label garment business contributed more to their economic success (Table 5.12D). The following two cases illustrate the operations of customer label garment suppliers and their marketing strategies.

Tak Sun Alliance Company Ltd

Tak Sun Alliance Company Ltd, a typical garment firm in Hong Kong, started as an exporter of customer label garments to Europe and the USA. The designs of the garments were specified by overseas customers. Since entering these markets, sales had steadily increased and the company in 1994 supplied customer label garments to over 30 buyers who are either agents, trading houses or major department stores. In 1991, sales of customer label garments accounted for approximately 27 per cent of the company's turnover by value (see Case 4, Appendix 2).

Tsui Hang Hing Garment Factory Ltd

Tsui Hang Hing Garment Factory Ltd had traditionally relied on the customer label garment business. Although the company in the late 1980s was able to produce some good quality garments, it refused to promote its own label. According to Cheung Hang-Seng, the owner of the company, promoting own label garments involved huge investment and high risk and therefore was not worthwhile. However, in 1991, the company changed its marketing strategy and promoted two of its labels, namely Lava and VV in China. These products accounted for 15 per cent of the company's total production in 1994. Cheung gave two reasons for this change. First, people in China generally considered Hong Kong made products to be superior to their locally made goods. Second, with a huge market in China, the average cost of promoting a label there was much lower. Since 1991 his products have been sold in Beijing, Shanghai, Huhan and other major cities (see Case 1, Appendix 2).

Overall, we can conclude that subcontracting is an important entrepreneurial strategy in Hong Kong's textile and garment industry. Engaging in subcontracting and customer label garment business, Hong Kong's textile and garment firms can maintain a high degree of flexibility, reduce costs, tackle seasonal impacts and receive the supply of parts or services which they are unable to produce.

SPATIAL ARBITRAGE

The availability of abundant low wage labour in the 1950s and 1960s was undoubtedly a major factor contributing to the dramatic growth of garment manufacturing in Hong Kong. This advantage has gradually been eroded over time. Rising labour and production costs in recent years have reduced the competitiveness of garments made in Hong Kong. On the other hand, China has an ample supply of cheap labour. In particular, significant wage differentials exist between Hong Kong and China. The difference in the wage rate levels in the garment industry between Hong Kong and Shekou (Guangdong) is shown in Table 5.13.

The wage differentials have attracted Hong Kong's textile and garment manufacturers to relocate their production to China. Led by Hong Kong companies, which now account for nearly 70 per cent of total foreign investment in China, the first wave of foreign investment was directed towards low capital and labour intensive projects, primarily in garment assembly for export. Some industry analysts

Table 5.13 A comparison of wage rates between Hong Kong and Shekou (Guangdong, China) in the garment industry, 1986

Occupation	Hong Kong	Shekou
Operative and craftsman	HK$2,550	HK$170+150 RMB
Skilled worker	HK$3,500	HK$170+220 RMB
Office worker	HK$3,000	HK$170+180 RMB

Source: Wong 1989, p. 27.

Note: RMB is the currency of China. According to the arrangement of the Special Economic Zone, in 1986, HK$170 was provided by Hong Kong manufacturers to the Labour Bureau of Shekkou for the payment of fringe benefits to work in Shekou involved in processing for Hong Kong's manufacturers.

felt that as much as 65 per cent of China's total garment exports were tied to Hong Kong's manufacturers.

My survey (Table 5.14A) reveals that in 1994 approximately 62 per cent of Hong Kong's textile and garment firms also operated on the mainland. Most of them participated in China's production in the form of joint ventures or contract export processing, whereby Hong Kong contractors supplied all required raw materials and paid the commissioned Chinese factory a processing fee, usually based on volume. Most joint ventures were valued at less than $1 million and even less in contract export processing ventures. The preferred cities were Shenzhen, Dongguan and Guangzhou, with which Hong Kong's manufacturers were familiar (1994 Field Survey of Hong Kong's Textile and Garment Industry). Lower production costs and geographical convenience were two other major considerations for choosing a location in China (Table 5.14D).

Relocating production to China was also a means to circumvent quota restriction. For example, in knitwear manufacturing, the process of panel knitting was usually undertaken on the Mainland. However, the linking and looping of panels into sweaters were carried out in Hong Kong, despite the fact that this latter stage was not particularly skilful or capital intensive. As a result, the import of semi-manufactured garments (mostly knitted panels) from China to Hong Kong increased rapidly and this partly explained the rapid rise in the share of Chinese garments in Hong Kong's retained imports (Sung 1991, p. 110).

There is another way to circumvent quota restrictions. The agents in Hong Kong can export Chinese garment under Hong Kong's quota. This can be done through two main channels. First, completed Chinese garments which are concealed under semi-manufactured items in containers are shipped from China to Hong Kong. This involves a risk because customs officers may examine the whole container. Second, completed Chinese garments can be imported by the retailers in Hong Kong. The garments are then resold to Hong Kong's manufacturers who label them as their own products. This method involves less risk and can account for part of the sharp rise in the import of completed Chinese garments. Sung (1991, p. 113) estimated that from 1980 to 1988 the amount of trade through this method was US$1,090 million or 29 per cent of completed Chinese garment

Table 5.14 Relocation of production activities

Aspects	Distribution (%)
A The company operates in other countries	62
The company only operates in Hong Kong	38
Total	100
No. of firms	[50]
$X^2 = 2.88$; df = 1; p > 0.1; Contingency coeff. = 0.2334	
B The company is one of the first group to move to China	
Yes	29
No	71
Total	100
No. of firms	[31]
$X^2 = 5.46$; df = 1; p > 0.02; Contingency coeff. = 0.3869	
C New market/location in China	
Yes	6
No	94
Total	100
No of firms	[31]
$X^2 = 23.52$; df = 1; p > 0.001; Contingency coeff. = 0.6567	
D Reasons to relocate to a particular location	
Presence of relatives/friends	14
Hometown or birthplace	19
Familiar with the place	17
Lower production cost	28
Geographical convenience	22
Total	100
No. of firms	[31]
$X^2 = 3.5$; df = 4; p > 0.5; Contingency coeff. = 0.3185	

Source: 1994 Field Survey of Hong Kong's Textile and Garment Industry.

imports, representing nearly 2 per cent of Hong Kong's domestic exports of garments. The operations of spatial arbitrage are further illustrated by the following three cases:

Tsui Hang Hing Garment Factory Ltd

Like many other manufacturers facing rising production costs in Hong Kong, Mr Cheung Hang-Seng, the founder and managing director, was alert to cost reduction opportunities. Following the open door policy in China, Cheung in 1985 began to subcontract parts of the production processes to the Frank Well Garment Factory, located in Fujian. Cheung owned a 55 per cent stake in this factory. In 1988 another joint venture in Hangzhou was formed, in which Cheung's company owned a 45 per cent share. By 1990 the company's investment in the Hangzhou factory amounted to Yn1,175,000. By similar arrangement, in 1990 the company controlled a printing factory (for garments) in Shenzhen. Altogether, by 1994, the company employed around 3,000 people in China. In contrast, the employment of his factory in Kwun Tong (Hong Kong) was reduced to only 30 people. The production in Hong Kong remained because the company could still utilise its quota in the Colony. However, as labour costs in Hong Kong kept rising, Cheung intended to close down the factory in Kwun Tong, leaving only an office there as a coordinating and sourcing centre.

Apart from China, Mr Cheung also established a factory in Mauritius (Africa). Taking the advantages of cheap labour, low tax rates and the Mauritius government's concession to allocate a full quota to the company, Cheung in 1991 invested US$668,000 to establish Tsui Hang Hing (Mauritius) Garment Factory Ltd. Moreover, unlike investment in China, exports from Mauritius to European countries were not subject to any quota restrictions. In 1994 Mr Cheung planned to invest in Russia and Vietnam (see Case 1, Appendix 2).

Topstyle Garment Factory Ltd: failure as a first mover

In early 1973, when China was still under the influence of the Cultural Revolution, the founder and the managing director of Topstyle Garment Factory Ltd, Lo Chiu-Hung, took an adventurous step to engage in processing trades in Shanghai. Being a first mover, Lo found that doing business with China's state enterprises was extremely difficult. Her investments during that time did not render her any benefit. Lo recalled one painful experience with China. State managers in China after a long time in isolation from the outside world did not know the significance of punctual delivery and quality control. A cargo of the company's finished products was urgently packed to beat the deadline for Christmas sales in the USA. Later, Lo was told by the county officials involved in the state enterprise that her cargo had not been arranged for delivery because the train had been diverted to transport mooncakes to Hong Kong for the mid-autumn festival. Consequently she lost several hundred thousand dollars and concluded that China was not yet ready for foreign trade. Subsequently she retreated to Hong Kong. This event illustrated that being a first mover may not be advantageous.

However, the Shanghai failure did not block her return to China. The lesson revealed that Shanghai was too far from Hong Kong and that communication was difficult. Therefore she considered other locations which were closer to Hong Kong. In 1977 she established a processing factory in Fujian and became involved in "compensation trades" in Guangzhou, Pangyu and Shuntak (all in Guangdong).

In 1987 the company established a garment factory in Pangyu county, Guangdong. In 1994 the company operated two factories there, with a total gross floor area of approximately 150,000 sq. ft and employed approximately 1,300 workers.

With the production and distribution being either subcontracted or relocated in China, the company retained its head office in Hong Kong where management, sales and marketing, finance and administration operations were located. Lo acted as an international coordinator (see Case 6, Appendix 2).

Goldlion (Far East) Co. Ltd

Following the success of Goldlion's business in Hong Kong, Tsang Hin-Chi planned to establish a subsidiary in the USA. However, the economic reform in China during the last decade disrupted this plan. With much lower production costs and a huge potential market on the Mainland, Tsang decided to invest US$1 million there. In 1989, he established a tie manufacturing factory – China Silverlion Ltd – in his home town, Meizhou (Guangdong). The factory occupied a total floor area of approximately 7,200 sq. ft, with four production lines employing 45 workers. The factory possessed a total production capacity of approximately 1,200,000 ties per annum on the basis of one shift of operation. In 1992 it manufactured 660,000 ties.

For Tsang, spatial arbitrage was not confined to manufacturing, it extended also to distribution. After the successful launching of counter sales in Hong Kong's department stores, Tsang applied the same concept to China and the South East Asian countries. The company established an extensive regional distribution network for its products in China, Taiwan, Indonesia, Singapore, Malaysia and Thailand. The two major centres were China and Singapore.

In China the company set up a subsidiary named Silverlion to promote sales. Silverlion was the principal wholesaler of products from Goldlion, though the latter also sold directly to customers in China, including a sole distributor for the city of Shenyang and the duty free shops in the five special economic zones. Goldlion had an office with a packing area in Guangzhou which was responsible for the coordination of the company's marketing and distribution activities in the country. The company had a total of approximately 460 wholesaler and retailer customers in China, with 32 in Guangzhou, 28 in Beijing, 17 in Shanghai, 11 in Tianjin, 11 in Chengdu, 8 in Dalian, 8 in Wuhan, 7 in Xian, 6 in Nanjing with reminder located in other cities.

In Singapore the company had approximately 90 wholesale and retail customers comprising apparel shops and department stores. In addition, the company operated 22 Goldlion counters in department stores, mostly located in popular shopping areas, comprising 12 on Orchard Road, four on Beach Road, two in Katong and four in other areas. The regional distribution of the total turnover is shown in Table 5.15.

In conclusion, garment manufacturers in Hong Kong are alert to cost reduction and profit opportunities. In recent years, they have relocated the garment production to mainland China to exploit cost differentials and the huge market there. However, moving to other locations requires substantial entrepreneurial learning, as illustrated in the above cases.

Table 5.15 Total turnover (HK$'000) of Goldlion (Far East) Ltd by region, 1988 and 1992

Regions	1988	1992
Mainland China	10,125	230,010
Hong Kong	66,199	140,941
Singapore	20,413	50,761
Others	3,558	40,374
Total	100,295	462,085
Gross profit	19,737	106,790
Net profit margin	15.9%	18.9%

Source: Case 5, Appendix 2.

ENTREPRENEURIAL STRATEGIES AND ECONOMIC PERFORMANCE

So far this study has shown that most manufacturers in the textile and garment industry adopted Kirznerian entrepreneurial strategies. This section will substantiate the argument that the success of the industry has been due principally to these strategies. Eleven criteria were employed to determine the kind of entrepreneurial strategy which a firm adopted (see Chapter 2). They are product novelty, customer label garment business, design specification, subcontracting, brand policy, patent protection, R&D, adoption of technology, spatial arbitrage and expected payback period. The economic performance of a firm was determined from Questions 27-31 of the questionnaire (see Appendix 1).

My survey reveals that the textile and garment industry was dominated by firms which pursued adaptive imitation strategies. About 78 per cent of the firms in 1994 adopted adaptive imitation strategies, another 18 per cent used intermediate strategies. Only 4 per cent of the firms employed creative innovation strategies (Table 5.16). Furthermore, those using adaptive imitation strategies could survive. Approximately 36 per cent of these firms reported that their business performances were either excellent or good. About 46 per cent of them replied that they could only manage to survive (i.e., marginal). The result is not surprising. Without any significant innovation, the profit margins in the industry will eventually vanish. Facing keen competition, quota protection and environmental regulation, some firms were even in danger of being driven out of the market.

Table 5.16 Entrepreneurial strategies and firms' performance (%)

	Excellent	Good	Marginal	Poor	Total	No. of firms
Adaptive imitation	10.3	25.6	46.7	15.4	100.0	[39]
Intermediate	44.4	33.3	22.2	0.0	100.0	[9]
Creative innovation	0.0	0.0	50.0	50.0	100.0	[2]

$X^2 = 11.28$; df = 6; $p < 0.05$; Contingency coeff. = 0.429

Source: 1994 Field Survey of Hong Kong's Textile and Garment Industry.

My survey also indicates that intermediate firms performed better. About 44 per cent of these firms had excellent performance while 33 per cent of them achieved good results. There were two firms using creative innovation strategies, but the performances were either marginal or poor, showing that these strategies were not viable, at least in the environment of Hong Kong. In an economic report prepared by the Hong Kong Government Industry Department in 1988, the companies were asked their opinions on the reasons for Hong Kong's economic success as a manufacturer of garments. They all agreed on the following factors: delivery on time, reaction to requirements, accommodation to change, high quality products, wide range of styles, low production costs in China, and the ability to take small orders. These factors are largely associated with Kirznerian entrepreneurial strategies. Note that the inclusion of high quality products implies that firms may not remain in the manufacturing of low value added clothing although they are still customer label garment suppliers.

For the textile industry, similar factors such as short lead time, delivery on time, reaction to requirements, accommodation to change, provision of a wide range of styles, and ability to accept small orders were noted (Hong Kong Industry Department 1992b, p. A133). In sum, this report reinforces our argument that successful textile and garment firms in Hong Kong did not adopt creative innovation strategies.

The following case reiterates my arguments. Though the Victory Garment Factory had already operated in Hong Kong for a long period, in an attempt to expand its business by adopting more innovative strategies, the company ended up in severe loss.

Innovation in garments manufacturing means fabric development, fashion design and label promotion. For Hong Kong's garment exporters, both fabric development and fashion design involve cultural factors which require local manufacturers to be familiar with tastes and preferences of foreign consumers. One way to tackle this problem is to establish a marketing office overseas and employ foreign professionals to deal with fabric development and fashion design. However, this involves very high costs and high risks. Therefore, Hong Kong's manufacturers seldom involve themselves in fabric development, fashion design and own label promotion, though they may have the capacity to do so. Instead, they produce customer label garments. Ng Mo-Tack, the owner of Victory Garment Co., attempted to adopt a more innovative strategy and hence failed.

In 1985 an American garment factory ran into financial problems and persuaded Victory Garment Factory to form a joint venture to promote Victory's own label garments in the USA. Since Victory Garment Factory possessed the kind of garment quota for exporting to the USA, Ng decided to have a trial.

The fabric development and fashion design activities were principally performed by its partner in the USA. An office with a 20,000 sq. ft warehouse in San Francisco was set up for promotion and distribution of its label garment "Victory". Aggressive marketing programmes which included an enlarged sales force and incentive schemes were launched. Initial success was recorded. Sales increased from HK$5 million to HK$9 million.

Later, due to personal reasons, the foreign partner withdrew and Ng decided to proceed independently. Having previously relied on the foreign partner, Ng was unfamiliar with the kinds of marketing and promotion strategies for the US market, especially those involving the culture and tastes of Americans. To tackle the problem, the company employed foreign senior designers and professional marketing teams for its marketing office in the USA. However, employing marketing personnel in the USA was costly. Though the marketing programmes achieved success in generating sales, it later proved to be financially burdensome for the company. Sales continued to increase but the costs required to support such sales growth escalated out of proportion, thereby contributing to substantial losses. Soon the company ran into debts of approximately US$2 million.

After reviewing the situation, Ng decided to return to a more conservative approach. The company reduced its reliance on its own label and concentrated on customer label garments. This also meant that the company only undertook garment manufacturing and left the selling and promoting activities to foreign buyers. Ng Mo-Tack admitted that this strategy was more practical and would be maintained in the future (see Case 9, Appendix 2).

In summary, both the survey and case studies showed that Hong Kong's textile and garment industry has been dominated by Kirznerian entrepreneurs engaging in small-scale enterprise, product imitation, subcontracting and spatial arbitrage. Specifically, pursuing imitation strategies, most of the textile and garment firms survived, though they might live on small profit margins. Only a few firms adopted more innovative strategies and their performances were not satisfactory, indicating that these were not practical in the environment of Hong Kong. Overall, it can be concluded that the dynamism in the textile and garment industry has been largely associated with Kirznerian entrepreneurship.

NOTES

1 Kwok (1978, pp. 141–2) reported that 88 per cent of the small textile firms were run by owner-managers and 78 per cent of these firms replied that the owner-manager was the principal decision-maker. Approximately 24 per cent of the small textile firms relied on verbal communication only while 38 per cent relied largely on verbal communication.

2 In a survey by Kwok (1978, p. 145), small textile manufacturers were asked to explain why they had not expanded in the last three years. Approximately 33 per cent of the firms mentioned that expansion might bring more problems and 24 per cent were satisfied with present size. About 9 per cent of the firms replied that if they expanded they would lose present advantages.

6

ADAPTIVE RESPONSE IN THE ELECTRONICS INDUSTRY

We have demonstrated that the economic success of the textile and garment industry has been associated with Kirznerian entrepreneurship engaging in small-scale enterprise, customer label garment business, product imitation, subcontracting and spatial arbitrage. In this chapter, we attempt to show that this argument also holds in the electronics industry, another major manufacturing activity in Hong Kong.

HONG KONG'S ELECTRONICS INDUSTRY

The development of the electronics industry in Hong Kong began in the 1950s. In 1958 Japan's Sony started assembling radios in Hong Kong under a subcontract arrangement. The Colony's first electronics company, Champagne Engineering Co., assembled over 4,000 radios a month for Sony (Henderson 1991, p. 80).

By 1960 Champagne and two other companies manufactured their own radios and exported to the USA. Taking advantage of cheaper labour at that time, exports to the USA increased fifteen-fold during 1960-1 (Henderson 1991, p. 81). By 1961, twelve firms operated in the Territory, of which two were joint ventures with American companies. The same year witnessed the establishment of the first semi-conductor firm, Fairchild, to manufacture transistors and diodes. By 1966, Fairchild's assembly plant in Kwun Tong, the Territory's industrial area, became the largest electronics firm in Hong Kong, employing about 4,500 workers (Hobday 1995, p. 1173). Fairchild was later joined by nine other American and two Japanese firms in semi-conductor production. The industry continued to grow and by 1987 it had become the Territory's second largest manufacturing industry, accounting for about two-thirds of Hong Kong's domestic exports (Henderson 1991, p. 84).

Within twenty years of its emergence in the early 1960s as a subcontracting assembler of transistor radios, the industry had grown to encompass the production of a wide range of consumer items such as TVs, VCRs, tape recorders, hi-fi equipment, computers, etc, as well as components such as semi-conductors, capacitors, condensers and transformers. By the late 1980s the industry had 1,200 factories employing more than 78,000 people (Henderson 1991, p. 87).

Unlike in the housing and real estate sectors, the Hong Kong government has not intervened directly in electronics manufacturing. It has been only indirectly

110

Table 6.1   Market locations of Hong Kong's electronics products

Market locations	Distribution (%)
Wholly overseas	40
Mainly overseas	32
Equally in both local and overseas markets	8
Mainly local	14
Wholly local	6
Total	100
No. of firms	[50]
$X^2 = 23$; df = 4; p > 0.001; Contingency coeff. = 0.5613	

Source: 1994 Field Survey of Hong Kong's Electronics Industry.

involved in the industry through the labour market. The Hong Kong government established vocational training schools and polytechnics to train qualified technicians and engineers. Such skilled labour enabled Hong Kong to develop into an advanced testing and design centre. Apart from this, the Hong Kong Productivity Centre, funded by the government, was established in the 1960s to assist manufacturers to develop their products. In short, like other manufacturing industries, the government's involvement in the electronics industry has been very limited.

The electronics industry in Hong Kong established itself as the second most important contributor to domestic exports. My survey reveals that, in 1994, 72 per cent of the manufacturers sold their products either wholly or mainly in overseas markets. Only 6 per cent sold their products wholly in Hong Kong (Table 6.1). In 1965 the share of the domestic exports of electronics products in the economy's manufacturing exports was only 4 per cent (Table 6.3). In 1992 the share increased to 25 per cent and the export value of electronics products was estimated at HK$60,291 million (Hong Kong Industry Department 1993, p. 25).

Table 6.2 shows the share of the exports absorbed by Hong Kong's principal markets. The USA was and remains an important market for Hong Kong made products. It accounted for nearly 25 per cent of the total electronics exports in 1992. However, Hong Kong has reduced its reliance on the US market. Instead, its trade relationship with China has increased. China has emerged as the second largest export market since its open door policy in the mid-1980s. The UK, Germany, Japan and Singapore were also major importers. Comparing 1992 with 1965, there had been a dramatic change in the export markets, showing the dynamics of Hong Kong producers in exploring new markets (Table 6.2).

ENTREPRENEURSHIP IN HONG KONG: OPPORTUNITY ARBITRAGEURSHIP

Virtually without any government support in R&D, the technological level of the electronics industry has logged behind South Korea and Taiwan (Chen and Wong 1989, pp 207–8). Hong Kong's manufacturers have survived by being alert to

Table 6.2 Market shares of the electronics exports from Hong Kong, 1965–92, selected years (% by value)

Countries	1965	1970	1975	1980	1985	1990	1992	Annual change (%) 1965–75	1975–85	1985–92
USA	75.5	71.4	48.2	42.0	45.4	28.8	25.3	−3.6	−0.6	−4.4
China				2.9	15.1	18.8	24.0	–	–	5.9
Singapore	1.2		3.4	3.2	2.1	6.8	12.4	–	−3.8	49.0
Germany	1.4	4.5	15.9	12.1	5.3	8.1	5.2	103.6	−6.7	−0.2
Japan	0.9	3.4	1.2	1.0	2.1	3.5	4.2	3.3	7.5	10.0
UK	13.2	5.2	5.3	8.5	5.2	4.5	3.9	−6.1	−0.2	−2.5
All others	9.0	14.3	26.1	30.4	24.8	29.9	25.0	19.0	−0.5	0.1
Total	100.0	100.0	100.0	100.0	100.0	100.0	100.0			

Source: Hong Kong Government Industry Department 1993 p. 59.

opportunities. The case of Luks Industrial Ltd serves as a good example. The growth of the company relied to a large extent on the ability of its founder, Mr Luk King-Tin, to identify market opportunities.

According to Mr Luk, South Korea and Taiwan have been Hong Kong's two major rivals. Mr Luk utilised the insight of *Sun Tsu Bing Fa* (a military strategy book in ancient China): "If you know thy enemies and know yourself, then you will win the battle", and avoided direct confrontation with rivals. In the 1980s the UK restricted the black and white TVs made in South Korea and Taiwan, but imposed no restriction on those made in Hong Kong. Therefore, Luks industrial Co. continued to produce and export black and white TVs to the UK, although they became a low value added product which many producers would not consider to be at all worthwhile .

Furthermore, colour TVs in the UK and certain European countries use the phase alternation line (PAL) system, but South Korea and Taiwan at that time produced TVs conforming to National Television System Committee (NTSC), mainly for the US market. So Mr Luk bought the PAL patent from Telefunken and manufactured colour TV and TV kits conforming to the PAL system which he exported to European countries. In this way he avoided direct encounters with South Korean and Taiwanese producers. In 1986 the export of Luks TVs to the UK represented approximately 30 per cent of the company's total turnover (*Luks Industrial Co. Ltd: A Company Profile*, p. 10).

Prior to 1986 the import of TVs to China was subject to high import duty, whereas the import of TV kits, a collection of components for the assembly of a TV, was subject to duty at much lower rates. So Mr Luk manufactured TV kits in Hong Kong and then sold them to Luks Shekou, or other Chinese concerns for final assembly, hence enjoying low customs duty. As a result, the company's total turnover in TV kits increased from approximately $40.4 million in 1981 to $205 million in 1985, a 500 per cent growth rate (*Luks Industrial Co. Ltd: A Company Profile*, p. 9).

Similarly, in 1986 the European Common Market initiated dumping accusations against Hong Kong TV manufacturers. In 1989 a special sales tax was imposed on the colour TVs made in China by Hong Kong firms. Faced with this, the company shifted its emphasis to the supply of production equipment and essential component kits, supplemented by the sale of complete TV sets. Furthermore, in the early 1990s, it established an assembly arrangement through the incorporation of a wholly owned subsidiary in the UK to assemble final TV sets for export to Europe (see Case 10, Appendix 2).

The above illustrations suggest that in the face of keen competition from South Korea and Taiwan and trade restrictions from developed countries, Hong Kong producers like Mr Luk can still survive due to their ability to identify profit opportunities and exploit narrow profit margins.

SMALL FIRMS, FLEXIBILITY AND SHORT-TERM PLANNING HORIZON

Unlike the textile and clothing industry which began with a group of experienced industrialists from Shanghai, the electronics industry started without any foundation at all, but has developed into a major manufacturing industry in Hong Kong. This achievement can be observed in the number of workers employed (Table 6.3). In 1961 there were only four electronics firms in Hong Kong, employing around 183 workers. By 1970 employment rose to more than 38,454 people and peaked in 1980. By 1992 the industry hired 60,653 people.

In terms of firm size, Table 6.3 shows that by 1970 electronics companies, employed on average around 160 people. The rapid growth in the number of factories during the 1970s and 1980s coincided with significant reduction in firm size. By 1992 the average size of an establishment was only 42 workers. This was largely associated with a growth in the subcontracting of the assembly of electronic components to the small family run factories, often employing no more than ten workers. Many of them operated in the informal sector (Henderson 1991, p. 87).

Table 6.3 Average size of Hong Kong's electronics firms, 1961–92

Year	No. of establishments	No. of employees	Average size by employment
1961	4	183	46
1965	35	5,013	143
1970	230	38,454	167
1975	490	53,833	110
1980	1,316	93,005	7
1985	1,304	86,115	66
1990	1,819	85,169	47
1991	1,633	71,466	44
1992	1,446	60,653	42

Source: Hong Kong Government Industry Department 1993, p. 54.

Moreover, most manufacturers have in recent years relocated their plants to China, resulting in shrinking production in Hong Kong.

Table 6.4   Distribution of electronics firms by number of persons employed (%)

	Distribution(%) of firms with plant located in	
Employment	Hong Kong	Hong Kong + China
1–9 person(s)	24	2
10–19 persons	24	9
20–49 persons	15	11
50–99 persons	15	4
100–99 persons	13	17
200 or over persons	6	56
Total	100	100
No. of firms	[46]	[46]

Source: 1994 Field Survey of Hong Kong's Electronics Industry.

My 1994 survey indicated that about 62 per cent of the firms employed 50 people or less for their plants in Hong Kong. However, their plants in China hired more workers. If the factories in China were included, 56 per cent of the firms in the survey employed 200 workers or more (Table 6.4).[1]

Hong Kong's electronics manufacturers maintain a small and very flexible capacity so that they can easily adapt to the changing needs of world markets, especially for the price slashing warfare and keen competition.[2] They could switch their product lines, say, from electronic calculators to notebook PCs, to cellular phones, in a matter of months (Engardio and Gross 1992, p. 67).

According to Thomson Lam, the president of Porro Technologies Ltd, the average product life cycle for most of the electronics goods was approximately eighteen months. If Hong Kong's producers reacted slowly, then they would be left with stockpiles of unsold items (Wilson 1991a, p. 38).

My survey in 1994 shows that only 24 per cent of the respondents in the last 12 months maintained the same products and same designs. About 76 per cent of them replied that they had changed product designs and models, of which nearly 16 per cent had also enlarged their product ranges (Table 6.5).

Table 6.5   Change in products or designs in the last 12 months

Product strategies	No. of respondents	Distribution (%)
Maintain same product and same design	12	24
Change in products and designs/models	6	
Change in designs/models only	38	76
Total	50	100

Source: 1994 Field Survey of Hong Kong's Electronics Industry.

Table 6.6 Lead time for product development and assembly in the electronics industry, 1988

Lead time for product development or assembly	Distribution (%)
Lead time for product development	
Less than 1 year	94
Less than 6 months	52
Lead time for product assembly	
Less than 6 months	77
Less than 2 months	28

Source: Hong Kong Government Industry Department 1991, Appendix IV–15

A survey by the Hong Kong Industry Department revealed that about 95 per cent of the electronics firms claimed that they could develop products in less than twelve months, while 52 per cent of them could do so in less than six months (Table 6.6). Furthermore, 77 per cent of the firms could assemble their products in less than six months while 28 per cent of them could do so in less than two months (Hong Kong Government Industry Department 1991, Section IV-58).

Furthermore, most Hong Kong manufacturers adopt a short-term view in production. This is especially true for small electronics firms (Cheung 1982). They do not make sales forecasts and decisions are made on an *ad hoc* basis. On the whole, the electronics manufacturers in Hong Kong do not make long-term commitments in any investment. Instead, they rush to the most popular products which have low value added, low profit margins but with a quick return.

My survey reveals that, in 1994, 32 per cent of the electronics manufacturers, at the time of planning their investment, expected to achieve break-even within five years, while only 10 per cent of them considered a payback period longer than ten years, illustrating the short-term view of Hong Kong manufacturers. About 50 per cent of them did not even have an expected payback period in their investment planning. For these producers, business would continue as long as profit existed (Table 6.7).

Table 6.7 Expected payback period

Expected payback period	Distribution (%)
5 years or below	32
6–10 years	6
>10 years	10
Do not know or no answer	52
Total	100
No. of firms	[50]

Source: 1994 Field Survey of Hong Kong's Electronics Industry.

A survey by the Hong Kong Government Industry Department showed similar results. When manufacturers considered adding new technology or machinery to their plants, most of them expected a payback period on those investments of less than three years (Hong Kong Government Industry Department 1991, Appendix IV–64).[3]

The importance of flexibility, rapid reaction and short-term view of planning is testified to by Mr Luk King-Tin, the founder and managing director of Luks Industrial Ltd. According to Mr Luk, Japanese producers have been well known for TV manufacturing. In terms of technology, Hong Kong's medium and small firms cannot compete with them. However, for a large Japanese firm like Hitachi, flexibility and adaptability have been restricted by its huge capital commitment. By contrast, Hong Kong's medium and small firms have been highly flexible and able to adapt quickly to changing market conditions. For instance, given the existing plant structure, they can reshuffle their production lines from making transistor radios to electronic watches within three months, or from electronic calculators to black and white TVs within six months, or from black and white TVs to colour TVs within nine months (*Economic Reporter* 1981, p. 19). Comparing internationally, Sung (1987, p. 48) reported that it took Hong Kong producers only three months to introduce a new electronics product, while the Japanese took five months and the Americans, eight months.

SUBCONTRACTING, OEM BUSINESS AND BRAND POLICY

Similar to the textile and garment industry, subcontracting is widely practised in Hong Kong's electronics industry. My survey indicated that, in 1994, 20 per cent of the electronics firms in the sample received orders other factories while another 24 per cent received orders from wholesalers or from other factories. Moreover, about 58 per cent of them subcontracted the production activities to other factories (Table 6.8).

Table 6.8C shows the reasons for subcontracting in the industry. A majority of the electronics firms used subcontracting to tackle labour shortage in Hong Kong. Insufficient capacity and seasonal fluctuations were also important factors. In short, the electronics firms used subcontracting largely for maintaining flexibility.

When the electronics manufacturers were asked whether subcontracting or vertical integration contributed to the success of the company, 42 per cent of them mentioned subcontracting (Table 6.8D). In their views, although vertical integration enabled them to have more control over production and earned larger profit margins, subcontracting had the advantage of less capital commitment and, more importantly, provided them with a higher degree of flexibility so that they could adapt rapidly to the changing economic conditions.

A form of international subcontracting is the original equipment manufacturer (OEM) business in which local manufacturers produce according to the requirements of the orders/contracts received from overseas companies. Despite the growth of design skills of some local firms, OEM business still accounted for a large proportion of total electronics output in Hong Kong (Hobday 1995, p. 1176).

Table 6.8 On subcontracting

Aspects	Distribution (%)
A Source of orders	
From wholesalers/trading agents	56
From other factories	20
From both	24
Total	100
No. of firms	[50]
$X^2 = 12.31$; df = 2; p > 0.01; C = 0.4399	
B Subcontracting to other factories	
Yes	58
No	42
Total	100
No. of firms	[50]
$X^2 = 1.28$; df = 1; p > 0.3; Contingency coeff. = 0.158	
C Reasons for subcontracting	
Insufficient capacity	25
Does not possess particular skills	11
Accepting rush orders	7
Seasonal reasons	11
Lower costs	11
Others	36
Total	100
No. of firms	[28]
Note: Multiple answers were sometimes given.	
D Contribution to the success of the company	
Subcontracting	42
Vertical integration	44
Not sure	14
Total	100
No. of firms	[50]
$X^2 = 9.03$; df = 2; p > 0.02; Contingency coeff. = 0.3911	

Source: 1994 Field Survey of Hong Kong's Electronics Industry.

My findings reveal that, in 1994, 66 per cent of the respondents had been and would continue to be OEM suppliers (Table 6.9A). They were followers.[4]

If a firm engages in OEM business, it does not need to promote its own brand. Many of the electronics firms in Hong Kong even specialise in no brand products. This fact is partly supported from my 1994 survey which found that nearly 41 per cent of the respondents had never established their own brand. Approximately the same proportion of firms responded that they had long established their own brands. Note that some firms produced as OEM suppliers but at the same time sold their own brand products (see Table 6.9B). A survey by the Hong Kong Industry Department shows that 28 per cent of the local electronics producers

Table 6.9 OEM business and brand policy

Items	Distribution (%)
A On OEM business	
It has been and continues to be an OEM supplier	66
It was previously but now no longer is an OEM supplier	2
It has never been an OEM supplier	31
Total	100
No. of firms	[49]
$X^2 = 17.5$; df = 2; p > 0.001; Contingency coeff. = 0.5092	
B On brand	
The company has never established its own brand	40
The company has established its own brand in recent years	19
The company has long established its own brand	41
Total	100
No. of firms	[37]
$X^2 = 3.90$; df = 2; p > 0.2; Contingency coeff. = 0.3088	
C Brand policy and the success of the company	
Produce as an OEM supplier	33
Promote the company's niche brand	31
Use both OEM and niche brand strategies	36
Total	100
No. of firms	[45]
$X^2 = 0.582$; df = 2; p > 0.8; Contingency coeff. = 0.1128	

Source: 1994 Field Survey of Hong Kong's Electronics Industry.

were involved solely in OEM business while 43 per cent of them were partially involved. About 51 per cent of the firms were partially involved in own brand products while only 8 per cent of them were solely involved in own brand business. Moreover, local firms mainly had their products distributed through overseas buying offices or importers (see Table 6.10). Not much effort had been devoted to marketing activities. They took a passive approach to the marketing of their products. This was particularly true for small local electronics firms (Hong Kong Government Industry Department 1991, Appendix IV-11, 18).

Being OEM suppliers, a number of firms also engaged in some innovations which did not require sophisticated technology. It was quite common for overseas firms only to provide some broad ideas about the requirements of the products, leaving the detailed design to be developed by OEM suppliers (*Economic Reporter* 1988b, p. 15). In this way, OEM suppliers could learn by doing and later were capable of building their own models. In other words, some of them could compete with well established foreign firms via imitation. This point will be further elaborated in Chapter 7.

Regarding whether OEM business or own niche brand contributed more to the economic success of the firms, nearly one-third of the firms in my survey mentioned OEM business, and a further third relied on both methods. This means

Table 6.10 Distribution channels for local companies

Distribution channels	No. of respondents
Overseas buying office/exporter	22
Own overseas sale office	14
Exporters	6
Trading firms	4
Manufacturer direct	3
No. of firms	29

Source: Hong Kong Government Industry Department 1991, Appendix IV–11.
Note: Multiple answers were sometimes given.

that they had been OEM suppliers and at the same time also sold their own brand products (Table 6.9C). In total, two-thirds of the firms used OEM strategy, showing the importance of this strategy in the electronics industry.

To illustrate further the significance of OEM business in Hong Kong's electronics industry, we examine the case of Termbray Electronics Ltd and S. Megga Telecommunications.

The insight of Mr Lee Lap, founder of Termbray Electronics Ltd, "We make it, you sell it", is worth noting and is indeed the secret of the success of most Hong Kong exporters. They shun grand marketing plans and multimillion dollar brand promotions. Instead they let the overseas buyers bear the risk of selling the products.

In 1984 Termbray Electronics Co. successfully secured its first order from AT&T to manufacture telephone sets and telephone answering machines designed by AT&T. Initially orders were only basic models, but the company later succeeded in obtaining contracts to manufacture upgraded and more complex products offering many features, including memory functions, speaker phones, liquid crystals and two-way recording functions. In the same year, the company set up another factory in Kwai Chung to expand its production capacity for OEM activities. In 1991 sales to AT&T accounted for approximately 84 per cent of the company's OEM sales and 60 per cent of the company's operating profit. In 1991 total turnover in the OEM business amounted to $601.9 million, with an operating profit of $97.2 million (see Case 3, Appendix 2).

Likewise, the success of S. Megga Telecommunication Ltd was built upon OEM business. In the late 1970s, when cordless telephones became popular in the USA, Leung Ray-Man, the owner of S. Megga, started to penetrate this market. At that time cordless telephones were largely monopolised by Japanese producers. In 1981, S. Megga successfully produced its first cordless telephone. Although initially the selling prices of these products were marginally higher than other local firms, when compared to Japanese products the products were still cheaper. Hence, S. Megga's telephones were able to enter the US market.

In 1982, after obtaining approval from the US Federal Communications Commission, the company sold cordless and feature telephones in the USA, Europe and Australia. In the following year, the company manufactured and sold

"Telehelper 1600" memory diallers and "Telehelper 600" speakerphones to AT&T for distribution in the USA under AT&T's brand name. In the same year, the company designed cordless telephones known as the "Nomad" series for the AT&T Group. Sales to AT&T grew dramatically from approximately HK$69 million in 1984 to HK$475 million in 1991. S. Megga became the major supplier of cordless telephones to AT&T. In 1990 the company received the OEM Quality Excellence Gold Award from AT&T. In 1991 it even sold cordless telephones with answering machine features to JVC, despite the fact that JVC was once a major supplier of cordless telephones.

TECHNOLOGY AND PRODUCT IMITATION STRATEGIES

As most electronics firms in Hong Kong are small in size, they have very limited resources and are unable to launch any original research and development. In 1973 expenditure on R&D in Hong Kong's electrical and electronics industry was estimated at HK$4,953,000, comprising only 0.5 per cent of value added (Sit *et al.* 1979, p. 41). Hong Kong's manufacturers in general are regarded as being followers and imitators rather than innovators (Sit *et al.* 1979, p. 40). They focus on the production of matured and low value added consumer products. The export figures indicated that only 25 per cent of the finished electronics was of high value added products such as computers and their related items (Hong Kong Government Industry Department 1991, Appendix IV–60).

Cheung's findings (1982) revealed that approximately 70 per cent of the small electronics firms seldom or never initiated product design. They copied or modified other products rather than designing new models.

In my 1994 survey, 36 per cent of the manufacturers responded that they did not need a formal R&D department. Two firms replied that they could afford to set up a formal R&D department but chose not to do so because it was not practical. About 18 per cent of the firms mentioned that, though they had a formal R&D department, R&D was not a priority (Table 6.11).

The survey also indicated that approximately 50 per cent of the electronics producers emphasised R&D. For them, R&D is mainly for imitation purposes.

Table 6.11 On R&D spending

R&D strategy	Distribution (%)
No, the company cannot afford	6
No, the company can afford but not an effective strategy	4
No, no need	26
Yes, but is not a priority	16
Yes, the company always places emphasis on R&D	48
Total	100
No. of firms	[50]

Source: 1994 Field Survey of Hong Kong's Electronics Industry.

Table 6.12 R&D by size of establishments and origin of investment

Sizes of establishments and origins of investment	% of establishments which carried out R&D regularly
A Sizes of establishments	
1–19 person	0
20–49	31
50–99	17
100+	41
All establishments	18
B Origins of investment	
Local	23
Overseas	6
Joint venture	43
All investment	18

Source: Hong Kong Government Industry Department and Census and Statistics Department 1991, p. 86.

The transfer of technology from overseas through formal arrangement, with the exception of foreign manufacturers which were generally supported by their overseas parent firms, was not widely practised by local manufacturers. In a study by the Hong Kong Industry Department (1991, Appendix IV–21), only five local electronics manufacturers reported having technical agreements with overseas companies. In another survey jointly conducted by the Hong Kong Industry Department and Census and Statistics Department (1991, p. 86), only 18 per cent of the electronics firms carried out R&D regularly. None of the firms with 1 to 19 workers engaged in R&D regularly. Furthermore, of the 18 per cent of firms that conducted R&D regularly, 43 per cent were joint ventures with foreign firms. About 23 per cent of them were local firms and 6 per cent were overseas companies, indicating that Hong Kong is not a centre for radical innovation (Table 6.12).

The technologies used in electronics production were not sophisticated. The firms largely employed non-skilled labour. In 1966 there were 20,322 workers in the industry, of whom more than 88 per cent were unskilled labour. None of the firms employed any technologist. This situation persisted in the 1970s and 1980s. In particular, in 1984, approximately 73 per cent of workers in the industry were unskilled labour. Nearly 20 per cent of them were technicians or craftsmen. Only 4 per cent of them were technologists (Lin and Tuan 1988, p. 174; Table 6.13; Figure 6.1).

The electronics firms adopted a product imitation strategy, in which production required only a low level of technological skill. My survey revealed that nearly 62 per cent of the electronics manufacturers copied and modified other products in the market. About 18 per cent of them copied exactly from other manufacturers without any modification. In total, 80 per cent of the respondents pursued an imitative strategy. Only 20 per cent of them aimed at new design products (Table 6.14C). Of the 31 firms that copied others with some modifications, four answered that they had previously attempted to design and produce completely new products but had failed.

Table 6.13 Skill levels of the electronics employees, selected years (% distribution)

	1966	*1974*	*1980*	*1984*
Technologist	0.0	1.5	2.4	3.9
Technician	4.5	6.3	10.7	11.7
Craftsman	7.3	16.7	10.0	9.3
Operative/unskilled	88.2	75.5	76.8	72.9
Total	100.0	100.0	100.0	100.0
Employment	[20,322]	[48,960]	[92,968]	[107,375]

Source: Lin and Tuan 1988, p. 174.

The argument that Hong Kong producers are mainly imitators gets further support from my survey. About 18 per cent of the electronics firms replied that their product designs were specified by buyers. In other words, they produced whatever customers demanded. This implies that the firms did not initiate new designs. Approximately 30 per cent of the firms in the survey answered that the designs were specified by themselves. Another 46 per cent replied that the designs were specified by both parties. This answer may indicate a degree of cooperation in design activities. But it may also refer to the situation that the firms performed two kinds of businesses at the same time, namely OEM products and company's own brand products. The designs of OEM products are specified by buyers while the

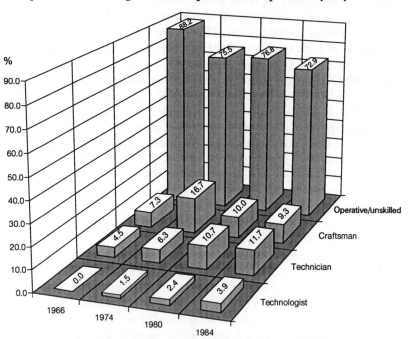

Figure 6.1 Skill levels of the electronics employees (% distribution)
Source: Lin and Tuan 1988, p. 174.

latter are specified by the firms themselves. For those replying that the product designs were specified by themselves or by both parties, we cannot determine whether the firms had been involved in any product innovation or adopted an imitative strategy (Table 6.14A). But when asked about the degree of novelty of their products, the result is clear. Over 96 per cent of the firms manufactured no unique designs of products or models (Table 6.14B).

Product imitation can be achieved through spin-offs. In Hong Kong this often occurs by means of spin-offs from multinational corporations in the Colony. As ambitious employees learn about the industry and the technology from foreign firms, they seek to establish their own business (Whitley 1990, p. 60). Many

Table 6.14 Product strategy

Aspects	*Distribution (%)*
A Design specification	
Mainly the company	30
Mainly buyers	18
Both the company and buyers	46
No answer	6
Total	100
No. of firms	[50]
$X^2 = 17.52$; df = 3; p > 0.001; Contingency coeff. = 0.5094	
B On product novelty	
The product is the first, or one of very few, of its kind both in Hong Kong and in overseas markets	2
The product is the first or one of very few of its kind in Hong Kong, but one of the many in overseas markets	2
The product is one of many in Hong Kong and in overseas markets	96
Total	100
No. of firms	[50]
$X^2 = 89.64$; df = 2; p > 0.001; Contingency coeff. = 0.8013	
C Product development policy	
Copy exactly from other manufacturers	18
Copy from others but with some modifications	62
Completely new product design	20
Total	100
No. of firms	[50]
$X^2 = 19.21$; df = 2; p > 0.001; Contingency coeff. = 0.5241	
D Patent Protection	
Use patent protection	40
Do not use patent protection	60
Total	100
No. of firms	[50]
$X^2 = 2$; df = 1; p > 0.01; Contingency coeff. = 0.1961	

Source: 1994 Field Survey of Hong Kong's Electronics Industry.

spin-offs are similar to the case of Li-Tung Electronics whose founders worked for seven years in NCR, an American firm in Hong Kong. In 1974 he and five other staff left NCR and invested HK$300,000 to set up a company to produce TV games and musical doorbells. Based on the knowledge and experience of their previous employment, this new venture was successful. In the first year their company produced and exported 50,000 TV games to the USA, valued at HK$3 million (*Hong Kong Economic Journal Monthly* 1990, pp. 96–9). This phenomenon is prevalent in Hong Kong's computer software industry. Newly employed programmers may spend around half a year developing a particular software programme in foreign firms. At the same time, they also have the opportunity to contact the company's customers. Within a year, the programmers resign and form a new company with several of their friends. The new firm takes away the clients from its former employer by selling similar but modified products at prices around 60-70 per cent cheaper (*Economic Reporter* 1991a, p. 20). Thus, keen competition is a common feature in Hong Kong's economy.

For those firms registering products at the patent office, their product designs must possess some degree of novelty. This implies that the firms are adopting an offensive technological strategy. On the other hand, if manufacturers pursue an imitative strategy, then patent registration may not be needed. We found that a majority of Hong Kong's manufacturers (60 per cent) did not use patent protection at all because they were followers who imitated products from other firms (Table 6.14D).

We have shown that most of Hong Kong's small electronics firms survived on the basis of Kirznerian imitation strategies. When they adopted a more radical innovative policy, they encountered many difficulties. This is illustrated by the experience of Dragon Precision Ltd which failed because of adopting offensive technological strategies.

In 1984 Sze Chak-Tong and his brother Sze Chun-Kuen established Dragon Precision Ltd. The factory was located at Cheung Sha Wan, an old industrial district, had a total gross floor area of 700 sq. ft and employed six workers to produce computer main boards for Apple and IBM compatible computers – XT, Turbo XT, 260 and 460 models (*Dragon Precision Co. Ltd: A Company Profile*). With long working hours, which are quite normal for small firms in Hong Kong, Sze's job ranged from looking for orders, supervision, day-to-day operations and delivery. Unlike other manufacturing firms in Hong Kong, the factory at that time produced solely for the local market where Sze's business connections were located.

During 1989–91 Sze expanded his business and rented a larger plant in Kowloon Bay, with a total gross floor area of 1,300 sq. ft, employing 30 people. Sze admitted that he was very ambitious at that time. Right at the beginning, obsessed with innovation and sophisticated technology, he established an R&D section, employing three electronics engineers to develop some uniquely designed products. But Sze found that the policy did not work. Even large Hong Kong firms would spend money on R&D only for the purpose of transferring overseas technology from their parent companies or modifying new product from other manufacturers.

Sze explained the costs and benefits of establishing R&D as follows. The company employed three graduate electronics engineers. Each trainee cost about HK$12,000 per month. Hence the total costs of employing three engineers for one year were approximately HK$400,000. Since the first year was largely a training period, results could only be observed at the end of the second year. So the total costs of employing three engineers for two years was approximately HK$800,000 to HK$1 million.

Despite the investment in R&D, it did not bring the company any benefits. According to Sze, the technological know-how in Hong Kong was normally six months behind Taiwan. Taiwan's manufacturers could obtain new advances in technology from their parent firms in the USA much sooner than local firms which had no affiliation with foreign companies. Because Sze's company had no technological support from any parent firm overseas, the so-called new models supplied by his R&D team were actually at the fully mature stage of the product life cycle and lagged approximately half a year behind international markets. Consequently, his products could not compete with those made in Taiwan. Therefore, in Sze's view, R&D was entirely worthless to his firm and was even regarded as counter-productive.

R&D may be useful in Hong Kong for well-established firms which are affiliated with foreign companies. Nevertheless R&D in those firms is aimed at adaptive imitation, not for any radical breakthrough in product designs. Indeed most Hong Kong firms are market driven, depending less on advanced technology and more on predefined product market guidelines to direct their business activities.

Sze soon found where the problems lay. Unable to compete with companies from South Korea or Taiwan, he redirected his production to products with slim profit margins but high turnover. Firstly he closed the whole R&D department so that the company operated on a very low R&D budget. In technology management, his firm now behaves as a follower and focuses on OEM business. Second, he discovered that his company had been vertically integrated to a large extent. Sze realised that if a firm expands mainly through vertical integration, it loses flexibility. For instance, if market signals call for a reduction of output, it is difficult for a vertically integrated firm to retrench workers. In order to maintain flexibility, he subcontracted production to China's enterprises, with the office in Hong Kong serving a consultancy function (see Case 8, Appendix 2).

It is worth noting that large electronics companies in Hong Kong spent money on R&D mostly for the transfer of technology or for imitation, not for technological breakthrough or designing brand new products. We can again cite S. Megga's case as example.

Compared to Dragon Precision Ltd, S. Megga Telecommunication Ltd is larger in size. Though the company had a formal R&D department with 50 engineers and technicians and was equipped with sophisticated testing instruments and computer-aided design systems, it did not aim to achieve technological breakthroughs. Instead, the department was intended: (1) to ensure that the performance of the company's products is compatible with the standards set by foreign regulatory authorities; (2) to update its technological know-how; (3) to improve the quality of existing products. For (2), the company also sent its engineers to various manufacturing firms worldwide including AT&T in the USA and JVC in Japan to obtain the latest technological skills. For (3), substantial research effort is devoted to improving product design, shortening product development time and minimising product development cost.

Currently the world is moving towards the second generation cordless telephones. But Leung chose to improve on the first generation model. He contended that the company had benefited more from improving the first model. Leung refused to move into the second generation model because a brand new product at an early stage of the life cycle has a limited market and is very risky. Therefore he preferred to wait until new models become popular and then enjoy the advantage of being a latecomer.

As noted in the theoretical chapter, imitation can be a very powerful strategy for competition in world markets. It allows firms in late industrialising economies to gradually catch up with advanced economies. This is shown by the dramatic development of a local Chinese firm, Vtech. According to the president, Allan Wong, the company's strategy focused on three principles, namely novel, quick and cheap. First, Vtech strove to improve the product design, with new models much more efficient than original ones from overseas. Second, the company could tailor products quickly to meet market needs. Wong claimed that he could make decisions within minutes and get things started. Third, the improved products were sold more cheaply than their rivals. On this, Wong proudly remarked that "to manufacture a computer is very easy, but to design it cost effectively is the name of the game".

To implement the three principles, the company established R&D centres in the USA, Canada, UK, China and Hong Kong. Their functions were to review constantly the marketplace for emerging trends and opportunities and to "adapt leading-edge technologies in order to create exciting and inventive consumer products". Wong admitted that only a minor portion of the R&D money was spent on new product design, while the bulk went into redesigning and improving products as well as making them easier and cheaper to produce. In these ways, the company adopted a defensive technological strategy (see Case 2, Appendix 2).

SPATIAL ARBITRAGE: ALERTNESS TO COST REDUCTION OPPORTUNITIES

To imitate and duplicate electronic products from multinational firms is easy but to produce them at competitive prices is difficult. Hong Kong's manufacturers obtained their competitive edge by being alert to cost reducing opportunities. In particular, when they experienced an erosion of cost competitiveness, they moved to lower cost regions. Previously they had shifted some of their production to countries like Indonesia, Thailand, Malaysia and Taiwan in order to reduce costs (Chen 1983, p. 91). In recent years, China accelerated its economic reforms. For Hong Kong's producers, this was a golden opportunity. Land is much cheaper in

China. Furthermore there are abundant supplies of labour and qualified engineers. More importantly, Hong Kong and China share a similar culture, which made mutual understanding easier. In general, people in China lack knowledge of world markets and modern managerial skills. On the other hand, Hong Kong producers suffer from rising production costs, especially in land rentals and wages.[5] In particular, it was claimed that in Hong Kong, an engineer with only post-secondary education cost more than HK$10,000 per month. In China, for the same amount of money, one could hire three engineers with university or postgraduate qualifications (*Economic Reporter* 1992, p. 20). The average wage of a technician in China is only HK$1,000 per month, far below the level in Hong Kong (*Hong Kong Economic Journal Monthly* 1991, p. 69). Furthermore, unlike Hong Kong, where experienced engineers would move to another firm for higher pay or to start their own business, employees in China were relatively more stable.

Hong Kong producers exploited these significant spatial price discrepancies to their advantage. It was reported that, in 1991, 85 per cent of the electronics firms moved their production to China, causing Hong Kong's entrepôt trade to increase by 46 per cent (*Economic Reporter* 1991b, p. 5). In my survey, 80 per cent of the electronics manufacturers relocated their production partially or fully to China (Table 6.15 A). A survey by the Federation of Industries (1992) showed that nearly 70 per cent of electronics companies in Hong Kong invested in the Pearl River Delta (PRD), which accounted for an average of 47.7 per cent of their total investments. In 1992, the average number of workers employed by each Hong Kong firm in the PRD was 905 and the total number of employees recruited in the PRD was 106,757. The average percentage of products finished/processed in the PRD was 78.9 (Table 6.16).

My survey showed that, in 1994, 84 per cent of the electronics firms indicated that they were not the first group to operate in China, neither were they the first group to operate in their chosen location (Table 6.15). Most Hong Kong manufacturers preferred locations such as Shenzhen, Dongguan and Guangzhou. All are in the Pearl River Delta region of southern China.

This result is consistent with the survey conducted by the Federation of Industries which revealed that nearly 56 per cent of the Hong Kong electronics manufacturers chose Shenzhen and 15 per cent of them chose Dongguan. Huizhou and Guangzhou were also popular locations (Table 6.18).

Most manufacturers chose a particular location because of geographical convenience. In particular, 46 per cent of the electronics firms in my survey chose Shenzhen because it is adjacent to Hong Kong. Production cost is also an important consideration (Table 6.15). A survey by the Federation of Industries shows similar results. Hong Kong's producers preferred the Pearl River Delta as a production base because of its geographical proximity to Hong Kong. Also they were more familiar with the environment in the PRD (Table 6.19).

Hong Kong's producers cooperated with China's enterprises either through technology licensing, subcontracting, joint ventures or by establishing a subsidiary firm in China. In the Pearl River Delta region, 36 per cent of Hong Kong

Table 6.15 On spatial arbitrage

Aspects	Distribution (%)
A The company operates in other countries	80
The company only operates in Hong Kong	20
Total	100
No. of firms	[50]
$X^2 = 18$; df = 1; p > 0.001; Contingency coeff. = 0.5145	
B The company is one of the first group to go to China	
Yes	16
No	84
Total	100
No. of firms	[50]
$X^2 = 23.12$; df = 1; p > 0.001; Contingency coeff. = 0.5623	
C New market/location in China	
Yes	6
No	94
Total	100
No. of firms	[50]
$X^2 = 38.72$; df = 1; p > 0.001; Contingency coeff. = 0.6606	
D Reasons to move to a particular location	
Presence of relative/friends	6
Hometown or birthplace	4
Familiar with the place	6
Many other companies operate there	2
Lower production cost	29
Large demand for the product over there	2
Geographical convenience	46
Others	4
Total	100
No. of firms	[48]
Note: Multiple answers were sometimes given.	

Source: 1994 Field Survey of Hong Kong's Electronics Industry.

Table 6.16 Investment of Hong Kong electronics firms in Pearl River Delta (PRD), 1992

Percentage of companies having investment in PRD	69.4
Percentage of companies planning to invest in PRD	8.1
Average percentage of PRD investment in total investment	47.7
Average no. of workers employed in PRD	905
Average percentage of workers employed in PRD	94.1
Total no. of employees recruited in PRD	106,757
Average percentage of product finished/processed in PRD	78.9
Percentage of PRD-made products which are sold in China	7.1

Source: Federation of Industries 1992, pp. 28, 77.

Table 6.17 Performance of Hong Kong's investment in Pearl River Delta, 1992

Categories	% of respondents
Excellent	6.7
Good	50.8
Fair	39.2
Poor	0.8
N/A	2.5
Total	100.0
No. of firms	[120]

Source: Federation of Industries 1992, pp. 28, 77.

Table 6.18 Favourable locations of Hong Kong's investment in Pearl River Delta, 1992

Location	Distribution (%)
Shenzhen	56.3
Dongguan	14.6
Guangzhou	5.7
Huizhou	15.2
Foshan	2.5
Jiangmen	0.6
Zhongshan	1.9
Zhuhai	1.3
Shantou	1.3
No answer	0.6
Total	100.0
No. of firms	[158]

Source: Federation of Industries 1992, p. 72.

Table 6.19 Reasons for choosing Pearl River Delta (PRD) as a production base

Reasons	Distribution (%)
Geographical proximity to Hong Kong	73
Attractive investment environment	6.9
Familiarity with environment in the PRD	8.2
Abundant land and labour supply	6.3
Absence of language barrier	1.3
To explore the large domestic market in the PRD	0.6
Having good relationship with local government or partner	0.6
No answer	3.1
Total	100.0
No. of firms	[159]

Source: Federation of Industries 1992, pp. 41, 74.

investments were in the form of wholly owned enterprises, 25.3 per cent were equity joint ventures and 20 per cent were processing trades (Table 6.20).

129

Table 6.20 Forms of investment chosen by Hong Kong electronics manufacturers in Pearl River Delta, 1992

Forms of investment	Establishments (%)
Wholly foreign-owned enterprise	36.1
Equity joint venture	25.3
Processing of imported raw materials	19.6
Cooperative joint venture	12.7
Mixed forms of investment	2.5
Compensation trade	0.6
Others (e.g. consignment and licence agreement)	1.3
Total	100.0
No. of firms	[158]

Source: Federation of Industries 1992, pp. 41, 73.

The investments in the PRD resulted in good returns. The Federation's survey revealed that more than 50 per cent of the Hong Kong electronics firms in China achieved good results, while 6.7 per cent of them had excellent results. Only 0.8 per cent of the respondents indicated that their business performances in the PRD were poor (Table 6.17). More in-depth case studies of the Hong Kong electronics firms operating in China are presented as follows.[6]

Termbray Electronics Co.

The economic reforms of communist China in the last decade have provided Termbray Electronics Co. with opportunities to establish manufacturing bases in the Mainland which has the attraction of lower overheads and an ample supply of labour. In 1984 Lee Lap, the founder of the company, set up a factory in his home town, Zhongshan, Guangdong, to concentrate on the production of single-sided and double-sided printed circuit boards. The plant had a total floor area of 60,000 sq. ft. In 1986 he set up another factory in Nantou, Shenzhen, for the manufacture of telephones and telephone answering systems designed by AT&T.

In early 1990 Lee began to relocate the manufacturing facilities for double-sided and multilayer printed circuit boards from the Tsuen Wan factory to Zhongshan, while the plant in Tsuen Wan was used as a headquarters.

In 1991 the construction of the factory's extension in Zhongshan was completed. The total floor area increased from to 263,000 sq. ft, employing 1,500 workers. Moreover, the installation of approximately $42 million worth of new machinery and equipment there significantly increased the company's capacity to manufacture more complex printed circuit boards.

Termbray's business continued to expand in China. A new factory was established in Guangzhou at the end of 1994. The land area of the new factory site was approximately 130,000 sq. m. In 1993 the company bought a whole set of advanced production facilities from a printed circuit manufacturing plant in Germany at US$3.5 million to be installed in the new factory. The new plant if operated at its full capacity could increase total printed circuit board production by 40 per cent (see Case 3, Appendix 2)

S. Megga Telecommunications Co.

Despite spending an equivalent of 6 per cent of total sales on R&D in 1992, almost as much as its Japanese rivals, S. Megga was unable to manufacture telephones and other electronics products significantly cheaply in Hong Kong. The situation improved after the company moved its production to China.

Production in China

The company's facilities in China which accounted for most of the company's total production in 1994 were located in Dongguan and had total a gross floor area of approximately 218,000 sq. ft. These factories were equipped with radio frequency testing equipment and auto-insertion, surface mount, automatic soldering and in-circuit testing machines to manufacture cordless telephones and feature telephones as well as satellite receivers. Apart from taking the advantage of much lower production costs in China, exports of cordless telephones and feature telephones manufactured on the mainland to the USA benefited from the most favoured nation (MFN) status granted to China by the USA.

Production in Malaysia

S. Megga also produced in Malaysia. S. Meggatel was formed as a result of a joint venture agreement in August 1991. S. Meggatel owned a piece of land in Klang, Malaysia, that occupied approximately 177,000 sq. ft in area. A factory was constructed on this site with a total gross floor area of approximately 66,000 sq. ft. It produced cordless telephones for AT&T.

S. Meggatel was granted pioneer status by the Malaysian Industrial Development Authority, which entitled the company to concessionary taxation in various forms. One of the concessions was taxation relief for a five-year period with a further five-year tax relief period which might be granted at the discretion of the relevant authorities upon meeting certain criteria. In addition, Malaysia was one of the countries eligible for the US Generalised System of Preferences (see Case 7, Appendix 2).

Vtech

Compared to other small manufacturers, Vtech was rather late in relocating its production activities to China to utilise the ample supply of low-cost labour and land there. However, Vtech's investment in the Mainland was large. Almost ten years after China implemented its open door policy, the company in 1987 invested HK$500 million in setting up an electronics plant in Dongguan, Guangdong. The plant occupied a manufacturing space of over 400,000 sq. m, with seven departments, employing around 11,000 people. The 21 production lines, supplying over 100 types of electronic toys, producing an annual turnover Y$3,000 million, were supervised by 100 local Chinese engineers and managers.

Apart from taking advantage of lower production costs in China, the company also enjoyed concessionary tariff terms when exporting Dongguan's products to the USA because China was granted most favoured nation (MFN) trading status. Vtech also cooperated with Lian Xiang Computer Ltd (Beijing) to market its educational computers in China (see Case 2, Appendix 2).

Luks Industrial Co. Ltd

In identifying opportunities in other regions, Mr Luk's strategy was unconventional. He focused his business on communist economies such as China, Vietnam and various Eastern European countries because these markets were unexploited. "In mature capitalist economies", Luk remarked, "one has to compete with many well established manufacturers. So if one tries to penetrate these markets, it is just like growing young trees in a big forest. The young plant would hardly receive enough nutrition. But for communist countries which have just pursued an open door policy, the markets remain unexploited and so possess high growth potentials." For this reason, Mr Luk actively sought to penetrate these markets.

The China connection

In September 1979 China announced its new economic policy and welcomed foreign investments. Mr Luk, with his Chinese background, immediately took the opportunity and invested in the mainland.

Lower production costs in China, combined with the lower import duties on TV kits, enabled the company to market its products more competitively in China than other importers. This was due to the fact that during the early 1980s Japanese manufacturers were hampered by the strength of the Japanese yen. Furthermore, Taiwanese and South Korean manufacturers had not yet established direct trade relationships with China.

In 1979 the company supplied production facilities and technical support to a factory in China to enable it to produce black and white TVs. In 1981 the company established its TV assembly line in Hong Kong to produce colour TVs to sell in Hong Kong and China. It also produced TV kits for China's markets.

In the same year the company established production facilities in China for the purpose of manufacturing colour TVs designed primarily for sale in China. It entered into an agreement with the Zhenhua Electric Industrial Corporation of China and the Shenzhen Electric Group to form a joint venture company named Huafa in which Luks held one-third of the equity. Huafa assembled and sold TVs from kits designed and supplied by Luks (*Luks Industrial Co. Ltd: A Company Profile*, p. 6).

Furthermore, in 1981, Luks Shekou, a wholly owned subsidiary of the company, was established in Shekou, a special economic zone in Shenzhen, Guangdong. In 1983 the subsidiary began to assemble colour TVs from kits supplied by the parent company for sale in China. Luks Shekou also undertook chassis subassembly work for the parent company.

In late 1986 the government of China introduced favourable foreign investment regulations (22 rules). The company's subsidiary firms, Luk's Shekou and the joint venture Huafa, had been helped by these new rules to obtain their necessary import licences (*Luks Industrial Co. Ltd Annual Report* 1987, p. 8). In 1992 sales of TVs to China accounted for approximately 44 per cent of their total sales.

Vietnam, the Eastern European bloc and Russia

Having succeeded in communist China, Luk took steps to invest in Vietnam which has a similar political and economic background. Vietnam has a huge population, and its government has recently provided incentives for industrial development via customs duties. Luk perceived that the company's development potential in Vietnam would be enormous.

In 1991 the company reached an agreement with the Donaco Electronics Factory of Vietnam to invest in joint venture factories to manufacture colour TVs, hi-fi equipment, electronic calculators, taperecorders, video tapes and related electronic products mainly for the domestic market. In 1993 the sales of colour TVs in Vietnam increased by 25 per cent and production was profitable (*Luks Industrial Co. Ltd, Annual Report* 1993, p. 6).

With ongoing political reforms and the gradual opening of Eastern European markets, Luk considered investing in those countries. In 1989 the company succeeded in penetrating the communist bloc and received orders for colour TVs from Russia (*Luks Industrial Co. Ltd Annual Report* 1989, p. 9). In mid-1991, the company entered into cooperative agreements with a German customer, HCM Electronic AKT Tientesellschaft, to establish a final assembly line for colour TVs within Poland for supplying Eastern European markets (see Case 10, Appendix 2).

ENTREPRENEURIAL STRATEGIES AND ECONOMIC PERFORMANCE

As argued in Chapter 5, Hong Kong's textile and clothing industry has been driven principally by Kirznerian entrepreneurship. So far, we also illustrate that most electronics manufacturers have adopted Kirznerian entrepreneurial strategies in the forms of OEM business, small-scale enterprise, short-term views on planning, product imitation, subcontracting and spatial arbitrage. The effect of an entrepreneurial strategy on the economic performance of the firm will be examined as follows.

The same eleven criteria previously applied in the textile or garment industry were employed here again to determine the entrepreneurial style of an electronics firm (see Chapters 2 and 5). Since the electronics industry by nature is more technology intensive than the textile and garment industry, it is not surprising therefore to find that the electronics firms in Hong Kong adopted more technology oriented strategies than the textile and garment firms. Table 6.21 reveals that 46 per cent of Hong Kong's electronics manufacturers adopted adaptive imitation strategies. Only 6 per cent used creative innovation strategies. Approximately 48 per cent of the firms adopted intermediate policies.[7]

As in the textile and clothing industry, the correlation between the kind of entrepreneurial strategies adopted and the economic performance of a company has been examined. Table 6.21 reveals that out of 23 electronics firms in the sample using adaptive imitation strategies, 10 (or 43.5 per cent) responded that their performances were "marginal". This is because followers or imitators can only earn very narrow profit margins. Only those making successful technological breakthroughs may earn huge profits. However, creative innovation strategies involve high risk and often fail in an environment such as Hong Kong.

In the survey there were three firms using creative innovation strategies. One manufacturer replied that his firm previously emphasised product novelty but the new products could not compete with those from other Asian NIEs. Another producer regretted having spent too much on R&D. Furthermore, his business was vertically integrated to such an extent that it encountered severe difficulties when there were declines in market demand. Later he relied on subcontracting to regain some flexibility. Overall, two (out of three) firms reported that their business performance was either poor or marginal. In general, we can conclude that creative innovative strategies were not widely adopted in Hong Kong. If they were used, the performances were not satisfactory, indicating that they were not appropriate strategies in a small open economy like Hong Kong's. Similarly, it was reported that the electronics firms in Taiwan that adopted creative innovation strategies had not been performing well. In 1992, the top four brand computer makers, namely Acer, Mitac, DTK and Copam which promoted their own brand of computer products in world markets ran into financial difficulties (*Forbes* 1993a, p. 49).[8]

Table 6.21 Entrepreneurial strategies and firms' performance (%)

Strategies	Excellent	Good	Marginal	Poor	Total	No. of firms
Adaptive imitation	8.7	47.8	43.5	0.0	100.0	[23]
Intermediate	54.2	29.2	16.7	0.0	100.0	[24]
Creative innovation	0.0	33.3	33.3	33.3	100.0	[3]

Note: $X^2 = 24.55$ df $= 6$ p > 0.05 Contingency coeff. $= 0.5739$.

Source: 1994 Field Survey of Hong Kong's Electronics Industry.

In conclusion, the findings in this chapter reveal that Hong Kong's electronics manufacturers largely adopted Kirznerian entrepreneurial strategies in the forms of small-scale enterprise, subcontracting, product imitation and spatial arbitrage. Creative innovation strategies were not practical in the environment of Hong

Kong. As local manufacturing firms learnt from the foreign firms and improved the product designs, Hong Kong was gradually catching up with advanced nations.

NOTES

1 Cheung (1983, pp. 384–405) argued that if a firm is viewed as a nexus-of-contracts, it is impossible to define the size of a firm.

2 Sung (1987, pp. 47–8) argued that flexibility is the source of Hong Kong's competitiveness and contributes to the economic success of Hong Kong.

3 Hobday (1995, p. 1176) recently remarked that the South Korean firms put little effort into medium or long-term research which aimed at producing products new to the work.

4 Hobday (1995, p. 1190) noted that OEM business accounted for a large proportion of consumer electronics exports for the four Asian NIEs during the 1970s and 1980s. For example, in Taiwan OEM business accounted for around 43 per cent of production in computers and related goods in 1989. The largest Taiwanese electronics firms, Tatung, exported around half of its output of colour TVs and PCs under OEM arrangements in 1991. Similarly, in South Korea, large firms such as Samsung depended on OEM for much of their consumer goods sales.

5 Under the pressure of lobbying groups, mainly industrialists, the Hong Kong government eventually agreed to import a certain amount of labour from China.

6 For an account of how RJP, one of the largest electronics firms in Hong Kong, transferred its manufacturing operations to China, see Hobday (1995, p. 1182).

7 The corresponding figures for the textile and clothing industry are 78 per cent, 4 per cent and 18 per cent (see Chapter 5).

8 It was reported that ACER still relied on OEM business for a large portion of its sales in 1993. In 1992 ACER pulled back from own brand investments to concentrate more on OEM business after sustaining heavy losses during the PC market downturn (Hobday 1995, p. 1176).

7

ENTREPRENEURSHIP, STRUCTURAL CHANGE AND CATCHING UP

This study has demonstrated the role of entrepreneurship in Hong Kong's manufacturing sector. Specifically, in the electronics, textile and garment industries, the manufacturers adopted Kirznerian entrepreneurial strategies in the forms of small-scale enterprise, product imitation, subcontracting and spatial arbitrage. Previous chapters also analysed how entrepreneurs mobilised resources in the manufacturing sector, both in and out of the Colony. This chapter will examine the effect of Kirznerian entrepreneurial activities on the structural change of the economy. The relationship between Kirznerian entrepreneurship and Hong Kong's catching up with developed nations will be discussed.

EFFECT ON STRUCTURAL CHANGE

It has been observed that economic growth is accompanied by continual structural changes, beginning by moving away from agriculture to manufacturing and later from manufacturing to services.[1] What has surprised economists is the rapidity and magnitude of such shifts associated with the economic growth in Hong Kong (Chen 1979, p. 28).

This ceases to be a surprise if we understand how Kirznerian entrepreneurs in Hong Kong operate (Chau 1993, p. 27). As a result of the arbitrage activities of the entrepreneurs, some production processes have been relocated to mainland China or other low cost regions. Also, some resources have been shifted from the manufacturing sector to the real estate, service and financial sectors. Each profitable move made by the entrepreneurs denotes an increase in the value of resources. This is the essence of economic growth. In short, with Kirznerian entrepreneurship as a propeller, Hong Kong's economy had been transformed in the 1950s and the 1960s from traditional fishing and agriculture to manufacturing, and then in the 1970s and 1980s to the finance and service sectors. It has evolved from a traditional entrepôt into an international trade and financial centre (Chau 1993, p. 16). In the manufacturing sector, Hong Kong has been integrated into new subregional division of labour with Japan serving as the epicentre (Chee 1991, p. 424).

Table 7.1 Number of firms by activities

Year	Manufacturing		Wholesale, retail and import/export trade		Restaurants and hotels		Finance, insurance, real estate and business services	
	Number of firms	Annual change %	Number of firms	Annual change %	Number of firms	Annual change %	Number of firms	Annual change %
1977	37,568		56,158		4,581		6,994	
1978	41,240	9.77	56,919	1.36	4,654	1.59	8,482	21.28
1979	42,282	2.52	60,133	5.65	5,022	7.91	9,638	13.63
1980	45,409	7.40	63,027	4.81	5,028	0.12	10,171	5.53
1981	46,729	2.91	68,810	9.18	5,258	4.57	11,563	13.69
1982	47,089	0.77	76,318	10.91	5,700	8.40	13,421	31.95
1983	46,817	−0.58	80,562	5.56	6,181	8.44	14,161	5.51
1984	48,992	4.86	85,515	6.15	6,832	10.53	14,651	3.46
1985	48,062	−1.90	94,545	10.56	7,309	6.98	15,532	6.01
1986	48,623	1.17	97,502	3.13	7,651	4.68	16,959	9.19
1987	50,409	3.67	102,396	5.02	7,993	4.47	18,806	10.89
1988	50,606	0.39	111,614	9.00	8,578	7.32	21,429	13.94
1989	49,926	−1.34	117,674	5.43	8,737	1.85	25,766	20.24
1990	49,087	−1.68	127,101	8.01	9,322	6.70	29,212	13.37
1991	46,276	−5.73	140,041	10.18	10,460	12.2	31,793	8.84
1992	41,937	−9.38	148,128	5.79	10,601	1.35	37,654	18.43

Source: Hong Kong Census and Statistics Department, *Hong Kong Annual Digest of Statistics*, various issues.

The changing economic activities of Hong Kong's economy for 1977–92 can be observed in terms of the number of establishments or workers employed in different sectors.

In 1977 there were 37,568 manufacturing establishments, employing more than 755,108 workers, with annual growth rates of 9.8 per cent and 8.2 per cent respectively. By 1992, though the number of establishments increased to 41,937, the number of persons employed declined to 571,181, with annual decreasing rates of approximately 9.4 per cent and 12.8 per cent respectively (Tables 7.1 and 7.2).

In contrast, there has been a significant increase in economic activities in the service sector. For the period 1977–92, in terms of the number of establishments, the wholesale, retail , import and export trades expanded from 56,158 in 1977 to 148,128 in 1992, resulting in an annual growth rate of 11 per cent, while the restaurants and hotels increased from 4,581 in 1977 to 10,601 in 1992, with an annual growth of approximately 8.8 per cent. The insurance, real estate and business services had the most impressive growth in the late 1980s and early 1990s. In particular, in 1992, this sector witnessed, in terms of the number of establishments, an annual growth rate of 18.4 per cent and in terms of persons employed, a growth rate of 9.7 per cent (Tables 7.1 and 7.2).

The structural change of the economy can also be analysed by the proportion of the employed labour force in different sectors of the economy or by the sectoral origins of a country's GDP. As clearly showed in Table 7.3, 7.4 and Figure 7.1, the primary sector has never been important in Hong Kong and has continued to shrink. In 1961, approximately 8.1 per cent of the total workforce was engaged in the primary sector, producing only 3.4 per cent of the economy's GDP. By the early 1990s, employment in this sector was reduced to only 1 per cent, producing

Table 7.2 Number of persons engaged by activities

Year	Manufacturing		Wholesale, retail and import/export trade		Restaurants and hotels		Finance, insurance, real estate and business services	
	Number of firms	Annual change %	Number of firms	Annual change %	Number of firms	Annual change %	Number of firms	Annual change %
1977	755,108		266,805		114,904		83,085	
1978	816,683	8.15	266,696	−0.04	118,006	2.61	98,225	18.17
1979	870,898	6.64	285,060	6.74	128,595	9.32	113,389	15.30
1980	892,140	2.44	308,911	8.42	132,002	2.33	116,000	1.75
1981	904,646	1.40	315,952	1.94	139,800	6.06	134,047	15.52
1982	856,137	−5.36	345,388	9.18	153,335	9.29	157,663	17.91
1983	865,073	1.04	357,076	3.48	163,276	6.48	164,453	3.80
1984	904,709	4.58	375,569	5.32	173,025	6.13	165,032	0.61
1985	848,900	−6.17	414,179	10.12	174,499	0.85	171,631	4.00
1986	869,753	2.46	431,544	4.23	179,220	2.71	185,702	8.20
1987	875,250	0.63	464,039	7.53	184,638	3.02	197,249	6.22
1988	844,575	−3.50	517,594	11.64	192,823	4.43	213,880	8.43
1989	802,983	−4.92	547,260	5.68	199,048	3.11	241,015	12.68
1990	730,217	−9.06	594,288	8.59	210,138	5.53	263,335	9.26
1991	654,662	−10.35	649,723	9.33	224,620	6.89	276,697	5.07
1992	571,181	−12.75	675,826	2.75	227,787	1.41	303,422	9.66

Source: Hong Kong Census and Statistics Department, *Hong Kong Annual Digest of Statistics*, various issues.

0.2 per cent of the economy's GDP. For each decade (i.e. 1961–71, 1971–81, 1981–91) employment in the primary sector decreased by nearly 50 per cent. This trend is not unexpected, given the geographical structure and factor endowment of the island economy (Chen 1984, pp. 7–8; Ho 1992, p. 32; Ho and Kuen 1993, pp. 333–51).

The most significant structural change in the 1960s was a substantial increase in the contribution of the manufacturing sector to the total product (Chen 1984, p. 8). For the two decades 1961–71 and 1971–81 approximately half of the population was engaged in the secondary sector, contributing more than 37 per cent of the

Table 7.3 Distribution of working population by sector, selected years (%)

	Primary	Secondary	Tertiary	Total
1961	8.1	49.0	42.9	100.0
1971	4.2	53.0	42.8	100.0
1981	2.0	49.6	48.3	100.0
1991	1.0	35.7	63.3	100.0
1961–71	−48.15	8.16	no change	
1971–81	−52.38	−6.42	12.85	
1981–91	−50.00	−28.02	31.06	

Source: Hong Kong Census and Statistics Department, *Quarterly Report on Household Survey*, Labour Force Characteristics, various issues.
Note: According to the Hong Kong Census Report 1991, the primary sector mainly comprises agriculture, fisheries and mining activities. The secondary sector mainly comprises manufacturing, construction, electricity, gas and water activities. The tertiary sector mainly comprises wholesale, retailing, import and export trade, hotel, restaurants, transport, telecommunications, finance, insurance, real estate, business services, community services, social services and personal services.

Table 7.4 Percentage contribution by sector to GDP

Year	Primary	Secondary	Tertiary
1959–60	3.4	36.7	59.9
1961–5	2.7	37.5	59.6
1966–70	2.1	37.6	60.3
1975	1.6	30.9	67.5
1978	1.3	26.7	72.0
1980	0.9	23.9	75.2
1983	0.6	22.7	76.7
1986	0.5	22.3	77.2
1988	0.3	20.4	79.3
1990	0.2	19.1	80.7

Source: Hong Kong Census and Statistics Department 1993,
Estimates of GDP 1966–1992, p. 31.

economy's GDP. Ho (1992, p. 32) argued that this was due mainly to the expansion of the export-oriented manufacturing industries such as textiles, clothing, plastics and consumer electronics during these decades. This study emphasised that such rapid transformation was largely attributed to Kirznerian entrepreneurship which emerged out of the unique environment of Hong Kong. Riedel (1974, p. 22) rightly remarked that "Hong Kong entrepreneurs are left free to do what they can do best ... [This] constitutes ... the Hong Kong model of industrialisation."

Another notable structural change in the 1970s was the emergence of Hong Kong as a fast growing financial centre in the Asian–Pacific region (Chen 1984, p. 8; Ho 1992, p. 34). Starting from 1970, the financial sector expanded and diversified rapidly with the emergence of financial institutions ranging from international merchant banks to small local finance companies. By the beginning of the 1980s, Hong Kong became host to scores of multinational banks, foreign exchange dealers, security houses and other non-bank financial institutions conducting a wide range of retail and wholesale banking services (Jao 1983; Australian Department of Foreign Affairs and Units 1992, p. 256). The contribution of financial services to the economy's GDP increased from less than 15 per cent in 1970 to around 23 per cent by the end of the decade (Ho 1992, p. 34). The financial services, together with wholesale, retail import/export trade, restaurants and hotels, transport and communications etc. contributed to nearly 60 per cent of the total GDP in 1961–70, utilising more than 42 per cent of the total workforce. In 1990, the tertiary sector accounted for nearly 80 per cent of the total GDP, employing 63 per cent of the total workers in the economy. Compared to the period 1961–70, this represented 33 per cent and 48 per cent increases respectively (Tables 7.3 and 7.4; Figure 7.1).

In contrast, starting from the early 1970s, the pace of manufacturing growth has contracted in relative terms. Its share in the total GDP declined from about 31 per cent in 1970 to less than 21 per cent in 1982 (Ho 1992, p. 35). As a result, the share

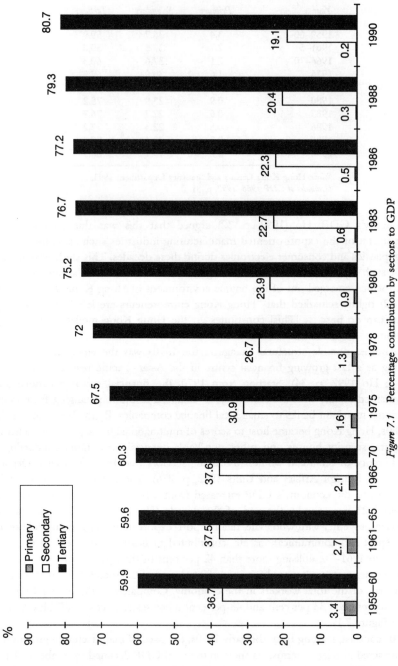

Figure 7.1 Percentage contribution by sectors to GDP

Source: Hong Kong Census and Statistics Department 1993, *Estimates of GDP 1966–1992*, p. 31.

of the secondary sector in the total GDP declined from about 37 per cent in 1966–70 to less than 20 per cent in 1990 (Table 7.4). Employment in the secondary sector also decreased from 49 per cent of the total labour force in 1961 to 35.7 per cent in 1991. The last decade (1981–91) witnessed a 28 per cent decrease in employment in this sector (Table 7.3). This trend clearly indicates that a process of "de-industrialisation" or "hollowing out" occurred (Ho and Kuen 1993, p. 336). Ho (1992, pp. 36–7) believed that it was the normal result of sustained economic growth in a fully employed economy. On the one hand, when entrepreneurs saw opportunities in the service sector which rendered them higher returns, they moved to this sector accordingly. On the other hand, some entrepreneurs relocated their production out of the economy to reduce the demand for the Territory's relatively scarce resources (Tan 1992, p. 38). As a result, the ratio of manufacturing to service employment changed from 1.1 to 0.35 between 1981 and 1991, and the ratio of re-exports (largely ex-China) to domestic exports increased from 0.5 to over 2.0 (Redding 1994, p. 74). In short, de-industrialisation is an inevitable consequence of Kirznerian entrepreneurial action in the economic development. The next section will take a closer look at the shifts in economic activities from the manufacturing sector to the service sector, made possible by Kirznerian entrepreneurship.

THE INCREASING DOMINANCE OF THE TERTIARY SECTOR

Entrepreneurship is not only confined to the manufacturing sector, it also operates in the such tertiary fields as retailing, transport, finance and real estate (Chau 1993, p. 26). It was argued that while South Korea and Taiwan have sophisticated manufacturing bases, Hong Kong has diversified significantly into the service sector (Chen 1989a, p. 36).[2]

The shift from one sector to another can be explained consistently by Kirzner's concept of entrepreneurship. When entrepreneurs perceive that other activities such as finance or services in the tertiary sector have higher growth potentials than the manufacturing sector, they will attempt to arbitrage. We illustrate this point by the following cases.

From manufacturing to property development: the case of Hongkong Land Ltd and Cheung Kong Holding Ltd

It was argued that there has been a tendency for Chinese entrepreneurs to gravitate towards a position of "rentier capitalists" as the strategy for survival (Redding 1991, p. 37). Chau (1993, p. 26) recently remarked that, in Hong Kong, it was in the property market that the mentality of merchant entrepreneurs found its fullest expression. Land in the Territory is a scarce resource. Due to its physical attributes, land in Hong Kong can only be increased through reclamation. Therefore, land has to be used more intensively, by either moving to higher value uses or constructing multi-storey buildings.[3] The change in the use of a piece of land requires imagination and alertness on the part of entrepreneurs. In Hong Kong, Chinese firms achieved growth via property development by acquisition of companies with substantial land holdings (Wong 1989, p. 144). This is evidenced by two classic acquisitions in the Colony.[4]

Dairy Farm Ltd owned a large piece of land at Pokfulam Road which is located at the fringe of the central business district. The land was used for cattle raising and milk processing. As Hong Kong's industrialisation proceeded in the 1960s, its population and economic activities grew. Therefore, the value of the land would increase if it was altered into a residential complex. However, the managing board of Dairy Farm was unaware of this and continued to operate its dairy business on the site.[5] The managing directors of Hongkong Land Ltd, a subsidiary of Jardine's Groups, saw the opportunity of developing the land into a residential estate. They perceived that the land was not adequately utilised and, therefore, that the shares of Dairy Farm were undervalued. In 1972, Hongkong Land succeeded in acquiring Dairy Farm and later converted the land into a huge residential block, Chi-Fu Gardens.[6] This entrepreneurial action brought considerable profit to Hongkong Land and at the same time raised the value of the site.[7]

Similar action was taken by Li Ka-Shing, managing director of Cheung Kong Holding Ltd. In the 1960s he saw that the supply of land in Hong Kong was limited, whereas population growth was unlimited. He reduced his manufacturing businesses and moved into property development (Rafferty 1991, p. 309). In the 1980s he perceived that the land owned by a British firm, Green Island Cement Co., possessed considerable development potential because it was located in Hungham, the city centre. If the land was developed into a residential estate it would yield a huge profit. After acquiring a 25 per cent stake in Green Island and joining the managing board of the company, in the 1980s, Li successfully converted the land in Hungham into a gigantic residential estate, Whampao Gardens (Guo 1990, p. 5).[8] The change in use of the land and its subsequent rise in value was not automatic, but was made possible by entrepreneurial insight. Otherwise the opportunity would have remained unexploited.

From a manufacturing factory to a trading firm: the case of Victory Garment Factory Ltd

Entrepreneurs are constantly alert to changing opportunities. Accordingly some manufacturing establishments have evolved into trading firms. For example, Victory Garment Factory, in 40 years of development, moved from one strategy to another (from private label garment to customer label garment), from one region to another (from Hong Kong to Guangdong), from one product to another (underwear, shirts, dresses).[9] Its development path fully illustrates the adaptability and flexibility of Hong Kong manufacturers. Currently, the company's office in Hong Kong has no actual manufacturing activities. It merely performs the functions of a headquarters, involved in sourcing, receiving orders, merchandising, etc.

In the future, the company plans to expand its business by establishing retailing chains in Hong Kong.

This method was successfully developed by another garment firm, Giordano (*Far Eastern Economic Review* 1993, pp. 72–6; Barnathan 1994, pp. 38–9). In short, Victory is now a trading firm more than a manufacturing firm. The boundary between a secondary and tertiary industry is increasingly blurred. The transformation of the company mirrors the structural change of the Hong Kong economy.

Diversification in the tertiary sector: the case of Tak Sun Alliance Co. Ltd

Clothing production is a very labour intensive business. As labour costs in Hong Kong are rising, profit magins from garment manufacturing are reducing. Aware of this, Ma Kai-Tak, founder and managing director of Tak Sun Alliance Company Ltd, diversified his investments into the less labour intensive businesses, namely trading, real estate, food and beverages, which are some of Hong Kong's major tertiary activities in the 1990s.

Through its subsidiary, the company engaged in trading a wide range of materials and apparel including textiles, knitwear and finished garments. These items were sourced from Hong Kong, China and South East Asia for sale to Europe and South Africa. In 1991 trading accounted for approximately 3 per cent of the company's turnover. The company intended to expand its retail networks by setting up a more extensive retail chain and department store counters in major shopping areas. Ma considered Hong Kong as a stepping stone for expansion in other affluent Asian countries.

Ho (1992, p. 169) argued that most garment manufacturers in Hong Kong nowadays become property developers, transforming their factory sites into commercial complexes, or investing in real estate. Tak Sun Co. was no exception. Apart from the property occupied by the company, it also held property investments which generated rental income. The portfolio of property investments comprised commercial properties located in Kowloon with an aggregate floor area of approximately 1,600 sq. ft. For the year ended 31 March 1991, the property investments generated approximately HK$344,000 of rental income for the company. Meanwhile, Ma intended to develop industrial and commercial properties in the high potential growth area in the Shenzhen Special Economic Zone in China.

The company had been involved in the food and beverage industry since 1985 and had invested in Ginza Development Company and Carrianna Chiu Chow Restaurant. Each of these companies owned directly or indirectly one of the well-known Carrianna restaurants in Hong Kong. These were located in prime areas of Wanchai and Tsim Sha Tsui and specialised in Chiu Chow cuisine. In 1991 the two restaurants contributed approximately 5 per cent of the company's total profits. Ma planned to open more Chiu Chow restaurants in Hong Kong, China and the South East Asian countries where the cuisine was popular.[10]

As a result of the shifts in Kirznerian entrepreneurial activities towards the tertiary sector, Hong Kong was transformed from a low wage, industrialising economy to a high wage, sophisticated serviced economy (Australian Department of Foreign Affairs 1992, p. 34).

CATCHING UP IN WORLD DEVELOPMENT: DAVID VERSUS GOLIATH

This study has argued that the outstanding performances of Kirznerian entrepreneurs in Hong Kong have enabled the economy to catch up economically with more advanced nations. This section further explains and illustrates this thesis. The analysis will first concentrate on the micro level, i.e. the catching up of the manufacturing firms. It is then extended to the macro level.

Catching up: evidence from local manufacturing firms

As mentioned in previous chapters, most local Chinese firms are small in size. They have survived by being alert to opportunities, flexible and adaptable to changing environments. Some enterprises have grown in size. Some have conducted joint ventures with foreign firms. Hong Kong producers have already discovered that they are able to obtain the know-how from multinational corporations which have taken advantage of Asia's low production cost (Engardio and Gross 1992, p. 67). As multinationals from developed countries invested in the Colony, local firms learnt foreign technologies and imitated their products.

It is well known in history that Japanese producers were not only able to copy other nation's products, but were able to change and perfect them in such a way that the replicated goods became typical Japanese models (Majumdar 1982, p. 115). Hong Kong's manufacturing firms have followed a similar path. The following example shows how they managed to catch up.

From customer label garment to own label garment: the case of Tak Sun Alliance Ltd

Ernst and O'Connor (1989, pp. 67, 88) argued that the Asian NIEs at first supplied finished products to foreign firms. Later they marketed the products under their own brand names. Local suppliers started out with simple products and gradually worked their way up to more sophisticated items, moving from customer label products to own label. Tak Sun Alliance Ltd is a typical example. It was traditionally involved in customer label garments which were made only against confirmed orders. Though the manufacture of customer label garments had its own advantages, its founder, Ma Kai-Tak, was well aware that by confining itself the company was unduly exposed to the marketing ability of others. Ma wanted to reduce this exposure. Previous involvement in customer label garment making provided Ma with sufficient technical knowledge in brand development. In 1977 the company created its own label garments, Cherry, and distributed them in the USA. The resulting sales encouraged the company to distribute its own label garments in the Netherlands. In 1991 approximately 90 per cent of the company's products sold in the USA and 71 per cent of those sold in Europe were own label garments. The own label garments business contributed to nearly 70 per cent of the company's total turnover. Moving away from customer label garments to own label garments reflected the improvement in the firm's capability. Ma's case also illustrates how firms in the Asian NIEs attempt to catch up with world fashions. In fact, Hong Kong garment manufacturers have moved up-market into fashion garments (Tan 1992, p. 143). They are now in the upper 30 per cent of the price range for clothing on sale in the USA. Clothing designed by Diane Freis, Judy Mann, Jenny Lewis, Ragence Lam, Eddie Lau and William Tang commands a premium in world fashion markets. It was believed that local designs were as good as those from Japan and much better than the those from the USA (Rafferty 1991, pp. 179–80).

The "no-brand-one-niche-product" strategy: the case of Termbray Electronics Co. Ltd

When caught in a squeeze between lower wage developing country competitors and the need to match the increasing technological sophistication of the industrialised economies, Hong Kong manufacturers shifted their focus to higher valued specialty niche products that required very quick responses to new fashions and market trends (Castells and Tyson 1989, p. 64). They tended to concentrate on one or two niche products which enabled them to boost quality and trim costs to unbeatable levels.

The expansion of Termbray Electronics Company did not rely on the manufacture of a diverse range of branded products. On the contrary, it focused on the strategy of producing no-brand-one-niche products.

With years of experience in the production of printed circuit boards, Lee Lap, owner of Termbray, in 1981 decisively invested $5 million to relocate his entire manufacturing plant to Tsuen Wan, one of Hong Kong's new industrial areas, to produce more complex printed circuit boards. The new plant occupied a total floor area of 30,000 sq. ft, employed 400 people, and produced high precision double-sided printed circuit boards for sale to a number of customers, including Atari and Commodore. In 1983 the company ceased production of its own brand name products in order to concentrate on printed circuit boards and OEM products.

In conjunction with technological developments in the computer industry which demanded more sophisticated high precision printed circuit boards, the company in 1984 commenced the manufacture of multilayer printed circuit boards. On the success of printed circuit boards business, Lee remarked: "I can never make computers like Commodore or IBM, but I can make printed circuit boards for them better than many other producers." By 1991, the company's total turnover in printed circuit boards amounted to HK$165.85 million, with an operating profit of HK$26.8 million. By 1994 the more advanced printed circuit boards were manufactured in Hong Kong while competitively priced printed circuit boards were made in China. This case shows that Hong Kong manufacturers at first learnt to make niche products and later produced them in the low cost regions so that they could compete in international markets.

The case of Vtech Ltd

Manufacturing firms in the Asian NIEs will not forever behave as pure imitators. As they learn from multinationals, they improve and modify their own products, undertake some innovation, establish their own brands, and more importantly, sell improved models at lower prices so as to compete with multinationals. Some local firms even threaten the original suppliers from advanced countries.

Two successful products of Vtech, namely educational toys and telecommunication equipment, can be used to illustrate how manufacturers in the Asian NIEs compete with American/European producers. In 1982 Texas Instruments Ltd of the USA successfully created three popular electronic educational toys which teach children spelling, conversation and numbers. Each sold for US$35. Once they appeared on the market, Vtech immediately imitated the production. More importantly, it combined all three functions into one item called Play Tech which sold for only US$30. The products soon undersold Texas Instruments and monopolised 60 per cent of the US market (*Vtech: A Company Profile* 1993, p. 5). This case illustrates the advantages of being a latecomer in exploiting commercial potential (Ernst and O'Connor 1989, p. 40).

Another successful example is the cordless telephone. Before Vtech, the market sold the standard 49 MHz models. Vtech improved the design and supplied the first digital 900 MHz cordless telephone with better sound quality and reliability. As a result, the company seized 70 per cent of the US market. In 1993, the company manufactured cordless phones for Phillips and Alcatel in Europe and AT&T in the USA as well as its own brands (*Vtech: A Company Profile* 1994, p. 9).

The watch industry

The catching up process can be further illustrated by the watch industry. Previously, Hong Kong's watch industry was only a small sector that produced watchbands, cases and some simple movements products. Making movements requires highly trained labour and very refined techniques. Some producers imported Swiss movements and combined them with locally made cases. It is generally admitted that Hong Kong at that time was far behind Switzerland and Japan in watch production.

Then came the technological innovation in watch manufacturing. With the development of LEDs (light emitting diodes) and LCDs (liquid crystal displays), electronic digital quartz watches came on to the scene. Hong Kong producers seized the opportunity. These techniques are simpler and easier to learn. More importantly, production can be done in small factories which fits perfectly into the requirement of Hong Kong's industrial structure, namely, small business and flexibility. Since the innovation, Hong Kong's watch industry continues to grow.

A wide range of new designs and models kept pouring into markets. Later, taking the advantage of lower production costs in China, the price of a watch came down to as low as HK$2 per unit. During this period, a number of major watch companies appeared. C.P. Wong's Stelux became one of the largest watch companies in the world (Woronoff 1980, p. 170). Hong Kong's export sales in watches rose from approximately 73 million units in 1979 to 329 million units in 1988, a 350 per cent increase in ten years. Hong Kong ranked number one in watch exports and was regarded as one of the three major watch production centres in the world (*Economic Reporter* 1990, p. 6).[11]

The whole catching up process of Hong Kong manufacturing firms was lucidly described by Woronoff:

> The foreign investors thought they were very clever in using Hong Kong's cheap and docile labour and they earned very handsome profits on their investments ... But surely, more and more local manufacturers were springing up, either former employees going into business on their own or a local industrialist who hired the necessary technicians to run a plant. Whereas Hong Kong was once dependent on foreign components to manufacture transistor radios, by mid-1960s it could do without them. In electronics ... Hong Kong was merely supposed to produce parts, which would be sent back to more mature industrial countries like America, Japan or Germany, to be assembled into highly sophisticated products. Oddly enough, soon locally made calculators, almost as good and certainly cheaper, were appearing on the market. Finished products began to include cassette-recorders, televisions, intercoms, memory telephones, home computers and all the latest gadgets, along with an increasing range of highly sophisticated parts and components, and ultimately the "chips". Moreover, many companies stopped being just subcontractors and began to sell under their own name.
>
> (Woronoff 1980, p. 170)

Catching up: some aggregate evidence

Catching up can be measured in terms of per capita income, real GNP growth, technological capability, and social indicators such as infant mortality, urban population, life expectancy, literacy rate, calorie intake, telephone–population ratio, TV–population ratio, doctor–patient ratio (see Hughes 1989; Heitger 1993). An index based on resource intensive categories which was developed by Finday et al. (1985, pp. 43–5) can be used to measure change in international competitiveness. A somewhat more sophisticated measurement, namely human development index and welfare index can also be applied to reflect change in living standard. The former incorporates indices such as life expectancy, educational attainment and real GNP per capita in purchasing power parity. The latter (developed by Kakwani and Subbarao 1992, p. 9) takes into account both the size and distribution of income within a country. In the following sections, Hong Kong's performance will be compared to the USA, Canada, Japan and Australia, other Asian NIEs (Singapore, South Korea and Taiwan), ASEAN-4 and China.

Technological capability

Previous chapters have illustrated how local manufacturing firms attempt to catch up with the multicorporations of advanced nations. Catching up can be partly reflected in technological capability. The overall picture of technological diffusion from multinationals to local Chinese firms can be observed from the statistics given by the Hong Kong Government Industry Department. In 1975, of the 236 foreign manufacturing establishments, half were foreign local–joint ventures. Of these, nearly 50 per cent had technical know-how arrangements, 24 per cent had management provided by foreign investors and 21 per cent had licensing arrangements provided by foreign investors. Thus, all of them could be considered as agents through which technology was transferred to Hong Kong (Hung 1984, p. 199).

According to another survey carried out by the same Department in 1989, of 605 manufacturing companies financed in part by overseas investments, 16 per cent reported that these same overseas investors had been involved in the transfer of one or more types of advanced technologies which included management information systems, computer aided design systems and material requirement planning software systems (Poon 1992, p. 216).

The other indicator is the number of patents registered. During the period from 1970 to 1982, there were around 7,900 patents registered with the Registrar General. About 98 per cent of them were made by foreign firms. This means, that almost all the patented goods or processes in Hong Kong since 1970 were introduced and used by foreign producers. Of these, American firms made up 42 per cent, the UK 15 per cent, Japan 14 per cent, Germany (West) 9 per cent, and Switzerland 7 per cent (Hung 1984, p. 199).

A study of multinational corporations in Hong Kong by Chen (1991, pp. 28–9) revealed that there was a positive correlation between the rate of technical progress and the percentage share of total foreign investment. In particular, the textile, garment and electronics industries in Hong Kong experienced relatively high rates of technical progress of 8 per cent, 7 per cent and 8 per cent respectively (see Table 7.5; Chen and Li 1991, p. 29).

A survey conducted in the late 1970s by Yamazawa and Watanabe (1988, pp. 221–2) revealed that the technological gaps in producing electronics products between Hong Kong and more highly industrial nations had been narrowed. Specifically, the technological levels of Hong Kong's electronic firms in manufacturing transistor radios, TV sets, semi-conductors, batteries, camera, desk and pocket calculators, and wristwatches were regarded by Japanese producers as more or less at their level. Some items might take less than five years to catch up with Japan (Table 7.6). A survey of Japanese makers of about 50 products in 1988 estimated catch up times of as little as three to five years for Hong Kong, even for

148

Table 7.5 Technical progress and foreign investment

Industry	Technical progress (%)	% share of total foreign investment
Textiles	8.07	14.7
Garments	7.02	4.2
Plastics and toys	2.91	4.0
Electronics	8.35	27.3

Source: Chen and Li 1991, p. 29.

Table 7.6 A comparison of Hong Kong's technological levels with Japan, 1978

Products	Technological levels
Washing machines	3
Refrigerators	3
Lighting fixtures	3
Communications apparatus	1
Transistor radios	4
TV sets	3
Computers	1
Electric instruments	2
Resistors and condensers	2
Semi-conductors	3
Batteries	4
Automobile, buses, vans, motorcycle	1
Camera	3
Boilers, valves, tanks, power shovels	1
Pumps	2
Effluent treatment devices	3
Agricultural machines, sewing machine	1
Desk and pocket calculators	3
Electronic cash registers	2
Wristwatches	3
Generators, transformer	1
Motor engines	4

Source: Yamazawa and Watanable 1988, p. 222.
Note: Technological levels are classified as follows: (1) means that it will take less than 10 years to catch up with Japan; (2) means 5–10 years; (3) means less than 5 years; and (4) means already reached the level of Japan.

such products as injection moulding machines, numerically controlled lathes and industrial robots. For some consumer electronic goods, Hong Kong was even more competitive than Japan (Australia Department of Foreign Affairs and Trade 1992, p. 139).

Though there is evidence that the technological gaps in producing certain consumer electronic products between Hong Kong and Japan have narrowed, Hong Kong's overall manufacturing technology has generally been regarded as not sophisticated and lagging behind the other Asian NIEs (Chen 1985, p. 37; Ng 1988, p. 39). Cheah and Yu (1995, pp. 4, 6) observed that "Hong Kong's international competitiveness is based principally on the export of unskilled labour intensive goods ... Although this competitive advantage has been eroded since the 1960s, it has not been surpassed by increased competitive advantage in the export of other (more technically sophisticated) goods." However, Hong Kong's economic performance does not rely solely on production capabilities. Its strength has been in business consultancy and service provisions (Deyo 1987, p. 244; Chen and Wong 1989, p. 227; Wade 1990, p. 333). With excellent communication networks, managerial skills, and a hybrid of Western and Chinese cultures, Hong Kong entrepreneurs have specialised in sourcing, quality controlling, testing, packing and coordinating functions.

Export ability and income gap

As a developing economy catches up with industrial countries, it will exhibit a capability to export. In terms of export performance, Hong Kong yielded a per capita export of US$24,590. This figure was much higher than the USA and OECD nations (see Table 7.8). Traditionally they have largely exported to the USA and European nations. Recently, Hong Kong's products have been able to penetrate the highly protected Japanese markets. Chen (1989a, p. 39) reported that in 1987 Hong Kong's exports to Japan increased in real terms by 42 per cent, while the increase in exports to all markets was only 23 per cent. By 1988, Hong Kong's exports to Japan, compared with the same period in 1987, increased in real terms by 22 per cent while only a 9 per cent increase was recorded for all markets.

As developing nations catch up with more advanced economies, the income gaps between them are also narrowed. Heitger (1993, p. 75) commented that for the decade 1960–70, relative per capita income in Hong Kong was about 24 per cent of the per capita income of the USA. By the 1970s it was able to double its per capita income and was on its way to catching up with the USA. For the decade 1970–80, Hong Kong's GDP per capita was around 37 per cent of the USA. Though in the 1980s, Hong Kong could only achieve an average growth rate of 4.3 per cent, its GDP per capita for the decade 1980–90 had increased to nearly 64 per cent of the USA (Heitger 1993, p. 77).

By the mid-1980s, the World Bank regarded Hong Kong as a middle income economy. In fact, by 1988, Hong Kong's GDP per capita reached HK$75,969 (US$9,740), clearly in the lower reaches of the high income economies. Comparatively, in 1987, Hong Kong's per capita income amounted to about 78 per cent of the UK equivalent (US$10,420) but higher than three OECD nations, namely Spain (US$6,010), Ireland (US$6,120) and New Zealand (US$7,750). Its neighbour, communist China, had a per capita income of only about US$290 (Ho 1992, p. 13). By 1992, the World Bank placed Hong Kong in the high income group, along with the USA and other OECD nations (Table 7.7). According to *Asiaweek* (1995, pp. 53– 4), Hong Kong's per capita income in 1995 reached US$21,670. Among the OECD countries, only Japan (US$21,090) and Germany (US$20,165) showed comparable performances, whereas Latin American nations such as Brazil and Mexico or South Asian nations, such as India, Pakistan and Sri Lanka were well below that level (Table 7.8 and Figure 7.2).

Table 7.7 Classification of selected economies by income, 1992–3

Low income group	China, Indonesia, Vietnam, India, Pakistan, Sir Lanka, Bangladesh
Middle lower income group	N. Korea, Malaysia, Philippines, Thailand, Colombia
Middle high income group	S. Korea, Brazil, Mexico
High income group	
OECD	Australia, Japan, USA, UK, France, Germany, Italy, Canada, Switzerland
Non-OECD	Hong Kong, Singapore, Kuwait, United Arabs

Source: The World Bank 1993, pp. 119–20.

Kakwani and Subbarao (1992) devised an aggregate welfare index to measure the changes in living standards of nations. Their study of 110 countries revealed that in the 1961–70 period, the poorest country (rank 1) was Burundi with an average welfare level of US$184, whereas the richest country (rank 110) was Kuwait with an average welfare of US$43,122. In that period, Hong Kong had an average welfare level of US$2,934, rank 81 (Kakwani and Subbarao 1992, pp. 8–11; Table 7.9).

With the exception of Bangladesh and Kuwait, all countries in other regions improved their welfare levels in the 1970s. Among 36 countries in Africa, nine had a fall in their welfare level in 1971–80 period compared to that in 1961–70. Hong Kong's welfare level had reached $5,413 and was promoted to rank 85. This represented an approximate 85 per cent change in welfare. In the 1981–90 period, Zaire became the country with the lowest welfare level (US$209). The USA had a welfare level of US$12,583, rank 108. Hong Kong's welfare level had reached US$9,729 and climbed up to rank 99. Comparing the period 1981–90 with the period 1971–80, this was a 80 per cent improvement in welfare level (Kakwani and Subbarao 1992, pp. 8–12; see Table 7.9).

In order to find out whether Hong Kong's performance over time is satisfactory or unsatisfactory, its progress is compared with respect to a benchmark performance. Kakwani and Subbarao (1992, pp. 20–2) analysed the performance of individual countries relative to the average performance of high income industrial market economies. For the period 1961–90, there were 62 countries whose performance was regarded as inferior. Of these 62 countries, 30 are located in Africa, and most of which have low incomes. A large number of inferior performers was also found in Central and South America. There were 15 countries whose performance was similar to the average performance of industrial market economies. Among these countries, Sri Lanka and Pakistan are in South Asia. Among nine East Asian countries, six had performed better than the benchmark. Hong Kong was one of them.

Social indicators

The process of catching up involves more than just technological improvement or attending higher income. There are other factors that may affect the gaps between the leaders and the followers and their ranks in the international income ladder.

Table 7.8 A comparison of living standards, selected countries, 1995

Country	Per capita GDP (US$)	GDP Growth (%)	Per capita export (US$)	Infant mortality	People per telephone	Urban population	People per TV	People per doctor	Life expectancy	Literacy rate (%)	Calorie intake
USA	24,750	4.5	1,920	9	1.3	76	1.2	420	77	95.5	3,671
China	2,428	11.4	100	31	45.4	29	32.3	809	71	80.0	2,703
OECD											
Australia	18,490	6.4	2,519	7	1.5	86	2.1	438	77	99.5	3,216
Japan	21,090	1.0	3,149	5	1.5	78	1.6	566	79	100.0	2,956
Germany	20,165	2.8	4,539	6	1.8	86	1.8	333	76	100.0	3,522
France	19,400	2.5	3,597	7	1.5	73	2.5	333	77	98.8	3,465
UK	17,750	4.0	3,253	7	1.9	89	2.3	611	76	100.0	3,149
Italy	18,070	3.7	3,069	7	1.9	70	2.4	210	77	97.4	3,504
Asian NIEs											
Hong Kong	21,670	5.5	24,590	5	1.5	95	3.6	866	78	90.0	2,857
Singapore	20,470	10.2	28,645	5	2.0	100	2.6	711	76	91.6	3,198
South Korea	9,810	7.7	2,065	8	2.3	76	4.8	855	72	96.8	2,852
Taiwan	12,315	6.1	4,184	5	2.4	56	3.1	910	75	92.4	3,036
ASEAN-4											
Indonesia	3,140	6.7	199	66	104.2	33	16.7	6,786	63	84.4	2,750
Malaysia	8,630	8.9	2,482	12	7.3	46	6.7	2,410	71	80.0	2,774
Philippines	2,660	4.3	201	40	52.5	45	20.8	1,016	65	93.5	2,452
Thailand	6,390	7.4	723	26	26.3	35	8.8	4,361	69	93.8	2,316
South Asia											
India	1,250	4.2	25.71	79	100.0	26	28.6	2,165	61	52.1	2,243
Pakistan	2,130	4.0	65.52	94	76.0	34	55.6	2,000	59	35.0	2,377
Sri Lanka	3,030	6.9	178	15	88.1	22	28.6	6,162	72	89.1	2,286
Latin America											
Brazil	5,470	5.7	256	52	10.0	78	4.8	847	66	82.1	2,751
Mexico	7,490	4.0	541	27	7.6	75	6.8	600	70	90.3	3,052

Source: The World Bank 1993, pp. 63–120, Tables 1–20; Asiaweek, 10 March 1995, pp. 53–4.

Notes: The per capita GDP has been adjusted according to the purchasing power parity which takes into account price difference between countries.

Infant mortality is the number of babies per 1,000 live births who die before reaching 1 year of age. Literacy rates refer to the population over 15 years of age.

Calorie intake is the average per person per day.

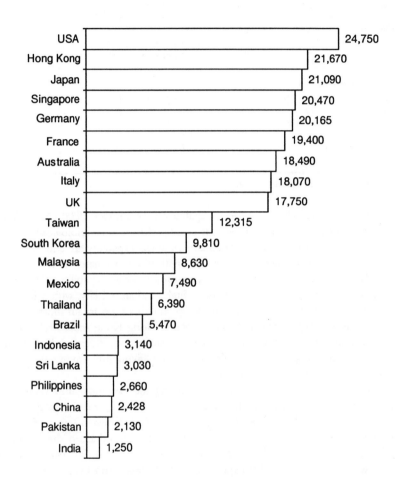

Figure 7.2 Per capita GDP, selected countries, 1995
Source: Computed from Table 7.8.

Table 7.9   Performance of Hong Kong in global development

A Welfare index

| Periods | Welfare levels | | Period | % change in welfare | |
	Value	Rank		Value	Rank
1961–70	2,934	81			
1971–80	5,413	85	1961–70 to 1971–80	84.5	104
1981–90	9,729	99	1971–80 to 1981–90	79.7	106

B Achievement indices

| Periods | Infant mortality rate | | Life expectancy at birth | | Literacy rate | |
	Value	Rank	Value	Rank	Value	Rank
1971–80	53.4	98	46.8	92		
1981–90	63.4	101	67.7	104		
1985					46	73.5

Source: Kakwani and Subbarao 1992, pp. 11, 25.

These factors are related to social capability (Abramovitz 1988). Accordingly, a country's potential for rapid growth is strong when it is technologically backward but socially advanced. Some determinants of social capability are educational level, communication networks, customs and institutions, to name a few. Table 7.8 presents the indices that reflect an economy's social capability. First, we can observe that Hong Kong in 1994 was a highly urbanised city, with a literacy rate of 90 per cent. In terms of four human capital indices (i.e. infant mortality, people per doctor, life expectancy and calorie intake) Hong Kong scored relatively high. Its communication facilities and leisure consumption, reflected by people per telephone and people per TV, also compared favourably among the advanced countries (3.6 and 1.5 respectively).

Further insights can be gained by observing the two most important achievement indices over time, namely life expectancy at birth and the infant mortality rate.[12] Kakwani and Subbarao (1992, pp. 23–6) found that in terms of the infant mortality rate, Mali was the country with the lowest value on the achievement index (7.6 in 1971–80). The index increased to 9.7 in 1981–90. The country with the lowest achievement in life expectancy at birth was Sierra Leone, with a value of 3.5 in 1971– 80 and 6.0 in 1981–90. At the other extreme, Japan was found to have the highest achievement in both infant mortality rate (70.2) and life expectancy at birth (79.6) in the 1981–90 period. In 1971–80, Hong Kong's infant mortality rate and life expectancy rate were 53.4 (rank 98) and 46.5 (rank 92) respectively, but improved to 63.4 (rank 101) and 67.7 (rank 104) respectively in 1981–90 (Table 7.9). Kakwani and Subbarao (1992, pp. 38–9) further noted that Hong Kong, together with Japan, had exceptionally good improvements in life expectancy in relation to their per capita incomes.

In terms of literacy rate, Kakwani and Subbarao (1992, pp. 24–6) revealed that Somalia in 1985 had a literacy rate of only 2.8 (rank 1) while most industrialised economies like the UK, Switzerland, Sweden, Japan, Germany, Italy, Canada and Holland scored 100 (rank 101.5). Hong Kong in 1985 scored 46 in literacy rate, rank 73.5 (Table 7.9).

In terms of human development index (which incorporates life expectancy, educational attainment and real GNP per capita in purchasing power parity dollar), Hong Kong also compares favourably with other countries (Cheah and Yu 1995).

To conclude, all major indicators revealed that Hong Kong is on its way to catching up with advanced nations. Hong Kong joined Japan and the other three Asian NIEs, Singapore, Taiwan and South Korea, as the most prosperous economies in Asia.[13]

NOTES

1 In particular, Clark (1940) and Fisher (1945) argued that, as countries experience economic growth, the numbers of workers employed in those areas of production closest to natural resources will decline relative to the numbers employed in the secondary sector, especially manufacturing, which will subsequently decline relative to the numbers employed in tertiary production.

2 Rafferty (1991, p. 168) wrote: "Hong Kong today is much more diversified than a mere manufacturing centre ... [it] is also a big financial centre involved in round-the-clock trading; has a strong service sector catering for tourists and business conferences, especially for people who want to see new ideas and a dynamic marketplace; and has an important communications role, keeping the Asia–Pacific region in touch with the rest of the world by means of air and shipping services and telecommunications."

3 The former Financial Secretary, Sir Philip Haddon-Cave, argued that the scarcity of land in Hong Kong had encouraged intensive development (Youngson 1982, p. 80).

4 Acquisition can be regarded as a form of arbitrage of the difference in organisational advantages. The benefits are sought through the restructuring of a company after takeover. When entrepreneurs discover that there are unused or underutilised assets in a company and that the value of its shares is undervalued, they will acquire the company. After restructuring, the assets are brought into a more efficient use, bringing impressive returns for acquirers. See Yu (1993).

5 For a company with a long history, Winter (1986, pp. 168–88) argued that its owners have made tremendous investments in physical and human capital. Such investments are of a highly specific and irreversible nature and become an organisational routine. For the owners, the investments are also a sunk cost. Past irreversible investments yield continuing benefits that sustain old methods. Hence, adopting a new method entails high opportunity costs. This consideration provides a basis for the persistent use of existing routines, no matter how inferior they are when compared to new alternatives. This phenomenon is described by Robertson and Langlois (1992b) as organisational inertia.

Furthermore, if a new method is attempted, it may often create a conflict of interests within the organisation. After assessing costs and benefits, "not to rock the boat" may be the best strategy (Winter 1986, p. 171). Hence, Nelson and Winter's evolutionary theory of the firm explains why an agent exerts a myopic overemphasis on short-term benefits and is reluctant to make a commitment to long-term investments which involve some fundamental change in routines. Williamson's (1985) concept of asset specificity associated with irreversible investment is consistent with this argument. For a treatment of acquisition in terms of subjectivist economics, see O'Driscoll and Rizzo (1985, pp. 76–9).

6 "Chi-Fu" means "get rich". This is an example of the money pursuing mentality of Hong Kong people. See Chapter 3 for a discussion of the issue.

7 This is the well-known case of the acquisition of a Chinese firm (Dairy Farm Ltd) by a British "hong" (Hongkong Land Ltd) in the business history of Hong Kong.

8 Unlike the Dairy Farm case, this is the acquisition of a British firm by a Chinese firm. This event represents the rising influence of Chinese entrepreneurs in Hong Kong.

9 See Chapter 5 and Case 9, Appendix 2.

10 Chau (1993, p. 26) described how the late shipping magnate, Sir Y.K. Pao, successfully moved from the shipping business to real estate as follows:

Sir Y.K. Pao came to Hong Kong from Shanghai as a young man. He chose shipping ... because his experience in China predisposed him to mobile assets which could escape (the Communist) confiscation. A man of modest means, he charmed his way to a bank loan for the purpose of his first ship. His subsequent success was due primarily to the niche he found in financing. He ordered ships from Japanese yards at low cost, taking advantage of the export subsidy of the Japanese government. The ships were immediately leased to Japanese shipping firms on long-term contract. With these contracts he obtained bank loans to finance the purchase of those ships. This way he was able to add to his fleet with little of his own money and at low risk. He discovered and exploited an important price discrepancy. He also knew when to leave the business. In the 1970s, he correctly sensed the coming shipping glut and shifted his interest to property, with even greater success. The two other big ship owners in Hong Kong were less fortunate. They were hit hard by the shipping slump of the 1980s.

11 For an excellent account of how the Hong Kong entrepreneur, David C.W. Yeh, developed his small toy factory, Universal Associated Co., into a multinational giant and eventually acquired the world famous British toy maker Lesney Group, see *Forbes* (1993b October, pp. 68–70).

12 For a discussion of the significance of these two indices, see Kakwani and Subbarao (1992, p. 5).

13 Rafferty (1991, p. 170) wrote:

The Territory has almost no natural resources. ... Yet today it can claim these achievements:
- Asia's leading financial centre and the third in the world after New York and London.
- Asia's largest gold trading centre.
- World's largest exporter of garments, toys and plastic products.
- World's largest exporter in volume of watches, clocks and radios.
- 18th among the world's trading nations (now about 12th).
- 20th among the world's exporters of domestic manufactures.
- World's third busiest container port, after Rotterdam and New York (today the busiest container port in the world).
- World's biggest single air cargo terminal.
- Highest living standard in Asia outside Japan.
- World's largest public housing programme.
- World's third largest diamond trading centre after New York and Antwerp.

8

LESSONS FOR DEVELOPING ECONOMIES

This study has explained and demonstrated the important role of entrepreneurship in the economic development of the Asian NIEs, with special reference to Hong Kong. It has been argued that the economic success of Hong Kong has largely hinged on Kirznerian entrepreneurship. Several significant implications can be drawn from our analysis.

AN ENTREPRENEURIAL APPROACH TO ECONOMIC PROBLEMS

Most economic advisers today are trained in conventional neoclassical economics. In their analyses, entrepreneurship, the engine of economic growth, has been neglected. Hence in development planning, they have seldom paid attention to the role of entrepreneurship. Consequently their policy recommendations often severely hamper entrepreneurial efforts (Kirzner 1985, pp. 36–9).

For instance, facing competition from other developing economies, most mainstream economists have advised the Asian NIEs to upgrade their technologies. In particular, in mid–1987, Mr S.K. Chan, the executive director of the Hong Kong Productivity Council (a government funded organisation), urged Hong Kong's manufacturers to switch to technology intensive areas as Hong Kong had lost its comparative advantage in labour intensive production (Rafferty 1991, p. 191). Professor Edward Chen (1985) also argued that Hong Kong's manufacturing industry could no longer survive based on existing technology. He was particularly concerned that the Territory's industrial technology level lagged behind that of Taiwan and South Korea. In another study, Chen insisted that, "with changing comparative advantage, Hong Kong has to diversify into higher technology and higher value-added products and industries" (Chen and Wong 1989, p. 208).

However, statistics showed that in the late 1980s ventures in Hong Kong were still in simple technology areas such as backing retail clothing franchises, rather than the sophisticated technology schemes (Rafferty 1991, p. 191). My study also revealed that most manufacturers in Hong Kong chose not to upgrade their technologies (see Chapters 4–6). In fact, it was reported that policies that attempted to speed up domestic technological acquisition in ASEAN had met with very limited success (Chng 1991, p. 242). These results are not surprising if we apply the entrepreneurial approach to the problems.

Apart from upgrading technologies, there are other measures which entrepreneurs can consider. Each solution has a set of constraints to be evaluated in terms of its feasibility. In fact, most private entrepreneurs in developing nations are not willing to take risks in investing in sophisticated technology production. The exploitation of technological opportunities requires imagination, risk taking and speedy decisions. If a technological judgement is wrong, the firm will go bankrupt (Hughes 1989, p. 141). A capitalist in Hong Kong once noted: "We've regretted past investments in high-technology. We've learnt a lot about why we shouldn't be investing in that field" (Rafferty 1991, p. 191).[1]

Furthermore, some local entrepreneurs might not even be interested in technological acquisition. Instead, they were satisfied to act merely as "comprador capitalists" or "merchant entrepreneurs" (Chng 1991, p. 242). As Ho (1992, pp. 159–60) remarked, Hong Kong can develop new product categories and markets whenever opportunities exist.[2] Such opportunities need not be entirely new markets or industries. They may have already existed for a long time and entrepreneurs simply rediscover them. Porter (1991, pp. 136–7) rightly pointed out that a lot of innovative opportunities often involve "ideas that are not even new – ideas that have been around, but never vigorously pursued". Therefore, as long as manufacturing firms can survive in competitive international markets, there is no harm staying in simple, traditional industries.

This study has already revealed that some manufacturers in Hong Kong explored profit opportunities in certain low value added products which many foreign firms did not consider to be worthwhile. Some manufacturers moved to other low cost countries, using unsophisticated technology. Others shifted towards the tertiary sector.[3] This is how Hong Kong could maintain impressive economic growth despite the fact that its export composition remained at the relatively low value added activities, with labour intensive and simple technology goods continuing to make up by far the largest share (Wade 1990, p. 332). Yet, we are not arguing that upgrading manufacturing technology is entirely unproductive. What this study contends is that upgrading technology is not the only path to economic development. The crucial point is that any policy recommendation on economic development should be based on analysis which incorporates entrepreneurship.

COMPARATIVE ADVANTAGE VERSUS COMPETITIVE ADVANTAGE

When the economic development of the Asian NIEs is viewed in terms of trade, most mainstream studies have utilised the theory of comparative advantage. For example, Balassa (1981) and Bradford (1987) argued that development is a process of adjustment in which countries move through different stages of comparative advantage. Ichimura (1988) and Dahlman (1989) analysed the economic growth of the Asian NIEs by examining their changes in comparative advantage structures. Research on the economic growth of Hong Kong has also been dominated by the neoclassical theories of comparative advantage.[4] In applying these theories, neoclassical economists neglect the fact that the creativeness of entrepreneurs can change the given resource situation of an economy and hence its comparative advantage. In this sense, Porter (1990, p. 65) was right to contend that "the principle of comparative advantage is limited in scope and fails to capture the determinants of economic success in the modern world economy". He recommended instead the concept of competitive advantage in analysing growth performance. In contrast to the comparative advantage approach which emphasises the optimisation of given resources, the competitive advantage approach pays attention to organisational learning, creative thinking and knowledge. As Porter (1990, p. 45) argued, the source of competitive advantage arises out of entrepreneurial perception or discovery of better ways to compete in an industry. The capability to identify competitive advantage also depends on culture (Casson 1990). Accordingly, both firms (micro level) or nations (macro level) can gain competitive advantage by conceiving new ways of conducting activities, employing new procedures, new technologies or different inputs (Porter 1990, p. 41).[5] In this sense, Porter's concept of competitive advantage fits better into our entrepreneurial paradigm.

In a review article, Warr (1994, pp. 1–14) argued that "the attack on the concept of comparative advantage rests partly on a false analogy – that between the determinants of the success of a single firm and the success of a nation". For Warr, while competitive advantage may be relevant for the performance of firms within a developing country, comparative advantage remains as salient as ever for the performance of the nation. As argued in Chapter 2 (the section on methodology), such a dichotomy is misleading. The performances of firms and nations are indeed two faces of the same coin. A clear and convincing exposition must shuttle between micro and macro levels in defining the problem and in explaining it (Mills 1963).[6] Indeed, the basic difference between the concepts of comparative and competitive advantage lies not on the analytical level, as Warr contended. Instead, they differ fundamentally in their approach. The former is essentially a neoclassical perspective while the latter is an entrepreneurial perspective. As will be discussed below, entrepreneurial strategies can be employed either by private firms or by government agencies. State intervention and planning also involve entrepreneurship and learning.[7]

THE FALLACY OF THE DEPENDENCY SCHOOL

Our findings challenge the arguments of the Dependency School, according to whose school of thought capitalist development is crucially dependent on the superexploitation of labour. Specifically, after World War II, transnational corporations had dominated the production and distribution of goods and services in developing countries. They established assembly plants and utilised cheap and unskilled labour. For the Dependency School, the ultimate objective of transnational corporations was to exploit the economic surplus in the forms of profits, interest, royalty payments and debt repayments from the developing areas (Dos Santos 1970). There was very little research and development for the transfer of the appropriate technology to the developing countries. On the contrary, the introduction of capital intensive investment by transnational corporations in the developing countries had aggravated the acute unemployment situation. As a result, the developing countries lost control over their economies. The general consequence was that minimal benefit accrued to the developing economies while maximum advantage accrued to the transnational corporations (Bhattacharya 1989, pp. 96–8). The theory concludes that it is impossible for developing economies to industrialise under the capitalist system. However, the industrial success of Hong Kong flatly contradicted these arguments (see also Deyo 1987, p. 15; Wu and Tai 1989, pp. 46–7). This study argues that relying on and learning from advanced capitalist nations can be useful development techniques. More specifically, by employing entrepreneurial strategies such as OEM business, small-scale enterprise, international subcontracting and product imitation, which are largely dependent on foreign firms, manufacturers in developing economies can compete in world markets and catch up with the economically more developed nations. The so-called dependence theory floundered on the economic performances of Hong Kong and other Asian NIEs.

THE ROLE OF GOVERNMENT IN ECONOMIC DEVELOPMENT

This study has shown that the economic development of Hong Kong has hinged largely on the dynamics of Kirznerian entrepreneurship and argued on similar grounds for the other three Asian NIEs. If entrepreneurship is so important in economic development, then what is the role of government? Like other economic activities, entrepreneurship can be passively or actively promoted by government. On the one hand, government can create an environment which facilitates the development of private entrepreneurship. On the other hand, government can act as an entrepreneur, govern the market and lead the direction of growth. In both cases, one may refer to them as "entrepreneurial states".

The Asian NIEs exhibit various entrepreneurial forms. In Hong Kong, the government mainly created an environment that facilitated the development of private enterprise. But in Taiwan and Singapore, apart from promoting private entrepreneurship, their governments also assumed certain entrepreneurial functions. In South Korea, like Japan, the government had even extended its full entrepreneurial role in industrial development to take the form of a senior partner (Henderson 1993, p. 105). In line with Wade (1990, p. 306), the Taiwan entrepreneurial state can be thought of as containing both the Hong Kong paradigm and the Korean or Japanese paradigm.

Luedde-Neurath (1988, p. 103) distinguished two kinds of government intervention, namely promotional and directive. The former aims to restore markets to their proper function. It seeks to provide public goods such as infrastructure, education, etc., which cannot be supplied efficiently in private markets. The latter aims to achieve predetermined results through conscious interference with market forces and selective application of incentives and/or controls. Following Luedde-Neurath, I refer to a government such as South Korea's, which intervenes on a large scale to make significant changes in investment and production patterns in an industry, as a "directive" entrepreneurial state, while a government such as Hong Kong's, which takes on a more passive role in industrial development, is a "facilitative" entrepreneurial state.

Hong Kong: the "facilitative" entrepreneurial state

Although Hong Kong has embarked on a more liberal economic policy in comparison with the other three Asian NIE, this should not be construed to mean that it has adopted a completely *laissez-faire* approach to economic management. Contrary to popular belief, Hong Kong's success has been aided by the government (Vogel 1991, pp. 68–72). Apart from building a legal, social and institutional framework necessary for the effective operation of markets, the government has taken initiatives in forecasting and planning most of the physical infrastructure, such as the new airport scheme, container terminals, cross-harbour tunnels, mass transit railway, highways, and public utilities such as gas, electricity, telecommunications, buses and trams.[8] However, the government did not undertake full ownership, though retaining some shares, of these enterprises. The provisions were tendered to and mainly owned by private companies. Henderson (1993, p. 95) rightly pointed out that only Hong Kong among the East Asian economies has not used state equity holding as part of a general development strategy.

Furthermore, the government has only been fully involved in the provision of basic necessity goods such as water, housing, education and rice, the supplies of which can influence social stability. Specifically, its public housing programme accommodated approximately 45 per cent of the total population (Yu and Li 1985; Li and Yu 1990). Castells (1992, p. 49) argued that the public housing programme has subsidised workers and allowed them to work long hours without putting too much pressure on their employers, most with little margin to afford salary increases. It has also provided a safety net for small entrepreneurs who took a chance in starting their businesses with few savings. Furthermore, the government has substantially intervened in land supply to the benefit of export competitiveness (Schiffer 1991, pp. 180–96; Henderson 1993, p. 100). It has also, as Henderson and Appelbaum (1992, p. 22) pointed out, "used land revenue as a budgetary mechanism to allow the delivery of a relatively extensive welfare system ... while maintaining low corporate and personal taxation". On the other hand, as a pro-business government, it has also repressed the labour movement and enacted labour legislation to make manufacturing industries more competitive. The Hong Kong government has left the remainder of economic affairs largely to the private sector. Particularly in manufacturing industries, the government has played only a catalytic role for development by motivating the people to exercise their entrepreneurial spirit (Soon 1994, p. 144). It has restrained itself from subsidising or protecting any industry and allowed private enterprises to function on their own. It can be concluded that the role of government in Hong Kong has been restricted to assisting entrepreneurs to pick the "right" industries by furnishing them with consultancy facilities such as the Hong Kong Productivity Centre and the Trade Development Council. Judging from this evidence (i.e. initiating planning in public works, providing social stability and creating an environment for business people to exploit opportunities), the Hong Kong government may be regarded as a "facilitative" entrepreneurial state.

It has been argued that government interference in the Asian NIEs was implemented with the aim of working with rather than against the market. In other words, it was primarily market sustaining rather than market repressing (Industry Commission 1990, p. 15; Tan 1992, p. 26; World Bank 1993, pp. 10, 84). Riedel (1988, p. 35) and Chia (1993, p. 34) concluded that "the dynamics of the Asian NIEs rests in the private sector". Based on my findings, these arguments are more correctly confined to the economic policies of Hong Kong than the other three Asian NIEs, where their governments have been substantially involved in economic affairs.

South Korea, Taiwan and Singapore: the "directive" entrepreneurial states

While Hong Kong's industrialisation has largely rested on private enterprises, the economic growth of Taiwan, Singapore and South Korea has owed much to government entrepreneurship.[9] Their development has been engineered by governments and they are prototypes of government-led growth (Deyo 1987, p. 17; Soon 1994, pp. 144–7). In contrast to the case of Hong Kong, these governments are classified as "directive" entrepreneurial states.[10]

Analogous to Johnson's theory of the developmental state, the "directive" entrepreneurial states define the growth, productivity and competitiveness of their economies (Johnson 1982, 1985).

Lichauco (1988, p. 111) argued that these three economies have regarded the state "not only as the source of economic policy, but also as the proprietor, entrepreneur and operator of industrial and commercial enterprises". These states have explored opportunities and set the direction for business to follow. Especially in South Korea and Taiwan, the state has consistently monitored world markets in search of export opportunities, and in order to identify new types of demand that it may then encourage companies to meet (Henderson and Appelbaum 1992, p. 22).

The approach of the directive entrepreneurial states has proceeded from the recognition that some industries and products are more important for the future growth of the economy than others, and they have attempted to concentrate scant capital in strategic industries. Some industries have accordingly been highly subsidised and directed by governments; others have experienced policy intervention only intermittently; the rest have been more or less left to take care of themselves within a broad framework of regulation (White and Wade 1988, p. 7).

Castells (1992, p. 38) argued that in the initial stages of the development process, the states (particularly South Korea) assumed entrepreneurial roles via public corporations and government investments. In the later stages, the governments steered the competitive process into higher wage, more sophisticated technology alternatives and away from labour cost reducing alternatives within or beyond the national territory. As a whole, mercantilist policies were employed to lever national economies into a higher niche in the world system (Deyo 1987, p. 18; Soon 1994, pp. 145, 148).[11] They have done this either by systems of constraints, such as controlling credit through the banking system (South Korea, Taiwan), and/or by rigging prices (South Korea, Singapore, Taiwan). For instance, in Singapore, manual labour costs since 1978 had more than doubled as a consequence of government induced increases in employer contributions to the Central Provident Fund (Henderson and Appelbaum 1992, p. 21).

In South Korea and Taiwan, laws were passed to discourage short-term speculative domestic or overseas investment and thus indirectly have ensured their flow into manufacturing. An extreme example is the South Korean law which forbade the export of sums of more than US $1 million without government permission (Amsden 1990, p. 22; Henderson and Appelbaum 1992, p. 21).

Government entrepreneurship and making winners

It was argued that the governments of Taiwan, South Korea and Singapore had been involved in altering market outcomes by industrial targeting to "pick winners". These winners were industries that might not emerge in the absence of government assistance. However, Wade contended:

> The governments of Taiwan, South Korea and Japan have not so much picked winners as made them. They have made them by creating a larger environment conducive to the viability of new industries – especially by shaping the social structure of investment so to encourage productive investment and discourage unproductive investment, and by controlling key parameters on investment decisions so as to make for greater predicability.
>
> (Wade 1990, p. 334)

The three entrepreneurial states have paid consistent and coordinated attention to the problems and opportunities of particular industries, based on a long-term perspective. In doing so, they have not only produced sizeable effects on the economy but also controlled the direction of the effects (Wade 1990, p. 343). These governments have routinely targeted industrial assistance at specific industries and even at specific firms. In some instances, the governments proposed a project to private firms and, through credit and financial guarantees, encouraged them to proceed. As in the mercantilist period, the governments sometimes even created a small number of interest groups, giving them monopoly rights in return for which they claimed the right to monitor them in order to discourage the expression of narrow demand. In this way, the states shaped the demands that were made upon them and hence maximised compliance and cooperation (Wade 1990, p. 27). In other cases, the governments simply initiated a project through a public enterprise (Wade 1990, p. 356).

In both ways, the governments have created industrial sectors that did not previously exist. Common examples found from all three states are steel, ship-building, transportation, petrochemicals and semi-conductors (Henderson and Appelbaum 1992, p. 22).

More specifically, in product and technology development, the states took initiatives about what products or technologies should be encouraged and put public resources and influences behind these initiatives. They have invested heavily in the creation and refinement of new technologies, usually by setting up govern-ment research and development facilities and then transferring the results to private companies without transferring development costs (Henderson and Appelbaum 1992, p. 21). It was reported that Taiwan's small firms were quite responsive to profit opportunities opened up by public investments; while South Korea's relatively more concentrated industry allowed the government to target its industry specific policies at a small number of firms each capable of substantial response (Wade 1990, p. 325). In South Korea, two examples are worth mention-ing. Hyundai Heavy Industries, now the world's largest shipbuilding company, was created on government instructions in the early 1970s with state subsidised credit, a protected domestic market for its products and a variety of technical assistance acquired from abroad (Amsden 1989, pp. 269–90; Henderson 1993, pp. 96–7). Similarly, semi-conductor production by Samsung, Goldstar and Hyundai was induced as a result of state pressure and support, the latter including the identification and funding of the acquisition of foreign technologies and technical assistance, heavily subsidised R&D and a protected domestic market (Henderson 1993, p. 97).

Export performance as a criterion

Entrepreneurial discovery implies selection. The governments selected new indus-tries with export potential and protected them. Wade (1988a, p. 155, 1988b, p. 53) reported that the central economic bureaucrats of the three countries "have been well aware of what might be called the Latin American fallacy; that indiscriminate support of any industrial investment would be sufficient to promote the right kind of industrialisation ... They seem to realise that mere protection was not sufficient to generate rapid growth. They have sought to couple protection with competition so as to ensure that the lethargy-inducing effect of protection was swamped by the investment-inducing effect."

To guide their directions, the Asian NIEs used export performance as the criterion (Henderson 1993, p. 98; Luedde-Neurath 1988, p. 99). The governments wanted these protected industries to start to export very soon. This export push approach provided a mechanism by which industry moved rapidly toward international best practice (World Bank 1993, p. 358). The link with export performance has helped to reveal mistakes. Furthermore, the emphasis on export performance or other indicators of international competitiveness provided government officials and private entrepreneurs with a "known principle by which the government would adjust to or adjudicate unforeseen contingencies and thereby helped them to enter transactions which they would not undertake if the governments' mode of response to unforeseen contingencies was unclear" (Wade 1990, pp. 335–6).

Hence, Castells (1992, p. 51) concluded that the economic competitiveness of the Asian NIEs does not seem to result from picking the winners but from learning how to win. Only those industries which could pass the crucial test of international competition could succeed in the long run. To illustrate this, entrepreneurial firms in Hong Kong have fully exposed themselves to international competition (Sung 1987, p. 48; Ng 1988, p. 35). The South Korean government tried to develop heavy industry behind tariff barriers in the 1970s By the early 1980s, the policy was discontinued to allow the industries to be exposed to international competition.[12] The export performances of most Latin American and Sub-Saharan African countries were disappointing, partly because their governments protected and tolerated negative value added industries for a long time (Wade 1990, p. 335).

Flexible, pragmatic and competent entrepreneurial states

Carroll (1992, p. 187) remarked that an interventionist government has to be alert and flexible, with a broad vision of what is essential to a prosperous nation. These are precisely the features of the entrepreneurial states in the Asian NIEs. They tended not to follow readymade textbook prescriptions. They were pragmatic and flexible, not only in the sense that no excessive trust was placed in liberal market policies but also in the sense that the dangers associated with state intervention were recognised (Luedde-Neurath 1988, p. 99). They behaved like private entrepreneurs in that, if economic policies were demonstrably incorrect, or inappropriate in the face of changed circumstances, they were quickly discontinued or reversed (Luedde-Neurath 1988, p. 99; Hong 1991, p. 160; Tan 1992, p. 26; Chia 1993, p. 12; World Bank 1993, pp. 86–7). For example, in the late 1970s and early 1980s, the Singaporean government embarked on a "wages correction policy", and increased wages across the board by substantial margins.[13] By the mid-1980s, this was found to be inappropriate. Immediately a wage freeze was implemented in order to get the economy out of recession (Chng 1991, p. 231; Tan 1992, pp. 26, 205; World Bank 1993, pp. 87, 120–121).

If government bureaucrats are not familiar with an industry, then they may be less proficient in identifying opportunities (Wade 1990, p. 335). Because of this, Taiwan, Singapore and South Korea have established institutional arrangements to avoid the pitfall of government officials taking the lead role in a new industry while knowing little about it. Government officials were involved in a policy network with sources of information much closer to the operating level of particular industries. Moreover, the custom of interaction between business and government leaders establishes that all parties know what is expected of them (Fallows 1994, p. 446). In South Korea, there has been close co-operation and consultation between the peak federations of business groups, the individual business groups, and the state owned or state influenced banks. In Taiwan, the Ministry of Economic Affairs and Council for Economic Planning and Development (CEPD) have been linked to public enterprises, publicly funded research and service organisations, and state banks (Wade 1990, p. 336; Tan 1992, p. 27).

Kirzner (1985, pp. 93–118) argued that entrepreneurial discovery is driven by profit incentive. In the public sector, such incentive is lacking. Therefore, he concluded that the public sector is unable to generate the same kind of entrepreneurial discovery as the private sector. Even worse, public choice theorists maintained that government officials may be lobbied or bribed by special interest groups and hence state owned enterprises often provide some unproductive activities which are contradictory to the public interest.

However, contrary to Kirzner's conclusion, the Asian NIE states have exhibited a high degree of entrepreneurship. Moreover, though they are not entirely immune from corruption, they have shown the ability to override special interests in the putative national interest. As Wade (1990, p. 337) reported, the government officials of the three countries in general were able to insulate themselves from the pressure of interest groups and aim at economic development as the priority goal. In a recent article, Leftwich (1995, p. 407) also argued that the entrepreneurial states "have generally been relatively non-corrupt and developmentally determined by contrast with the pervasive corruption from top to bottom in so many developing societies". These phenomena require an explanation.

According to Wade (1990, pp. 337–9), all three states have evolved out of a serious military threat from outside or from other communal groups in the countries, which has raised the prospect of the leaders' demise if they do not assert the state's order throughout the society. In other words, a "hard state" is required. Unlike democratic societies where public policy decision is heavily influenced by the interest groups, the hard states can ignore private demands without affecting their legitimacy. Hence, Wade (1990, p. 339) concluded that "in this kind of political regime, the bureaucracy can more easily demonstrate competence and remain 'clean' because it is neither caught between and penetrated by struggling interest groups nor subverted from above by the politics of rulers' survival".

The "facilitative" roles

While the three governments have taken initiatives in many economic affairs and exerted "directive" entrepreneurial styles, this does not imply that they have ignored the efforts of private enterprises. After all, they are not socialist economies. In fact, all the governments are anti-communist. The three nations are essentially market economies in the sense that the means of production are mostly privately owned, and profits are mostly privately appropriated (White and Wade 1988, p. 6). Economic activities remain largely in private hands and companies engage in competitive relations with one another (Henderson and Appelbaum 1992, p. 19; Henderson 1993, p. 88). For example, though South Korea is regarded as the most mercantilist state among the three economies and the role of public enterprise has been impressive, a large share of its growth has originated in the private sector. Jones and Sakong (1980, pp. 166–7) found that "despite the pervasive activity of the government's visible hand, the bulk of decisions leading to production are still taken in the private sector". Therefore, heavy government intervention in the three states should not be taken as indicative of either blindness or an anti- business bias (Jones and Sakong 1980, p. 194).

Apart from assuming the "directive" role of entrepreneurship, some government policies are structured to be supportive of entrepreneurial endeavour.[14] First, all three states have maintained social stability, law and order. Opposition political movements were repressed, and later brought under control by the states so that businesses can function normally (Castells 1992, p. 52). Anti-labour legislation banning oppositional trade union activities was imposed. As a result, labour costs in the three economies have been restrained to a lower level. This provided their manufacturing industries with competitive edges over the USA and Western Europe (Henderson and Appelbaum 1992, p. 17; Rodan 1992, pp. 77–89).[15]

Second, the governments had provided physical infrastructures such as highways, telecommunications, transportation and dams, and invested in education which is essential for development. In particular, they emphasised engineering, technical and vocational education (Industry Commission 1991, p. 1; World Bank 1993, p. 14).

Third, the three states have encouraged entrepreneurs to exploit their talents. Industrialists have virtually been guaranteed against nationalisation of their enterprises. Anyone who wishes to initiate new productive combinations is in no sense discouraged by bureaucratic impediments (Jones and Sakong 1980, p. 193). Though protection had been given to certain industries, the governments did not intend to attenuate competition (McCord 1991, pp. 107, 113).

Fourth, policies were carefully structured to attract foreign capital. In fact, foreign direct investment has been essential for the development of the three economies, though the governments of South Korea and Taiwan have been more selective in inducing the kinds of investments for their national interests.

In summary, the growth experiences of the Asian NIEs reveal a combination of government and private entrepreneurial efforts and preferences (Jones and Sakong 1980, p. xxxii; Wade 1990, p. 27). The economic success of these regimes has derived from their abilities to combine a high degree of government entrepreneurship with strong encouragement to the private sector (Mackie 1988, p. 289). It can be concluded that government can play important roles in economic development. It can either create an environment conducive for private entrepreneurs to exploit opportunities or directly assume the entrepreneurial role to promote economic growth.

THE EMERGENCE OF NEW NIES IN THE FUTURE

Using Hong Kong as an illustration, this study argues that Kirznerian entrepreneurship is important for developing nations to catch up with advanced nations. There was a time when Hong Kong and other Asian NIEs served as "Japan's manufacturing backyard" (Arrighi *et al.* 1993, p. 64). The arrangement had provided opportunities for the Asian NIEs to achieve high rates of economic growth and to catch up with Japan and the Western nations. The Asian NIEs have become a significant economic influence in the world and have acted as a nucleus or centre in the promotion of other developing countries' catching up (Chen 1989a, p. 216). They have not only provided the experience and a model of how Kirznerian entrepreneurial strategies work, but will also be able to play a practical role in facilitating the spread of the East Asian way of industrialisation to other developing countries.

The Asian NIEs have played and will increasingly play this important role through:

- passing on the opportunities of their low value added industries and production processes to the other developing countries;
- actually facilitating production in other developing countries through direct investment or joint ventures;
- providing market access for other developing countries.

It is conceivable that nations such as Thailand, Malaysia, Indonesia and the Philippines take up the manufacture of labour intensive goods, become OEM suppliers, and imitate and learn from the Asian NIE multinationals. This means that they are on their way to catching up with the Asian NIEs via Kirznerian entrepreneurship. Consequently, another tier of NIEs may emerge. The Asian NIEs were the first tier to emerge in the 1960s. The second tier of NIEs in Asia may consist of ASEAN-4 and China (Yamazawa and Watanabe 1988, pp. 203–24; Chen 1989a, pp. 227–8; Tan 1992, p. 147).

The possibility for other countries in Latin American, Africa or Middle East nations, with cultures entirely different from the Asian NIEs, to employ Kirznerian entrepreneurship to emulate the East Asian "miracle" deserves careful scrutiny. In particular, some scholars argued that the economic performances of the Asian NIEs rest heavily on conditions so unique as to be unreproducible (McCord 1991, p. 5). Others argued that in order for an East Asian economy to be taken as a model of development for other countries, all aspects of its historical growth must be applicable, for non-economic events cannot be neatly separated from economic processes (Soesastro 1985, p. 115).

Avoiding easy historical generalisations and being cautious about deriving "lessons" from past experiences, this study argues that there is still a possibility for nations with cultures significantly different from the Asian NIEs to be new industrial economies. We have argued that in the Asian NIEs Kirznerian entrepreneurial strategies take a slightly different form in each country. We are fully aware of the fact that the Asian NIEs are not homogeneous. For example, Hong Kong, though in many ways resembling other Asian NIEs, differs from them significantly in other aspects. First, in terms of international division of labour, each of the Asian NIEs has occupied a distinct niche in the international product cycle. Second, the role of foreign capital in the four Asian NIEs is very different. Singapore has actively recruited multinational corporations. Hong Kong has treated both domestic and foreign businesses in a generally *laissez-faire* manner. Taiwan has limited foreign capital to certain key export sectors and promoted linkages with the internal economy. South Korea has strongly regulated MNCs and pushed the eventual "indigenisation" of the industries in which they were allowed (Ernst and O'Connor 1989, p. 65; Clark and Chan 1992, p. 204). Third, the political differences among the Asian NIEs are also quite substantial. South Korea and Taiwan are generally cited as the best examples of "hard" developmental states among the four (Clark and Chan 1992, p. 204; Chia 1993, p. 3). Fourth, Hong Kong's manufacturing industry has been dominated by small and medium enterprises but South Korea has larger scale operations than the other three (World Bank 1993, pp. 161–3). Fifth, it is well known that the industrialisation of Hong Kong was largely the result of indigenous entrepreneurship. However, the industrialisation of Singapore was largely attributed to the efforts of multinational entrepreneurship (Lee and Low 1990, pp. 26–30; Nyaw 1991, p. 197). Redding (1994, pp. 94–5) argued that the international network of commercial subcontracting and OEM manufacturing in Hong Kong contrasts sharply with the Singapore pattern of production via foreign investment. Furthermore, Lichauco (1988, p. 109) claimed that it is socialism which distinguished Singapore from Hong Kong. Sixth, the two city-states, Singapore and Hong Kong, have virtually no agricultural activities but Taiwan and South Korea have substantial rural sectors. The list is by no means exhaustive. Despite the significant variation in institutions, structures and policies, however, it can be argued that all four Asian NIEs have successfully achieved impressive economic growth via varying forms of Kirznerian entrepreneurship.

The development experiences of Hong Kong and the other Asian NIEs imply that differences in culture, political background or physical structure are not necessarily barriers to achieving economic success via Kirznerian entrepreneurship. Instead, success depends on whether the environments of developing economies can incubate Kirznerian entrepreneurship. Hence McCord was correct in remarking that

A recreation of Asian NIEs' example in other parts of the world does not depend on unique cultural factors, receptive social structures, or particular political systems ... If a nation encourages entrepreneurial tendencies, follows policies that eliminate obvious structural obstacles, and provides a stable government that is reasonably free of arbitrary dictatorial methods, there is every reason to expect that it can too can move forward within the constraints imposed on all nations by world economic conditions.[16]

(McCord 1991, p. 182)

This study reiterates that Kirznerian entrepreneurship is one important factor in assisting developing countries to catch up. It has argued that the Asian NIEs have relied on the dynamics of Kirznerian entrepreneurship which is either promoted by their governments or assumed directly by the states. Our proposition that the economic growth of developing countries hinges on Kirznerian entrepreneurship is not limited to the Asian NIEs. The critical issue is whether those developing countries can successfully develop Kirznerian entrepreneurial strategies compatible with their backgrounds so as to exploit international market opportunities. In fact, as McCord (1991, p. 182) remarked, the Asian NIEs model of development has already been emulated in some regions of Latin America, South Asia, Central America, and, increasingly, in the former Soviet bloc. This trend is particularly evident in countries such as Chile, Costa Rica and the Ivory Coast that have already forged economic links with the Asian NIEs.

Unfortunately, many Third World countries have failed to promote Kirznerian entrepreneurship. Some states did take up a leading role in industrialisation but they could not insulate themselves from the rent seeking activities of special interest groups. Others did not use export performance as a criterion of intervention (Wade 1988b, pp. 32, 58; White and Wade 1988, p. 9). Even worse, as Wade (1990, p. 350) pointed out, certain African nations, such as Kenya in the late 1980s, exhibited the characteristics of vampire states. Their rulers were described as "predatory, in the sense that their efforts to maximise the resource flow under their control erode the ability of the resource base to deliver future flows". In short, in those countries, Kirznerian entrepreneurship has been severely choked off and the economies have remained in stagnation.

The role of foreign aid

It was argued that the Asian NIEs generally benefited in the 1950s to 1970s from US financial, economic and military assistance, good preferential access for their exports to the large US market, and the benign world trading environment during their period of rapid economic growth (Parry 1988, pp. 98–106). In particular, the two most successful East Asian economies, South Korea and Taiwan, received disproportionate amounts of foreign aid prior to rapid growth (Riedel 1988, p. 24). Hence, it is argued, other developing countries will not benefit from these advantages and consequently cannot expect to be as successful as the Asian NIEs even if they adopt similar development strategies.

However, aid can hardly be taken as a sufficient condition for the superior economic performance of the Asian NIEs. Several other countries had received similar or even larger amounts of aid per capita but had not used it as effectively (Wade 1990, p. 83). For example, the USA had poured aid into its three major recipients – Israel, Pakistan and Egypt – but there were no noticeable economic improvements in those areas (McCord 1991, p. 116). On the other hand, the main contribution of aid in Taiwan and South Korea seemed to have been political and economic stability rather than growth per se (Riedel 1988, pp. 24–5; McCord

1991, p. 116). For Hong Kong and Singapore[17] it was presumably their ability to make good use of the resources that counted more than anything else and aid was not a necessary condition for growth. Similar to the argument of tariff protection in infant industries, if the nation that receives aid cannot build up a competitive edge, develop its entrepreneurship and let its industries pass the crucial test of international competition, even larger amounts of aid will not enable it to industrialise.

International protectionism

Some scholars, notably Robin Broad and John Cavanagh, argued that it is highly unlikely that any more NICs would emerge in the near future because the international economic environment was no longer favourable. In particular, world trade was slowing down and protectionism in developed countries was on the rise (McCord 1991, p. 145; Tan 1992, p. 152). It is generally thought that growing protectionism will restrict the opportunities for international trade and transfer of technology, particularly when imitating and copying are important means of improving the technological level of developing countries.

It is true that protectionism may affect the development of Kirznerian entrepreneurship, but the influence seems to be exaggerated. The reasons are as follows. First of all, international protection is generally imposed upon more prosperous developing countries such as the Asian NIEs. Special favourable treatment is normally given to least developed countries. Hence those least developed countries can still enjoy unique advantages (McCord 1991, p. 147). To be sure, they have to utilise this opportunity to develop Kirznerian entrepreneurship. Furthermore, motivated by cheaper labour as well as to circumvent trade protections, multinationals from advanced nations will increase their direct investments in developing countries, thus providing Third World manufacturers with more chances for learning and imitating (McCord 1991, pp. 147, 175). More importantly, once a regulation is imposed to protect local markets, it will remain unaltered for a long period. Rapid technological innovation may reduce the effectiveness of regulation (Lam and Lee 1992, pp. 120–1).[18] In fact, protectionism tends to have less influence on entrepreneurial nations. For when a quota or restriction is imposed on a certain export industry, manufacturers will immediately explore other opportunities where they have competitive edges. This has been evidenced in the Hong Kong manufacturing industry (see Chapters 4–6).

Finally, in the dynamic world environment, opportunities always exist. For instance, growing international protectionism has threatened trade opportunities but the recent liberalisation of most communist countries has provided a new wave of opportunities for entrepreneurs. In short, market opportunities, the result of the creative power of entrepreneurs, will never be exhausted. Whether a developing nation can catch up with advanced nations depends on whether it can promote entrepreneurship to identify and exploit such opportunities.

NOTES

1 In addition, Hong Kong will be returned to communist China in 1997. Therefore, the Hong Kong government was reluctant to risk itself in sophisticated technology business or to initiate capital intensive projects as the Singaporean government did.

2 Porter (1990, p. 73) argued that chance events, if favourable, can play an important part in enabling firms to take advantage of new opportunities and to excel in international competitiveness. Based on this argument, Tan (1992, p. 78) argued that "the Asian NIEs did benefit from some favourable developments which were largely outside their control. Just at the time when they reached a level of development which enabled them to embark on export-oriented industrialisation, a number of important changes took place in the international trading system. In a sense, the Asian NIEs happened to be at the right place, at the right time, and were able to seize on opportunities which were not open to other less developed countries." However, it must be emphasised that economic success does not depend on sheer luck, but on entrepreneurial alertness to chances (Kirzner 1979, p. 180). This means that the ability to seize opportunities, the function of entrepreneurs, is extremely important in economic development.

3 In particular, Wade (1990, p. 333) argued that "Hong Kong's restructuring success has been in finance rather than in industry, led by the major banks."

4 Some well-known studies are Riedel (1974), Chen and Wong (1989) and Ho (1992).

5 In other words, Porter had implicitly put forward a subjectivist approach to economic problems which is the method employed by the Austrian School of economics. For a review of subjectivist economics, see O'Driscoll and Rizzo (1985).

6 Majumdar (1982, p. 34) argues that any model of dynamic competitive advantage should be oriented to the micro level behaviour of corporations.

7 For an exposition of planning as learning, see De Geus (1988).

8 In Hong Kong, the establishment of the Independent Commission Against Corruption (ICAC) in 1974 has effectively eliminated corruption in both the public and private sector. This is particularly beneficial for less-well-connected small business owners and for foreign businessmen not familiar with the local art of bribery (Chau 1993, p. 28).

9 For an account of the role of government in the economic development of Japan, see Johnson (1982); for South Korea, see Jones and Sakong (1980), Mukerjee (1986) and Amsden (1989); for Taiwan, see Wade (1990); for Singapore, see Rodan (1989; 1992, pp. 77–89), Lee and Low (1990). For a comparative analysis of the state and economy of the Asian NIEs, see Castells (1992, pp. 33–70).

10 Johnson (1985) and White (1988) referred to the Asian NIEs as developmental states. Building upon Johnson's distinction between plan rational states and plan ideological states, Henderson (1993, pp. 85–114) referred to them as plan rational economies while Wade (1988a, b, 1990) argued in terms of a "guided market economy".

11 For an account of how the governments of the east Asian economies applied mercant-ilism and nationalist economics, see Lichauco (1988).

12 The World Bank (1993, pp. 98–9) argued that using exports as a performance yardstick generated substantial economic benefits. A firm's success in the export market is a good indicator of economic efficiency.

13 Lichauco (1988, p. 109) argued that Singapore is a heavily socialised economy where the government is extensively involved as proprietor, entrepreneur and manager of commercial and industrial enterprises.

14 It is this aspect of government policies that partly lead the free market economists to misunderstand that all the Asian NIEs have virtually pursued market sustaining policies. For example, referring to the East Asian miracles, Chen (1979, p. 185) claimed that "state intervention is largely absent. What the state provided is simply a suitable environment for the entrepreneurs to perform their functions."

15 However, the importance of cheap labour in accounting for the economic success of East Asia should not be overstated. For further explanation, see Henderson and Appelbaum (1992, pp. 17– 18).

16 Here the statement "reasonably free of arbitrary dictatorial methods" can be interpreted as what Johnson (1982) termed plan rationality, pursued by the dictatorial governments of the Asian NIEs.

17 According to Riedel (1988, p. 25), Hong Kong did not receive much aid, but did get undisclosed amounts of mainland and overseas Chinese capital in the 1950s; Singapore borrowed heavily in the early 1960s from the World Bank and the Asian Development Bank, but on relatively hard terms.

18 Lam and Lee (1992, p. 120) further argued that under the strategy of guerrilla capitalism, the Chinese manufacturers in Asian NIEs were able to stay one step ahead of protection measures. Therefore, it was neither practical nor feasible for the Asian NIEs' trading partners to stem the flood of imports effectively through regulation, given the length of time it takes for regulations to be changed.

9

CONCLUSIONS

To explain the growth performances of the Asian newly industrialising economies, most orthodox economists employed Harrod–Domar growth models and neo-classical theories, with technological factors embodied or disembodied in the aggregate production function. However, their quantitative methods which endea-voured to optimise given resources had severe limitations. As Kirzner remarked:

> an economy that can successfully stimulate efficient allocation of resources is no guarantee that it can perform similarly with respect to the entrepreneurial activity required for growth. ... For a long time economists discussing growth virtually ignored entrepreneurship. And for a world in which entre-preneurship in the discovery of new resources (or in the discovery of new uses for already known and available resources) is seen as having no scope, the distinction between allocation and growth is deeply flawed.
>
> (Kirzner 1985, pp. 79–80)

Accordingly, applying the non-entrepreneurial neoclassical paradigm to explain the Asian economic "miracle" in general and Hong Kong's success in particular did not yield a convincing result. Unable to find a solution, some scholars in econom-ics hailed non-economic factors such as Confucian culture to explain East Asian economic growth.

Stemming from dissatisfaction with the orthodox treatment, this study provides an alternative explanation of the Asian economic "miracle". In particular, this study proposes an entrepreneurial framework for the economic development of the Asian newly industrialising economies, with special reference to Hong Kong. This approach centres on entrepreneurs who discover opportunities, coordinate resources and bring about the transformation of the economies.

This study began with the introduction of two modes of entrepreneurship, namely Schumpeterian and Kirznerian. While the Schumpeterian mode exerted a revolutionary impact on developed nations, the Kirznerian mode has had an evolutionary impact on developing economies. The former, as a creative response in economic history, generated a development discrepancy in the world economy, while the latter, as an adaptive response in economic history, attempted to narrow the development gap. Applying the concept of Kirznerian entrepreneurship to

174

explain the economic development of Hong Kong, this study begins by arguing and illustrating that Hong Kong has been an entrepreneurial society. It further contends that the environment of Hong Kong has been conducive to the development of the Kirznerian mode of entrepreneurship. The major arguments of this study are that the economy has been driven principally by Kirznerian entrepreneurial strategies in the forms of small-scale enterprise, subcontracting, product imitation and spatial arbitrage. Moreover, Kirznerian entrepreneurial activities have brought about the structural transformation of the economy. Outstanding economic performances resulting from these entrepreneurial activities have enabled Hong Kong to catch up with early industrialised economies in the dynamic world environment.

HONG KONG IS AN ENTREPRENEURIAL ECONOMY

The society of Hong Kong has had a tradition of approving profit seeking. The legitimacy of entrepreneurship has been well established and people in the Territory have always been keen to start their own businesses. This study reveals that both the number of enterprises and the company formation rates, after controlling for population size, were higher in Hong Kong than in the USA, another often cited entrepreneurial economy. The number of new firms established each year has consistently outweighed the number of failures, so that the total number of firms keeps rising. In addition, the names of many outstanding Hong Kong entrepreneurs frequently appear in international journals and business/finance magazines which helps to reinforce the premise that Hong Kong has long been an entrepreneurial society.

But why has Hong Kong been flooded with entrepreneurs? A related question is whether entrepreneurs can be trained. This is still a controversial issue.[1] In fact, many countries currently have programmes that teach and assist people to start small businesses. Some business schools provide courses specifically to train entrepreneurs. This study contends that the environment of Hong Kong has facilitated the development of private enterprises. The Hong Kong government has created an milieu for entrepreneurs to exploit their potential. Its policies encompassed an easy access to business, a relatively small public sector, and free mobility of capital and human resources. Apart from government policies, other factors, such as a society with different ethnic groups and a hybrid of traditional Chinese and Western cultures as a result of British colonisation, are also important.

THE HONG KONG ENVIRONMENT HAS INCUBATED KIRZNERIAN ENTREPRENEURSHIP

While the Hong Kong environment has facilitated the development of private enterprises, this study further argues that Hong Kong's unique political, economic and cultural features have incubated the Kirznerian mode of entrepreneurship which has enhanced the economic success.

The political uncertainty of Hong Kong's future has compelled investors to take a short-term view in their investment planning. Although the Territory's sovereignty was somewhat settled by the Sino-British agreement in 1984, its future still depends on the political development of China, in particular the stability of Deng's leadership. The uncertainty concerning the survival of the free market economy and the status quo after 1997 has constantly haunted investors. Facing this dilemma, Hong Kong's manufacturers have opted for some investment projects with a short payback period – a form of Kirznerian business strategy.

In terms of economic structure, given the small domestic market, Hong Kong's manufacturers have aimed at exporting. For this reason, they have to be keenly alert to change. Furthermore, in order to adapt to international business fluctuation, they have kept production flexible, operated on a small scale and avoided huge capital commitments. Little government assistance on research and development on the one hand and a multitude of foreign technologies available for application on the other have also encouraged local manufacturers to adopt product imitation strategies.

The flexible price and wage structures in Hong Kong have induced a subcontracting system in which every small profit opportunity can be exploited. This form of Kirznerian entrepreneurship can be widely adopted because the Territory virtually has no price control authority, no influential labour union, and no minimum wage legislation.

Another important factor that has promoted Kirznerian entrepreneurship in Hong Kong is its culture. The combination of Western values with traditional Chinese culture has incubated a unique form of managerial strategy and organisation called "entrepreneurial familism" which allows Hong Kong's manufacturers to tackle problems arising in the Territory. Chinese entrepreneurs in Hong Kong have managed their businesses like a family. It is argued that familism has facilitated the development of small innovative enterprise and also partly led to the evolution of a subcontracting system. More importantly, the family as a business unit builds in some flexibility for Hong Kong's firms to adjust quickly to the external world.

HONG KONG'S ECONOMY AND KIRZNERIAN ENTREPRENEURSHIP

My case studies and survey further support the argument that the majority of Hong Kong's manufacturers have adopted Kirznerian entrepreneurial strategies in the forms of small-scale enterprises, product imitation, spatial arbitrage and subcontracting. This implies that the Hong Kong economy has been propelled principally by Kirznerian entrepreneurship.

Small firms

A major characteristic of Hong Kong's industrial structure is that each industry includes only a few large undertakings and numberous small concerns whose activities are largely responsive to buyers' orders, especially to those from original equipment manufacturers or to subcontracting orders from either their larger counterparts or their peers.

Hong Kong's small-scale enterprises possess several distinctive features. They are able to handle small jobs. Some factories even manage a multiplicity of small jobs at the same time. They do not specialise too much, so that they can pick up the production of different types of products more quickly. Moreover, most of them deliberately keep the size of their enterprise small because they are afraid of problems which might appear with expansion as well as losing the advantages of being small. Hence, small firms in Hong Kong often overload themselves, resulting in rush orders, overtime work and late delivery. Small firms have no quality control department, but rely heavily on workers for this function.

It is important to note that in Hong Kong the proportion of small firms has exhibited a clear tendency to increase at the expense of larger businesses over time. The average size of Hong Kong's industrial undertakings, which was small by most international standards in the beginning, actually became smaller over a period of rising prosperity.

Therefore, the arguments that the dominance of small and medium enterprises is only a characteristic of an early stage of industrialisation, and that they will decrease gradually as an economy industrialises, do not seem to apply in Hong Kong. Such a phenomenon also refutes the argument that small factories have no hope of competing with foreign products and that economic development should be promoted with the concept of "the bigger the better".

Product imitation

This is the most popular form of Kirznerian entrepreneurial strategy in Hong Kong's manufacturing industry. On the one hand, small firms with limited resources are unable to launch any research and development. On the other hand, there is a plentiful supply of sophisticated technology from overseas. Hong Kong's manufacturers can acquire the technical know-how from foreign multinational corporations which have taken advantage of Asia's low production costs. In other words, local manufacturers find that it is more economical for them to adopt product imitation strategies, to be followers and adaptors rather innovators.

In the early stages of Hong Kong's industrialisation, most firms were original equipment manufacturer (OEM) suppliers. They produced according to the requirements of the orders received from the overseas companies. They did not place emphasis on R&D. Through OEM arrangements, they learnt, imitated, perfected their methods of production and later were capable of building their own models. Others started initially as employees in multinational firms. After several years of work experience, they left and set up their own companies. By selling similar products at lower prices, they competed with previous foreign employers. A strategy of product imitation which involves learning and modification has enabled Hong Kong's firms to catch up with advanced nations.

Subcontracting

When Hong Kong manufacturers produce for export houses or for overseas companies via OEM business, they are in fact involved in international subcontracting. If local firms cannot produce in certain areas or when orders exceed their own capacities, they will subcontract to others. If they can only manage part of the job, they will also subcontract the rest upstream or downstream. Thus, using the subcontracting method, manufacturers can exploit small profit margins which cannot be earned otherwise, as long as they are able to identify such opportunities. Further to this, subcontracting in Hong Kong is mainly a short-term relationship for a convenient deal. By utilising local factories in the manufacturing of parts, firms in Hong Kong undertake one production process or even share in the completed production of finished goods. Hence some flexibility can be built in. In extreme cases, manufacturing firms in Hong Kong may have no production site at all. All they have is an office for administration and coordination. Owners subcontract all jobs to others from the orders they receive. They exploit profit margins by providing their managerial and marketing services to foreign buyers and sellers. Their efforts have unintentionally made Hong Kong an important international coordinating centre. This phenomenon was illustrated in the textile/garment and electronics industries (see Chapters 5, 6 and Yu 1995a).

Spatial arbitrage

To imitate products from multinationals is easy but to produce them at competitive prices is the name of the game. Encountering an erosion of cost competitiveness, most Hong Kong manufacturers have relocated their production activities to lower cost regions, such as Indonesia, Thailand, Malaysia and China in order to maintain profit margins. In the textile, garment and electronics industries, most firms have moved their production to China, causing Hong Kong's entrepôt trade to increase. Forms of cooperation with China have included technology licensing, subcontracting, joint ventures or the establishment of subsidiaries there. Shifting production to other regions is also used for circumventing quota restrictions. This has been generally practised in the textile and garment industries where an export quota was enforced. As a result of the outward processing trades in the Pearl River Delta, the relationship between China and Hong Kong has evolved into the so-called "Store in the front (Hong Kong), workshop at the backyard (Pearl River Delta Regions)" (Feng 1991, p. 499). This arrangement has combined China's cheap labour and more sophisticated technology with Hong Kong's marketing and managerial skills. Consequently, Hong Kong has developed into a regional coordinating, testing and sourcing centre.

Entrepreneurial strategies and economic performance

This study found a strong correlation between the entrepreneurial strategies and the economic performance of the manufacturing firms. The findings from the

178

electronics, textile and garment industries broadly supported the thesis that the success of Hong Kong's manufacturing industry has been hinged largely on Kirznerian entrepreneurship. A majority of the manufacturing firms in the 1994 survey adopted imitative strategies, though many of them survived on a very small profit margin. Innovative strategies were seldom adopted in Hong Kong and when they were the performances were not satisfactory, indicating that these strategies were not practical in a small open economy.

KIRZNERIAN ENTREPRENEURIAL ACTIVITIES AND STRUCTURAL CHANGE IN THE ECONOMY

Like many developing countries, Hong Kong in its early stage of development was characterised by a relatively large population of unskilled labour but limited capital. When local entrepreneurs perceived profit opportunities in labour intensive production such as transistor radios and apparel, they would engage in these activities. Once they discovered a fall in demand for their output, they would, if possible, rapidly move to other products which used similar techniques and raw materials, thus causing intra-firm shifts in economic activities.

As industrialisation proceeded, labour and land costs in Hong Kong rose. Facing competition from other regions where production costs were even lower, some manufacturers moved towards high value added products, with more sophisticated designs. Others attempted to establish their own niche brands. But a majority chose to relocate their production activities to other countries such as China. This involved regional shifts in economic activities. As manufacturers retained the production of some high value added products domestically and shifted the production of labour intensive industries to other regions through such arrangements as joint ventures, subcontracting, etc., Hong Kong has developed into a regional coordinating and sourcing centre. A sophisticated spatial division of labour has emerged.

Kirznerian entrepreneurship has not only been confined to manufacturing industry, but also exerts its influence on other sectors (Chau 1993). If entrepreneurs perceive that they can earn higher profit margins in the tertiary sector, they will revise their investment plans accordingly. Resources are then drawn from manufacturing activities into banking/finance, real estate, hotels and transport activities.

As a result of the arbitrage activities of Kirznerian entrepreneurs, some production processes have been moved to China or other low cost regions. Some resources have also been shifted from the manufacturing sector to the real estate, service and financial sectors. Each profitable move made by the entrepreneurs denotes an increase in the use value of resources. This is the essence of economic growth. In summary, with Kirznerian entrepreneurship as a propellant, Hong Kong's economy was transformed from traditional fisheries and agriculture into manufacturing in the 1950s and the 1960s, and then to a finance and service sector in the 1970s and the 1980s. It has evolved from a traditional entrepôt into an international trade and financial centre. In the manufacturing sector, Hong Kong has been integrated into the subregional division of labour with Japan serving as the epicentre.

HOW HONG KONG CAUGHT UP WITH DEVELOPED NATIONS

With entrepreneurship at the centre of analysis, an overall picture of how Hong Kong has caught up with advanced nations can now be drawn. Hong Kong in the mid-nineteenth century was only a barren island with hardly a house upon it (Rafferty 1991, p. 94). It did not possess any natural resources. For many people, it scarcely had any use at all. Yet entrepreneurs saw things differently. The British merchants first came to the Colony and engaged in Far East trading and shipping activities. Some local Chinese compradors were involved in the China trade.

After World War II, Hong Kong possessed a population of cheap and unskilled labour. Taking advantage of low labour costs, indigenous entrepreneurs started to manufacture labour intensive goods which required simple technology such as plastics, textiles, footwear and transistor radios. Because of the small domestic market and limited technological skill, local producers were content to participate in the original equipment manufacturer business and produced for overseas firms. Some of them sold their output to export houses. This is the origin of the export oriented industrialisation. The strategy in short involved the mass production of standard items which were merely copies of items designed overseas. Like the early industrialisation of Japan, local manufacturers at that time entered into production that was no longer economically viable in the more advanced industrial economies.

But Hong Kong's economic progress did not cease there. During the same period, multinational firms from early industrialised countries invested in the Colony to take advantage of the low production costs. They largely engaged in textile and electronics production. The growth of foreign direct investment in the manufacturing sector was most dramatic in the 1970s. Multinational corporations have exerted rather large economic impact on the Colony.

As multinational firms moved in, local firms learnt their skills and imitated their products. According to their abilities to absorb foreign technology, local manufacturers modified and gradually created some new designs. From a large reservoir of knowledge, they adopted foreign technology to local circumstances and improved on it. When imperfections arose, they made changes rapidly. When a strategy was no longer useful, it would be abandoned immediately. In short, they took full advantage of being latecomers. Later, some of them spent money on R&D and moved away from pure copying. By trial and error, eventually some firms established their own brands. More importantly, by selling improved designs at lower prices, local producers had even threatened the original suppliers from advanced countries. They are now able to compete in world markets. Consequently, Hong Kong has emerged as one of the most prosperous economies in East Asia.

POLICY IMPLICATIONS

Having explained and demonstrated the important role of entrepreneurship in the economic development of Hong Kong, several implications have been drawn. First, this study has highlighted the importance of the entrepreneurial approach to economic problems. It has argued that any policy recommendation on economic development should be based on the analysis that incorporates entrepreneurship. Second, the principle of comparative advantage is limited in scope and fails to capture the determinants of economic success in the modern world economy. Instead, the competitive advantage approach which emphasises organisational learning, knowledge and creative thinking is a more appropriate tool in analysing the growth performance of both firms and nations. It also fits better into the entrepreneurial paradigm. Third, our findings challenge the validity of the arguments of the Dependency School. Fourth, the growth experiences of the Asian NIEs revealed that government can play an important role in economic development. Government can either facilitate private enterprises by creating an environment for them to exploit profit opportunities, as in the case of Hong Kong, or directly assume the role of entrepreneurship to promote economic growth, as in the cases of South Korea, Taiwan and Singapore. Fifth, our argument that the economic growth for developing countries hinges on the Kirznerian mode of entrepreneurship is not limited to Hong Kong or other Asian NIEs, though such entrepreneurship may appear in different forms. The crucial point is whether these countries can successfully develop Kirznerian entrepreneurship so as to exploit international market opportunities. Sixth, this study has downgraded the role of foreign aid in economic development. It has argued that if the country that receives aid cannot build up its competitive edges, develop entrepreneurship and pass the crucial test of international competition, even larger amounts of aid would not enhance development.

Finally, this study has argued that though the rise of international protectionism may restrict the opportunities for international trade and transfer of technology, the problem is often exaggerated. In the future, new NIEs will still emerge because in the dynamic world development process market opportunities, the result of the creative power of entrepreneurs, will never be exhausted. Whether a developing nation can catch up with advanced countries depends on whether it can promote entrepreneurship to identify and exploit opportunities. For even a tiny city economy like Hong Kong can emerge into one of the world's most dynamic business centres.

NOTES

1 In particular, D.C. McClelland (1961) argued that the "need for achievement" (n Ach), a motivate variable for entrepreneurship, can be developed deliberately in individuals. However, Brockhaus (1982, p. 42) disagreed about the effectiveness of individual training in n Ach. See Gilad (1986, pp. 189–210).

APPENDIX 1

A SURVEY OF HONG KONG'S MANUFACTURING INDUSTRY 1994

A Firm size, product and flexibility

1 What are the major products of your company? _____

2 For how long has your company existed? _____ years

3 Excluding yourself, how many people are currently working in your company?
Hong Kong: _____ Mainland China: _____

4 Where do you sell your products?
   (a) Wholly overseas
   (b) Mainly overseas
   (c) Equally in both local and overseas markets
   (d) Mainly local
   (e) Wholly local

5 When you planned to invest in this business, within what period of time did you
expect to reach the break-even point? _____ years

6 During the last 12 months, have you ever changed product or design?
   (a) No, maintain the same product and the same design
   (b) Yes, change the product: from _____ to _____
   (c) Yes, change the design: major change or minor change?

B On product imitation

7 Who specifies product designs?
   (a) Mainly your company
   (b) Mainly contractors/buyers
   (c) Both your company and contractors/buyers

8 Which of the following best describes your product position?

    (a) Your product is the first, or one of very few, of its kind both in Hong Kong and in overseas markets

    (b) Your product is the first or one of very few of its kind in Hong Kong, but one of the many in overseas markets

    (c) Your product is one of many both in Hong Kong and in overseas markets

9 Which of the following strategies does your company now adopt?

    (a) Copy product exactly from other manufacturers

    (b) Copy product from other manufacturers, but with some modifications

    (c) Completely new product designs

Did you use this same strategy since the establishment of the company? (Yes/No)

In your experience, which of the above can contribute more to the economic success of your company? Why?

10 Have you ever used patents/copyrights to protect your product/design?

    (a) Yes (b) No

11 Is your company among those that try to be leaders in adopting new production techniques/skills from overseas?

    (a) Yes (b) No

Why? _____

C On research and development

12 Does your company have a formal R&D department and employ more than one engineer or technician specifically to deal with product development?

    (a) No, the company cannot afford

    (b) No, the company can afford but this is not an effective strategy

    (c) No, the company does not require this

    (d) Yes, but R&D is not a priority

    (e) Yes, the company has a strong emphasis on R&D

13 In your experience, is it worth investing in R&D?

    (a) Yes (b) No (c) Not sure (d) Not applicable

Why? _____

D On subcontracting

14 What are the sources of orders for your products?

    (a) Orders come directly from buyers (e.g. wholesaler, retailer or trading firm)

    (b) Orders come from other factories (local or overseas)

15 What is the proportion of your total order/jobs from contractors (other factories)? _____ per cent

16 Do you subcontract out part of your production?
(a) No   (b) Yes, state the percentage _____

17 If "yes" in Question 16, what is/are the reasons? (may answer more than one)
(a) Labour shortage
(b) Insufficient capacity
(c) The firm does not possess particular skills
(d) Accepting rush orders
(e) Others _____

18 In your experience, which of the following can contribute more to the economic success of the company?
(a) Subcontracting
(b) Vertical integration

Why? _____

E   On spatial arbitrage

19 Does your company operate in other countries?
(a) No, it operates only in Hong Kong
(b) Yes, it also operates in _____
If it operates in mainland China, state the province/city _____

20 Was your company the first in your industry to start business in that country?
(a) Yes   (b) No   (c) Not applicable

21 What are the reasons for your company to operate in that country? (may answer more than one)
(a) Presence of relatives or friends
(b) That place is your hometown or birthplace
(c) Familiarity with the place from previous experience
(d) Many other companies have established operations there
(e) Lower production cost
(f) Large demand for the product over there
(g) Geographical convenience
(h) Not applicable

22 In what form does your company operate in other countries?
(a) As a wholly owned subsidiary of the Hong Kong company
(b) As a joint venture with a company from that country
(your share is _____ per cent)

(c) Through subcontracting of production

(d) Not applicable

Why? _____

F   On brand strategy

23 Has your company ever been an original equipment manufacturer (OEM)/ customer label product (CLP) supplier?

(a) Yes, and still continues to be an OEM/CLP supplier

(b) Yes previously, but now no longer is an OEM/CLP supplier

(c) No

24 Have you established and promoted your own brand or niche product?

(a) No (if no, do you intend to do so in the future?)

(b) Yes, all the way

(c) Yes, but only recently

25 What is the share of your own brand/label in your total production?

_____ per cent

26 In your experience, which is more important for the success of your company?

(a) Operate as an OEM/CLP supplier

(b) Produce a niche product under your company's own brand

Why? _____

G   The performance of your business:

27 What is the annual turnover of your business now? $ _____

What was the annual turnover of your business in your first year of operation?

28 Compared with the first year of operation, the current profit level has:

(a) Improved a lot

(b) Improved marginally

(c) Remained the same

(d) Decreased

29 How do you rate the performance of your current business?

(a) It is a success

(b) It is just managing to break even

(c) It is not performing well

30 What are your future plans? (may answer more than one)

(a) To form joint venture with overseas producers

(b) To establish business operations in China

(c) To cease business operations

(d) To continue business operations without any change

(e) To become a listed company in the stock market

(f) To merge with another company

(g) No future plan yet, will act according to the changing situation

(h) To introduce new models/product

31 Have you ever experienced a business failure?

(a) Yes   (b) No

If yes, the reasons are _____

APPENDIX 2

CASE 1 TSUI HANG HING GARMENT FACTORY LTD

Founder: H.S. Cheung

Address: 2/F Hewlett Centre, 52–54 Hoi Yuen Rd, Kwun Tong

This case illustrates how a typical garment factory in Hong Kong survived by employing Kirznerian entrepreneurial strategies. In its early stage of development, Tsui Hang Hing Garment Factory was involved solely in the customer label garment business, spent little on R&D and focused on low value added products. As the business grew, a design department was established to keep up with world fashions. The company later promoted its own label garments in China. Facing the pressure of rising costs in Hong Kong, the company moved most of its production activities to the mainland, leaving the office in the Colony as a sourcing and ordering centre. Tsui Hang Hing Co. and other manufacturing firms have enhanced a structural change of Hong Kong's economy.

Mr H.S. Cheung is a Fujian-born Chinese. Before he started his business, he was employed as a worker for more than ten years in a garment factory in Hong Kong . This work experience was very useful for developing his garment business in later days. In 1982, he perceived a profit opportunity in sportswear production. Utilising his $10,000 savings, Mr Cheung set up a garment factory in Tai Kok Tsui, one of Hong Kong's industrial areas. At that time the factory was small and therefore could not handle a large number of orders. Overtime work was frequently undertaken.

After the establishment of the first garment plant in 1982, the company steadily expanded. The annual turnover grew from HK$100,000 in the first year to HK$200 million in 1993, with production plants in Fujian, Shenzhen and Hangzhou in mainland China, and Mauritius in Africa. His production lines in sportswear could be described as one of the largest in the world. The company in 1994 produced two main groups of garment: sportswear (shorts 58 per cent, jackets 4 per cent, pullovers and pants 26 per cent) and casual wear (6 per cent).

Export-oriented strategy

In the early development of the company, Mr Cheung accepted any order, domestic or overseas. He soon found that the local market was very limited. What he encountered were mainly import/export companies, or foreign agents in Hong Kong. Consequently, he received orders largely from foreign buyers and his business became export oriented. By 1994, nearly 96 per cent of the company's products were exported, of which 53 per cent to Holland, the UK, Germany, France, Belgium and Austria, 21 per cent to the USA and 18 per cent to China.

Alertness and flexibility

The success of Tsui Hang Hing Garment Factory was mainly attributable to the entrepreneurship of Mr Cheung. The company did not encounter any severe financial losses. From the information provided by Mr Cheung, we can highlight two main reasons for this.

First, Mr Cheung was always alert to change. Because export-oriented business is particularly vulnerable to international business cycles, Cheung needed to pay much attention to changing economic and political conditions of world markets. Hong Kong is an open economy with excellent communication facilities. Thus Cheung could obtain this information very quickly. Subsequently precautionary action could be taken and damage to his company due to international shocks could be reduced to a minimum. The adjustment to the changing environment also implied that the company moved to a new direction in garment production.

Another method which Mr Cheung employed to tackle business fluctuation was to diversify his buyer orders over 30 countries. The largest buyer would not exceed more than 10 per cent of the total orders. This practice was widely adopted by other producers in Hong Kong. To build in some flexibility, the factory also subcontracted part of the production activities to other factories. In 1994, the subcontracting activities of the company represented around 10 per cent to 15 per cent of total production.

Customer label garment business

Like many other Hong Kong manufacturers, Tsui Hang Hing Factory began as a customer label garment manufacturer. In other words, the firm produced garments which bore the labels of foreign companies. Producing for overseas customers continued to be a major direction of the company. As a customer label garment supplier for many years, the firm gradually learned to produce clothing with standards and styles accepted by foreign consumers.

Product strategy

The company adopted product imitative strategy. It competed with other local manufacturers by building up a professional image to gain foreign buyers' confidence. The company did not have a formal R&D department, but had a design team with ten specialists. The team attempted to catch up with world fashions. Every year it created a new list of sportswear and casual wear. Each new line of fashion took approximately six months to complete. The design team worked closely with the marketing department to make sure that their garments fitted into world markets. The design and marketing team frequently visited Europe and the USA to understand the market trends and communicate with potential buyers.

Marketing policy

Having relied on customer label garment business, the company did not need to promote its own labels. According to Mr Cheung, own label promotion involved huge investment and high risk, and therefore was not worthwhile. However, in 1991, he changed the marketing strategy and promoted two of his company's labels, namely Lava and VV in China. In 1994, these garments accounted for nearly 15 per cent of the company's total production. Cheung gave two reasons for the change in marketing strategy. First, with the huge market in China, the average cost of promoting there was much lower. Second, people in China generally considered Hong Kong made products to be superior to locally made goods. Since 1991 his products have been sold in Beijing, Shanghai, Huhan and other major cities in China.

Spatial arbitrage

In recent years garment production in Hong Kong has suffered from rising rentals and labour costs, and even worse, quota restriction. Like many other manufacturers, Mr Cheung was alert to cost-reducing opportunities. Following the open door policy in China, he began to subcontract parts of his production processes in 1985 to the joint venture in Fujian, namely the Frank Well Garment Factory. Mr Cheung owned a 55 per cent stake in this factory. In 1988 another joint venture in Hangzhou was formed, in which Mr Cheung's company owned a 45 per cent share. By 1990, the company's investment in the Hangzhou factory amounted to Yn1,175,000. By a similar arrangement, the company in 1990 controlled a printing factory (for clothing) in Shenzhen. Altogether, in 1994, the company employed around 3,000 people in China. In contrast, employment in the factory in Kwun Tong (Hong Kong) was reduced to only 30 people. Some production in Hong Kong remained because the company could still utilise the quota available in the Colony. However, as labour costs in Hong Kong kept rising, Mr Cheung intended to close down the plant in Hong Kong, leaving the office solely as a coordinating and sourcing centre.

Apart from China, Mr Cheung also established a factory in Mauritius (Africa). Taking advantages of cheap labour, low tax rates and the Mauritius government's concession to allocate a full quota to the company, Cheung in 1991 invested US$668,000 to establish Tsui Hang Hing (Mauritius) Garment Factory Ltd. Unlike China, exports from Mauritius to the EEC are not subject to any quota restriction.

Cheung was not the first to set up plants in China or Mauritius, but certainly the company was not a late entrant. In 1994 Mr Cheung planned to invest in Russia and Vietnam.

In sum, Cheung employed Austrian entrepreneurial strategies. The company produced customer label garments, spent few resources on R&D, did not promote its own label garments, and focused on low value added products. As the business grew, a design department was established with an aim of catching up with world fashions. The company also promoted its own labels in China. This means that the company moved away from purely imitative strategies. Facing the pressure of rising costs in Hong Kong, the company relocated most of its production activities to China, leaving the office in Hong Kong as a sourcing and ordering centre.

CASE 2   VIDEO TECHNOLOGY GROUP (VTECH)

Founder: Wong Chi-Yun, Allan

Address: 23/F Tai ping Industrial Centre, Block 1, 57 Ting Kok Rd, Tai Po

---

Vtech's competitive strategies included:

- utilisation of foreign technology,
- relocation of production activities to China;
- use of Hong Kong as a coordinating and management centre.

The company

Video Technology Group (Vtech) was established in 1977 by Allan Wong and Stephen Leung, with paid up capital of HK$300,000. The company's annual turn-over grew dramatically from US$600,000 in 1978 to US$565 million in 1993. In 1986 Vtech became a listed company in Hong Kong. In 1992 the company gained a concurrent listing on the London and Hong Kong stock exchanges. By 1994 the company ranked as the largest manufacturing outfit in Hong Kong's electronics industry. It was a leading producer of electronic educational toys and the biggest personal computer maker in Asia outside Japan, South Korea and Taiwan. The company also made cellular and cordless phones and satellite receivers. In less than two decades Vtech had evolved from a small manufacturer of single-chip micro-processor video games into one of the world's most comprehensive consumer electronics firms.

The entrepreneur

Allan Wong comes from a family involved in the import/export business. Part of the commodities traded included electronics products. In his youth Allan Wong showed great interest in electronic engineering. Like many Chinese families in

Hong Kong, Wong's parents wanted their son to receive a good education. Wong received his first engineering degree from the University of Hong Kong and a masters degree in electrical engineering from the University of Wisconsin, USA.

After graduation, Wong was employed as an electronics engineer for three years at NCR, a computer maker in Hong Kong. Wong thought that "it's always better to work for yourself than for someone else". In 1977 he perceived that the single-chip microprocessor that had just appeared overseas could be applied to many fields. Only a few specialists in Hong Kong were familiar with this kind of technical application and productions cost were much lower. Wong quit his job and set up a small electronics factory, Vtech. Initially it produced electronic games and later educational toys and personal computers.

Allan Wong's career path is typical among new generation entrepreneurs in Hong Kong in the last two decades. That is, with a university degree and several years of work experience in related fields, ambitious young people spin off from their employers to set up their own companies. Vtech is a successful case. In 1991 Allan Wong was named "Hong Kong outstanding young industrialist".

Product strategy

The company has engaged in some OEM production. In 1984, Vtech began with the manufacture of satellite receivers on an OEM basis and captured a significant slice of the OEM telecommunications market in the US and Europe. However, unlike many small manufacturing firms in Hong Kong, the company has not relied solely on such business. Vtech also developed its own niche brands. By 1994, 90 per cent of the company's output belonged to its own brands. Some major brands were Vtech, Playtech, Laser and PC Partner.

On product development, Wong's strategy relied on three principles, "novel", "quick" and "cheap". Vtech strove to improve the design, with new models which were much more efficient than original products from overseas. The company could tailor products quickly to meet market needs. Wong claimed that "they can make decisions within minutes and get rolling". He further remarked that "to manufacture a computer is very easy, but to design it cost effectively is the name of the game".

In summary, the company pursued imitative strategies. Whenever brand new products emerged overseas, the company quickly imitated them and supplied the same markets with new improved models at much cheaper prices than the originals.

The novel–quick–cheap principle can be illustrated by the company's two most successful products, namely educational toys and telecommunication equipment. In 1982 Texas Instruments in the USA successfully created three popular electronic educational toys which teach children spelling, conversation and numbers. Each sold for US$35. Once they appeared on the market, Vtech immediately imitated the production. More importantly, it combined all three functions into one called Play Tech that sold for only US$30. The products soon undersold the Texas Instruments toys and in 1994 captured 60 per cent of the US market. This case fully demonstrates the advantages of being a latecomer.

Since product life cycles for these kinds of products were shorter, Vtech's speed in developing new models was of particular importance. The company was able to bring 30 new products to market each year.

Another successful example is cordless telephones. Before Vtech, the market sold the standard 49 MHz units. Vtech improved the design and supplied the first digital 900 Mhz cordless telephone with better sound quality and more reliability. As a result, the company seized 70 per cent of the US market. In the 1990s, the company manufactured cordless phones for Phillips and Alcatel in Europe and AT&T in the USA as well as its own brands.

R&D and product development

To implement the novel–quick–cheap principle, the company maintained a rigorous commitment to R&D. In 1991, it put US$18 million, or about 4 per cent of the company's annual turnover, into R&D. By 1994 the R&D department employed 600 people. However, only a minor portion of the R&D money was spent on new product design, the bulk went into redesigning and improving products as well as making them easier and cheaper to produce.

The company had R&D centres in the USA, Canada, UK, China and Hong Kong. Their functions were to review the marketplace constantly for emerging trends and opportunities and to "adapt leading-edge technologies in order to create exciting and inventive consumer products". With the help of these R&D centres, Vtech produced approximately 65 new products a year, resulting in average growth in sales of 50 per cent over the past five years. Most of the products had patent protection both in Hong Kong and overseas. The management of technology can be summarised by the following statement from the company:

> Innovation does not happen by chance. At Vtech, every innovation our R&D experts achieve is a response to a specific product development challenge. And to help our experts meet those challenges, we promote a responsive and interconnective intelligence link between marketing and product development teams around the world that is integral to staying one step ahead of the competition. We believe our R&D teams are well equipped to set new standards and meet head-on the demands of the future.

> (*Vtech: A Company Profile*, p. 13).

Vertical integration

Innovation requires coordination among departments. Therefore, for innovating firms vertical integration is preferred. Vtech was a largely integrated manufacturer, able to handle virtually every aspect of production and assembly from plastic injection moulding to printed circuit board assembly. The company only subcontracted around 10 per cent of its production processes to other smaller factories which specialise in those activities. Allan Wong claimed that the company's success was attributable to its commitment to vertical integration. Vtech's vertically integrated manufacturing capability allowed the entire process to be completed in-house. For example, in personal computers, every step, from the highly complex design and development of their own LSI circuits and ASIC chips, to printed circuit boards assembly and plastic and metal casing, was coordinated to create a highly efficient and cost-effective production process. In electronic toys and games, virtually the entire production assembly process from plastic moulding production to sophisticated electronic components insertion was conducted in-house to ensure that the highest quality standards were delivered.

Spatial arbitrage

Compared with other small manufacturers, Vtech was rather late in relocating its production activities to China to utilise ample supplies of low cost labour and land. However, Vtech's investment there was large. Almost ten years after China had implemented its open door policy, the company in 1987 invested HK$500 million in setting up an electronics plant in Dongguan, southern China. The plant occupied a manufacturing space of over 400,000 sq. m, with 7 departments, employing around 11,000 people. The 21 production lines, supplying more than 100 types of electronics toys, with annual turnover Yn3,000 million, were supervised by 100 local Chinese engineers and managers.

Apart from taking the advantage of lower production costs in China, the company also enjoyed concessionary tariff terms when exporting Dongguan's products to the USA because China had been granted most favoured nation (MFN) trading status. Vtech also cooperated with Lian Xiang computer Ltd (Beijing) to market its educational computers.

The company's dilemma

Not all went well for Vtech and Allan Wong admitted that personal computer operations had lost money in recent years. Vtech in 1994 controlled 1 per cent of the world PC market, accounting for 55 per cent of the company's total turnover. In particular, the US market, which accounted for approximately 75 per cent of the company's sales of personal computers, suffered keen competition from other smaller producers, some from less developed countries. It resulted in an operating loss for this product line during the first half of 1992. Market analysts commented that Vtech was overexposed in the competitive PC market. When a company grows to a certain size, too much dependence on certain products will reduce flexibility. Because the company lost ground to some smaller producers from other late industrialising nations, it was therefore forced to take steps to upgrade its range by introducing products of a higher specification to cater to sectors of the US market. As a result, the company faced the same situation as

Japanese producers where competition comes from manufacturers in late industrialising economies.

The Vtech lesson

Despites the difficulties in PC operations, Vtech had been a success. The company emerged from a small microprocessor to become a multinational firm. Mr Wong summarised his Vtech's experience into what he called a Hong Kong's model:

Foreign technology + Hong Kong management + production in mainland China

This formula is fully consistent with our arguments. That is, Hong Kong's manufacturers utilise foreign technologies and China's cheap labour to produce cheap improved electronic goods for overseas markets. The activities are coordinated by outstanding entrepreneurs who, given the excellent international communication network in the Colony, are able to grasp market opportunities and respond rapidly to change and arbitrage for profit. Their efforts contribute to Hong Kong's dynamics.

CASE 3 TERMBRAY ELECTRONICS CO. LTD

Founder: Lee Lap

Address: 18–22 Lam Tin St, Kwai Chung, New Territories

Termbray's case illustrates how the founder, Lee Lap, employed Austrian entrepreneurial strategies to expand his business. These strategies included:

- OEM business;
- one-niche product;
- production in China.

The entrepreneur: an immigrant from China

It is widely known that the early industrialisation of Hong Kong was partly attributed to a group of immigrants from China when the communists took over the mainland in 1949. The continual influx of immigrants due to a series of political upheavals in China sustained such a trend. Lee Lap and his company provide us with an illustration of how Austrian entrepreneurship has contributed to Hong Kong's economic growth.

Lee Lap was born in 1943 in Zhongshan, a county located at the Pearl River Delta of southern China. The Great Leap Forward movement initiated by Mao Tse-Tung in 1957 caused general famine in China. In 1963 Lee decided to cross the border illegally to try his luck in the Colony. He successfully obtained permanent residency status in Hong Kong. Reluctant to be hired as a cheap labourer, Lee struggled to start his own business. In 1968 he invested $3,000 in the electronics industry and set up a one-man workshop, Termbray Co., in Mongkok (Kowloon Peninsula) to manufacture single-sided printed circuit boards.

A printed circuit board consists of insulating material on which electronic circuits are printed by application of photographic, chemical and electroplating processes. Virtually every piece of electronic equipment requires at least one printed circuit board which is used as a compact base to make electrical connection between the various components. If sales in electronic equipment increase, demand for printed circuit boards will also increase.

As the business grew, Lee hired several workers. In the first year of operation, he earned HK$10,000 profit. Unable to afford additional staff, overtime work in the factory became a normal phenomenon. According to Lee, he worked almost 365 days a year and sometimes stayed up to 20 hours per day or even overnight in the factory to beat delivery dates.

During the 1970s, when there was a growing demand in consumer products such as transistor radios, calculators, telephones and hi-fis, Termbray's sale in printed circuit boards continued to grow. Apart from local sales, the company also exported to Singapore. In 1972 Lee established a larger factory in Kwun Tong, with a total floor area of 5,000 sq. ft, employing 20 workers.

In 1974 Lee set up his own plastic tooling and injection moulding facilities to produce plastic castings for radio and audio equipment. By 1975 Lee had earned his first million dollars. By 1977 the company manufactured clock radios, hand-held, television and musical games and distributed them under the company's brand name principally for export to Europe and the USA.

OEM business and the no-brand-one-niche product strategy

However, further development of the company did not rely on the manufacture of a diverse range of branded products. On the contrary, it has adopted two strategies, namely no-brand-one-niche products and OEM business.

Regarding the first strategy, Hong Kong manufacturers have tended to concentrate on one or two niche products which has enabled them to boost quality and trim costs to unbeatable levels.

With years of experience in the production of printed circuit boards, Lee knew his competitive edges. In 1981 he decisively invested $5 million to relocate his entire manufacturing plant to Tsuen Wan, one of Hong Kong's new industrial areas, to produce more complex printed circuit boards. The plant occupied a total floor area of 30,000 sq. ft, employing 400 people, and produced high precision double-sided printed circuit boards for sale to a number of customers including Atari and Commodore. In 1983 the company ceased production of its own brand products in order to concentrate on printed circuit boards and OEM products.

In conjunction with technological development in the computer industry which demanded more sophisticated high precision printed circuit boards, the company in 1984 commenced the manufacture of multilayer printed circuit boards. On the success of his printed circuit boards business, Lee remarked: "I can never make computers like Commodore or IBM, but I can make printed circuit boards for them better than many other producers." In 1991, the company's total turnover in printed circuit boards amounted to HK$165.85 million, with an operating profit of HK$26.8 million. By 1994 the more advanced printed circuit boards were manufactured in Hong Kong while competitively priced printed circuit boards were made in mainland China.

Regarding the OEM business, Lee's insight, "We make it, you sell it", has been the secret of success for most Hong Kong exporters. They have shunned grand marketing plans, multimillion dollar brand promotions. Instead they have let the foreign brand owners take the risk of selling the Hong Kong made products in overseas markets.

In 1984 Termbray Co. secured its first order from AT&T to manufacture telephone sets and answering machines designed by AT&T. Initially contracts were to produce only basic models but later, the company was successful in obtaining orders to manufacture upgraded and more complex products offering many features, including memory functions, speaker phones, liquid crystal displays and two-way recording, etc. In the same year the company set up an additional factory in Kwai Chung to expand its production capacity for OEM business. By 1991, sales to AT&T accounted for approximately 84 per cent of the company's OEM sales and 60 per cent of the company's operating profit. The total turnover of Termbray Co. in the OEM business amounted to HK$601.9 million, with an operating profit of HK$97.2 million.

In short, the company relied on two main production lines: printed circuit boards for local and overseas buyers and OEM products for the USA and European markets. The distribution of two kinds of business in 1994 is summarised in Table A2.1.

Table A2.1 Turnover and operating profits of Termbray Electronics Co. Ltd, 1994

Products	Turnover		Operating profits	
	HK$million	*Share (%)*	*HK$million*	*Share (%)*
Printed circuit board	165.8	17.4	26.8	21.4
OEM business	601.8	80.0	97.0	78.0

Spatial arbitrage

The economic reforms in China during the last decade provided the company with opportunities to establish manufacturing bases there which had the attraction of lower overheads and an ample supply of labour. In 1984 Lee set up a factory in his home town, Zhongshan, Guangdong, to concentrate on the production of single-sided and double-sided printed circuit boards. The plant had a total floor area of 60,000 sq. ft. In 1986, he set up another factory in Nantou, Shenzhen for the manufacture of telephones and telephone answering systems designed by AT&T.

In early 1990, Lee began to relocate the manufacturing facilities for double-sided and multilayer printed circuit boards from the Tsuen Wan factory to Zhongshan, while the plant in Tsuen Wan was used as a headquarters.

In early 1991, the construction of the factory's extension in Zhongshan was completed. The total floor area of the factory there increased from 60,000 sq. ft to 263000 sq. ft, employing 1,500 workers. Moreover, the installation of approximately US$42 million worth of new machinery and equipment significantly increased the company's capacity to manufacture more complex printed circuit boards.

In the 1990s Termbray's business in China continued to expand. In 1993 the company bought a whole set of advanced printed circuit manufacturing equipment from Germany at US$3.5 million to be installed in the new factory in Guangshou. The land area of the new factory site was approximately 130,000 sq. m. The new plant if operating at full capacity could increase printed circuit board production by 40 per cent.

Conclusion

Lee's case illustrates several strategies for business expansion in Hong Kong. First, as an original equipment manufacturer supplier, he focused on the production of OEM products, mainly telephones, for US and European buyers and hence saved all the promotion jobs. Second, he concentrated on one niche product, namely, printed circuit boards, in which he was able to undersell his competitors. Third, by relocating production to China, he could effectively lower costs. Above all, Lee's ability to respond efficiently and swiftly to customers' changing needs, to exercise effective cost and quality control for both the company's printed circuit boards and OEM business, and to meet customers' required delivery dates were the secrets of Termbray's success.

CASE 4   TAK SUN ALLIANCE LTD

Founder: Ma Kai-Tak

Address: 26/F Kwai Hing Centre, 300 Cheung Sha Wan Road, Kwai Chung, New Territories

The expansion path of Tak Sun Alliance Ltd consisted of:

- moving from custom label garments to own label garments;
- subcontracting;
- production in South Africa;
- diversification into service activities.

Ma Kai-Tak and Tak Sun Alliance Ltd

Tak Sun Alliance Ltd, found by Ma Kai-Tak in 1973, was principally involved in the design, manufacture, distribution, and retailing of jeans and other casual wear.

A typical self-made entrepreneur, Ma kai-Tak shaped his own career path with endurance. Without a strong educational background and formal training in garment manufacturing, Ma succeeded in expanding his jeans business from a company with only 50 workers into a conglomerate of more than 80 local and overseas companies. This achievement earned him the name "King of Jeans" in the local garment industry.

However, Ma had no pretensions to such success when he first came to Hong Kong in 1967. His primary concern then was to survive. With help from his relatives, he found a labouring job in a garment factory at a daily wage of HK$5.50. A firm belief in hard work and a persistent desire to learn motivated him to climb the industrial ladder. Soon he was promoted to the positions of garment technician, supervisor and factory manager. In 1967 he established Tak Sun Garment Factory. When asked what made him start his own business, his answer was Hong Kong's environment. "Hong Kong is a place of opportunity," said Ma, "if one wants to try his ideas and is willing to work hard, the chance of success is very high."

Initially, the company's garments were manufactured for Hong Kong based importing houses and agents, including those of major European department stores, for sale as customer label garments. As the volume of orders increased over the years, the company's product range also grew. By 1973 the company's business was reorganised and expanded to include casual wear such as overalls, shirts, jackets and shorts. Subsequently, Tak Sun Alliance Ltd was formed to take over the business of Tak Sun Garment Ltd's business.

From customer label garments to own label garments

Like many other manufacturers in Hong Kong, the company started as a producer of customer label garments for export to Europe and the USA. Usually the designs were specified by customers. Since entering these markets sales had steadily increased and in 1994 the company supplied customer label garments to over 30 customers, including agents, trading houses and major department stores. In 1991 sales of customer label garments accounted for approximately 27 per cent of the company's turnover.

Customer label garments were made only against confirmed orders. Though the customer label garment business had its own advantages, Ma was well aware that in confining itself, the company was unduly exposed to the marketing ability of others. Ma wanted to reduce this exposure. Previous involvement in customer label garment business provided him with sufficient technical knowledge in brand development. In 1977, the company created its own label garments, Cherry, and distributed them in the USA. Resulting sales encouraged the company to distribute

Table A2.2   Turnover of Tak Sun Alliance Ltd

Product	Turnover in 1991 HK$million	Share %
Own label garments	331.6	70
Customer label garments	130.8	27

own label garments in the Netherlands. By 1991, approximately 90 per cent of the company's products sold in the USA and 71 per cent of those sold in Europe were own label garments. Turnover of the own label garments amounted to $331.6 million, around 70 per cent of the total turnover. The figures are summarised in Table A2.2.

Subcontracting

To enhance the company's competitiveness and increase its production capacity and access to quotas, the company in the 1980s subcontracted with independent manufacturers to produce own label garments. In 1994 own label garments were manufactured by the company as well as by 28 independent manufacturers overseas to the company's specifications for sale in the USA and Europe. Own label garments manufactured for the company by independent manufacturers represented approximately 76 per cent of the total value of own label garments sold. None of these manufacturers accounted for more than 11 per cent of external contracting. According to Ma, the policy of subcontracting with independent manufacturers allowed for greater flexibility in pricing and delivery times, reduced fixed overheads, lessened the impact of seasonal sales fluctuations and helped to alleviate stringent quota restrictions on goods produced in Hong Kong for import to the USA.

Through its subsidiaries in the USA, the company subcontracted with independent manufacturers in Latin America, the Caribbean, Asia and the USA for the supply of own label garments for sale in the US market. Furthermore, through its subsidiaries in Europe, the company subcontracted with independent manufacturers in Europe and Asia for the supply of own label garments to the European markets.

For own label garments sold in Hong Kong and other parts of Asia, the company subcontracted with independent manufacturers in Hong Kong and Thailand. In addition, all knitwear for sale as own label garments was subcontracted to independent manufacturers as the company did not have knitwear manufacturing facilities. By 1991, approximately 36 per cent and 97 per cent in terms of value of own label garments distributed in the USA and Europe respectively were sourced from independent manufacturers.

For those activities which required facilities that the company did not own, such as label making, embroidery and washing, and orders beyond its capacity which might occur during peak seasons, the company subcontracted to independent manufacturers. In general, urgent orders, garments subject to strict customer requirements and fancy fashion wear were subcontracted in Hong Kong, while large volume orders for garments with simpler designs were subcontracted overseas. All orders processed by the subcontractors were monitored by the company's senior staff.

Spatial arbitrage

Expansion of the company's manufacturing base began in 1983 after Ma identified South Africa as a favourable garment manufacturing site. Investment there enhanced the company's ability to cater for different export markets and allowed for greater flexibility in pricing. However, an unexpected event in 1984, the US-led economic sanctions, adversely affected the company's operations. This led the company to phase out its South African operations and to establish a factory in Lesotho where garment manufacture was not subject to economic sanctions. In 1990, after the economic sanctions on goods manufactured in South Africa were lifted, the company re-established a new factory. The company's factories in Lesotho and South Africa manufactured customer label garments for export markets as well as for sale to the domestic market in South Africa. In addition, the Lesotho factory also manufactured own label garments for sale in the USA.

Towards the tertiary sector

Clothing production was a very labour intensive business. Aware of rising labour costs and consequently decreasing profit margins, Ma diversified his investments into less labour intensive businesses, namely trading, real estate, food and beverages, which were the main tertiary activities in Hong Kong during the 1990s.

The company engaged in trading a wide range of materials and apparel including textiles, knitwear and finished garments, through its subsidiary. These were sourced from Hong Kong, China and South East Asia for sale to Europe and Southern Africa. In 1991 trading accounted for approximately 3 per cent of turnover. The company intended to expand its retail network by setting up a more extensive chain and department store counters in major shopping areas in Hong Kong and Kowloon. Ma considered Hong Kong to be a stepping stone for expansion to other affluent Asian countries.

The company also invested in the property market. The portfolio of property investments comprised commercial properties located in Kowloon with an aggregate floor area of approximately 1,600 sq. ft. The project generated approximately $344,000 of rental income for the company. Ma intended to develop industrial and commercial properties in the high potential growth areas in Shenzhen Special Economic Zone in China.

The company had been involved in the food and beverage industry since 1985 and had invested in Ginza Development Company and Carrianna Chiu Chow estaurant. Each of these companies owned directly or indirectly one of the well-known Carrianna restaurants in Hong Kong located in prime areas of Wanchai and Tsim Sha Tsui respectively and specialising in Chiu Chow cuisine. In 1991 the two restaurants contributed approximately 5 per cent of the company's profit. Ma planned to open more Chiu Chow restaurants in Hong Kong, China and South East Asian countries where Chiu Chow cuisine is popular.

Conclusion

Like many other entrepreneurs in Hong Kong, Ma Kai-Tak started his garment business from a penniless foundation. After many years of hard work, Ma became one of the successful industrialists in the Colony. His company largely adopted Austrian entrepreneurial strategies, focused on customer label garments, though it later also promoted own label garments. This shift signified a higher capability of the company to penetrate high value added markets. Both subcontracting and spatial arbitrage enhanced the company's competitiveness and access to quotas. To look for a higher return on investments, Ma diversified into trading, real estate, food and beverages. In short, entrepreneurial activities such as Tak Sun Alliance Ltd have contributed to the structural change of the economy of Hong Kong.

CASE 5 GOLDLION (FAR EAST) CO. LTD

Founder: Tsang Hin-Chi

Address: 5 Yuk Yat St, G/F-8/F Wai Shun Industrial Building Tokwawan, Kowloon, Hong Kong

---

This case shows how the manufacturer succeeded by imitating the styles of foreign products, by adopting the retail strategies of overseas firms, by subcontracting the works to independent manufacturers and by performing spatial arbitrage.

The entrepreneur and the company

Goldlion (Far East) Company Ltd was engaged principally in the production and marketing of men's apparel such as ties and shirts under the Goldlion brand name. The company was founded by Tsang Hin-Chi who was born in Meizhou, Guangdong, in 1934. A graduate of Zhongshan University, Guangzhou, Tsang emigrated to Hong Kong in 1963. In 1968 Tsang commenced a small home-based manufacturing operation for ties in Kowloon. At that time he normally worked from 6.00am to 12.00 midnight.

Initially, Tsang aimed at the production of low-priced ties. He estimated that if the ties were sold at $58 a dozen, there would be $20 net profit. But soon he found that his ties had no buyers, so he switched to a high quality product. To begin with,

APPENDIX 2

Table A2.3 Turnover and gross profit of Goldlion (Far East) Co. Ltd

	1988	1992	Annual change %
Turnover (HK$'000)	100,295	462,085	90
Gross profit (HK$'000)	19,737	106,790	110

Source: Goldlion (Far East) Co. Ltd, New Issue, September 1992, p. 2

he bought four famous brand ties made in Europe and replicated their styles. With quality and design almost the same as foreign labels, he sold his ties to shops in Tsimshatsui and Central, Hong Kong's densest business districts, with an initial sale target of 60 ties per day. He found that this kind of imitative strategy paid.

In 1970 he established a factory, Goldlion (Far East) Ltd in Tokwawan. Tsang and his assistants frequently travelled to France, Germany (West), Italy, Austria and Switzerland to learn the technique of producing and marketing ties, bringing home some of the latest fashions and designs. Over time the quality of the company's products improved. Furthermore, he successfully established trading relationships with local major department stores and Hong Kong Daimaru department store. In 1987 the company began to produce men's shirts. The company continued to expand. The turnover and gross profit for 1988 and 1992 are shown in Table A2.3.

Fashion development: imitation of styles

Tsang remarked that the success of Goldlion (Far East) Co. was attributed to the borrowing foreign ideas strategy which has been widely adopted by Hong Kong manufacturers. He implemented this strategy through his "four quick principles": "Quick design, quick sampling, quick production and quick marketing". Specifically in the tie market, France and Italy possess many first-class designers and every day supply world markets with new designs and styles. The company simply sent its staff overseas and adopted these new designs via paying a license fee. In the Hong Kong factory their designs were modified into Goldlion's products and quickly put into mass production. In this way, Goldlion could guarantee a fast supply of new styles. Hence Tsang's "four quick principles" enabled the company to catch up with world fashions. In 1994 Goldlion supplied the world markets with ties of 20,000 different colour designs.

Marketing strategy

Brand promotion is important in the necktie market. In 1971 the company launched a newly designed tie labelled "Goldlion". In the same year it stepped up its public promotion campaign by participating in the television sponsorship of the Chinese national table tennis team exhibition in Hong Kong and of US President Richard Nixon's visit to China in 1972. In 1973 counter sales were

202

commenced in local department stores. In 1986 the company promoted its products in China under the label Silverlion. Taking the advantage of "Hong Kong fever" in China after the adoption of the open door policy, the promotion of the label was very successful.

Subcontracting

Apart from producing ties, the company also manufactured shirts and other clothing items. All garments sold were subcontracted to outside manufacturers. In order to ensure quality and to control costs, the company sourced its own raw materials and accessories for shirts and T-shirts which were then provided to subcontractors for processing. In 1992 the company worked with 17 subcontractors for its garment products based mainly in Hong Kong. A major problem in subcontracting is quality control. For Goldlion, commercial production of the company's garments by subcontractors would only commence after production run samples were checked for quality, design and colour. For all garments manufactured by subcontractors in Hong Kong and Macau, the company's merchandising staff undertook online inspection. Finished products would also be rechecked on delivery to ensure that all specifications and quality requirements had been met.

Spatial arbitrage

Manufacturing

Following the success of Goldlion in Hong Kong, Tsang attempted to establish a subsidiary in the USA and penetrated markets there. However, the economic reform in China over the last decade disrupted his American plan. With much lower production costs in China and a huge potential market there, Tsang decided to invest US$1 million. In 1989 he established a tie manufacturing factory, China Silverlion Ltd, in his home town, Meizhou (Guangdong). The factory occupied a total floor area of approximately 7,200 sq. ft, with four production lines employing 45 workers. The factory had a total production capacity of approximately 1,200,000 ties per annum on the basis of one shift of operation. In 1992 it manufactured a total of 660,000 ties.

Sales and marketing

Apart from selling its products through 130 wholesalers and retailers such as trading companies, department stores and apparel shops, the company operated 34 Goldlion counters in department stores in Hong Kong's popular shopping areas. The idea of counter sales was taken from other famous foreign brand products in Hong Kong. The Goldlion counters sold Goldlion products within department stores with a standard design and layout in accordance with the company's specification. All Goldlion counters were managed by the company's uniformed sales staff. The company was responsible for the decoration, fitting out and management of the counters while the department stores provided the floor area, which usually ranged from 200 sq. ft to 600 sq. ft for each counter. The revenues derived were shared between the company and the department stores on a predetermined basis with the stores guaranteed a minimum payment.

Standard retail prices were set by the company for the products on all counters and in other retail outlets and this uniform pricing policy was generally expected to be adhered to. The aim was to gain retail customers' goodwill by giving them confidence that they would not pay different prices for the same products in the same region.

Following the successful launch of counter sales in Hong Kong's department stores, Tsang extended the concept to China and South East Asian countries. An extensive regional distribution network was established for products in China, Taiwan, Indonesia, Singapore, Malaysia and Thailand. The two major regions were China and Singapore.

In China the company set up a subsidiary, Silverlion Company, to promote sales and to be the principal wholesaler of Goldlion's products. In addition, Goldlion also sold directly to customers in China, including a sole distributor for the city of Shenyang and the duty free shops in the five Special Economic Zones. The company had an office with a packing area in Guangzhou which was responsible for the coordination of company's marketing and distribution activities in the country. There were approximately 460 wholesale and retail customers in China, with 32 in Guangzhou, 28 in Beijing, 17 in Shanghai, 11 in Tianjin, 11 in Chengdu, eight in Dalian, eight in Wuhan, seven in Xian, six in Nanjing, with the remainder located in other cities.

In Singapore, the company had approximately 90 wholesale and retail customers comprising apparel shops and department stores. In addition, the company in 1994 operated 22 Goldlion counters. These were located in popular shopping areas, comprising 12 on Orchard Road, four on Beach Road, two in Katong and four in other areas. The regional distribution of total turnover is shown in Table A2.4.

Table A2.4   Goldlion's total turnover (HK$'000) by region, 1988 and 1992

Regions	1988	1992
Mainland China	10,125	230,010 (49.8%)
Hong Kong	66,199	140,941 (30.5%)
Singapore	20,413	50,761 (10.9%)
Others	3,558	40,374 (8.8%)
Total	100,295	462,085
Gross profit	19,737	106,790
Net profit margin	15.9%	18.9%

Source: Goldlion (Far East) Co. Ltd, New Issue, September 1992, p. 12

Conclusion

The case of Goldlion (Far East) illustrated how a hardworking entrepreneur built up his necktie empire. Pursuing an imitative strategy, he created a policy of "four quick principles" to catch up with world fashions. Later, by subcontracting the manufacture of shirts and other menswear, he was able to enlarge the product range. He also adopted the concept of counters to boost sales in department stores. Having performed successfully in Hong Kong, he then extended the strategy to China and other South East Asian countries.

CASE 6 TOPSTYLE GARMENT FACTORY LTD

Founder: Lo Chiu-Hung

Address: Unit E, 9/F Lladro Building, 72 80 Hoi Yuen Road, Kwun Tong, Hong Kong

Topstyle's case reveals how Lo acted as an international coordinator in silk garment production. Utilising different kinds of spatial arbitrage techniques, such as processing trade agreements, subcontracting or establishing subsidiary factories in China, the "Hong Kong made" products were sold to the USA and Europe through marketing agents overseas. The office in Hong Kong performed a headquarters role, engaging in planning, sourcing and testing. This case also highlights some of the difficulties of a first mover.

Introduction to the company

Topstyle Garment Factory Ltd in the 1990s designed and manufactured a wide range of silk and non-silk garments including blouses, shirts, shorts, jackets and dresses for ladies. The silk garments were distributed under customer labels or the company's own labels to an extensive customer base which encompasses boutiques, department stores, specialty stores and other retail outlets. The company's principal market is the USA, which is also the single largest market for Hong Kong's silk garment exports.

The founder

Lo Chiu-Hung was born in Hong Kong in 1946. She came from a business family. Her grandfather was a wholesaler in clothing and her father was a merchandiser at the Swire Group, one of the four big "hongs" (British trading firms) in Hong Kong. At the age of 19, after graduating from a private business college, she was hired by an international trading firm, McCrory International. Not willing to work under other people, she decided to start her own business. With HK$9,000, she set up a trading company, Edlan International, to export children's wear. However, she soon found that the business potential was quite limited so she closed down Edlan and in 1969 set up another firm, Mountain Industries, to engage in the design, production and sale of garments, primarily ladies' knitwear, from Hong Kong to the USA. As business grew, Mountain Industries also manufactured ladies' blouses. Mountain Industries was renamed Topstyle Garment Factory Ltd.

One niche product: specialisation in silk garments

Because the silk garment business had no quota restriction on imports to the USA and only few factories in Hong Kong at that time manufactured silk garments, Lo in the mid-1980s began to develop, manufacture and market silk garments in response to their increasing popularity in the USA. Building upon her experience in garment production, the company was able to make a rapid and smooth transition into the production of predominantly silk garments. In 1991 approximately 72 per cent of the company's products were made of at least 70 per cent silk with the balance being garments of cotton, wool, rayon and other materials. Nearly all of the company's garments were made from washable silk and in 1994 the principal products were ladies' blouses and co-ordinates (that is, a blouse with a matching shirt or trousers and a jacket).

Subcontracting of distribution activities

Initially Lo attempted to market garments directly in the USA. In 1980 she set up her own marketing office in Los Angeles to promote the company's own label garments. However, high marketing costs associated with the promotion of its own labels led the company to adopt a new approach. She closed down the US office and appointed agents instead. This strategy proved to be successful.

Sales to US customers introduced by marketing agents were made directly by Katony Corp on a commission base. This distribution centre, located in New Jersey, provided the company with a greater ability to deal with rapid changes in the inventory requirements of US customers as trends altered.

Another distribution centre appointed by the company was Sunny Leigh Inc., located in New York. Sunny Leigh was a traditional buying centre for large department stores from all over the USA. It covered the important markets of New York State, Chicago, Boston, Dallas, Miami, San Francisco, Los Angeles and many other big cities. Since 1986 the company had been the sole supplier of silk garments to customers of Sunny Leigh. During the year 1990–91, 67 per cent of the company's turnover was made through Sunny Leigh.

According to Lo, subcontracting of distribution works in this way enabled the company to minimise its marketing costs while securing maximum market coverage.

Processing trade in China

In early 1973 China was still under the influence of the Cultural Revolution. Lo took the adventurous step of engaging in processing trades in Shanghai. Being a first mover, she found doing business with China's state enterprises was extremely difficult and her investments during that time received no benefits. She recalled one painful experience of trading in China. After a long-term isolation from the outside world people in China did not understand the significance of punctual delivery and quality control. A cargo of the company's finished products was packed to meet urgent Christmas sales in the USA. Later she was told by county officials involved in the state enterprise that her cargo was not arranged for delivery because the train had been diverted to transport mooncakes to Hong Kong for the mid-autumn festival. In consequence she lost several hundred thousand dollars and concluded that China at that time was not yet prepared for foreign trade. Subsequently she brought her business back to Hong Kong. This case fully illustrated that being a first mover may not be advantageous.

However, the Shanghai failure did not block her return to China but the lesson proved that the city was too far from Hong Kong and business communications were difficult. Therefore she considered other locations closer to Hong Kong. In 1977 she established a processing factory in Fujian and became involved in compensation trade in Guangzhou, Pangyu and Shuntak (all in Guangdong).

Subcontracting of production activities

In the 1970s Mountain Industries undertook its own production as well as subcontracting some manufacturing processes to other smaller manufacturers in Hong Kong.

In 1992, utilising cheap resources in China, the company subcontracted approximately 40 per cent of its production to seven regular subcontractors there. According to Lo, these arrangements enabled the company to minimise its overheads while maintaining flexibility in its own production scheduling. To ensure quality of output, the fabrics used were purchased by the company and delivered directly to the subcontractors' factories. The company had a team of 12 full-time employees stationed at various factories to supervise the subcontracting work.

Establishing factories in China

In 1987 the company established a garment factory in Panyu county, Guangdong, and manufacturing activities were mainly conducted there. By 1994 the company had two factories in operation with a total gross floor area of approximately 150,000 sq. ft and employed a total workforce of approximately 1,300.

With the production and distribution either subcontracted or relocated in China, the company retained its head office in Hong Kong where management, sales and marketing, finance and administration operations were located. Lo acted as an international coordinator.

CASE 7   S. MEGGA TELECOMMUNICATIONS LTD

Founder: Leung Ray-Man

Address: 1 Kwai Hei St, S. Megga Industrial Building, Kwai Chung, New Territories

---

The development strategy of S. Megga Telecommunications Ltd was in many ways similar to Termbray Electronics Co. (Case 3), in the sense that it also relied on OEM business, established one niche product and relocated production to mainland China. As a latecomer, the company adopted a defensive technological strategy. This case also illustrates the difficulties of promoting brands in China.

The founder

Leung Ray-Man was born in Hong Kong in 1943 and shortly afterwards migrated to Canada. At the age of 12 he returned to Hong Kong to receive high school education and later studied industrial engineering at Seattle University. In 1967, when many Hong Kong residents were leaving the Colony due to the political upheaval, Leung returned to engage in the import/export trade. In 1972 he saw a profit opportunity in electronic watch manufacturing. He estimated that producing a watch in Hong Kong cost only US$3.50 but it could be sold overseas at US$47. He then established S. Megga Electronics Factory Co. to produce super-thin electronic watches of only 4mm thickness. The business brought Leung considerable profits. After earning HK$9 million, he moved to cordless telephones. Operating in Kwai Tak Industrial Centre in Kwai Chung, New Territories, his business at that time was largely involved in the development of cordless and feature telephones.

In 1994 the company's factory at Kwai Chung occupied a total gross floor area of approximately 144,000 sq. ft. By 1991, the company's total turnover amounted to HK$500 million with approximately HK$400 million in cordless telephones, HK$63 million in feature telephones, HK$4.5 million in other communication products and HK$22.9 million in electronic products such as satellite receivers, facsimile machines, and pain relief healthcare machines.

OEM business and brand policy

The company was mainly involved in the development and production of cordless telephones. In 1991 the business accounted for approximately 80 per cent of the company's total turnover. S. Megga's development strategy is in many ways similar to Termbray, that is, the company had been an OEM supplier for US firms and focused on establishing one niche product. Later, the company even promoted its own brands in mainland China.

APPENDIX 2

OEM business

In the late 1970s, when cordless telephones became popular in the USA, Leung attempted to penetrate those markets. At that time, cordless telephones were largely monopolised by Japanese producers. In 1981 S. Megga Co. successfully produced its first cordless telephone. Although initially the selling prices were marginally higher than other local firms when compared to Japanese products, US buyers found S. Megga's products cheaper.

In 1982, after obtaining approval from Federal Communications Commission (US), the company sold cordless and feature telephones in the USA, Europe and Australia. In the following year the company manufactured and sold Telehelper 1600 memory diallers and Telehelper 600 speakerphones to AT&T for distribution in the USA under its brand name. In the same year the company designed cordless telephones known as the Nomad series for AT&T. Sales to AT&T grew dramatically from approximately HK$69 million in 1984 to HK$475 million in 1991 and S. Megga became one of their major suppliers. In 1990 the company received the OEM Quality Excellence Gold Award from AT&T. In 1991 it even sold cordless telephones with answering machines to JVC, a major manufacturer of cordless telephones.

S. Megga's brands in China

Though China experienced remarkable economic growth in the early 1990s, its infrastructure and telecommunications remained primitive. Leung observed that "the big market there will be in things like multi-hand sets. One line would serve all the families living in a block through extension numbers". S. Megga was well placed to provide such services. In 1990 it obtained approval from the Ministry of Posts and Telecommunications to sell the cordless and feature telephones under its own brand name of ZETA.

However, promoting its brands in China also involved certain difficulties. "To sell in China, we go through a lengthy and costly approval process while others do so in the black market", said Leung. Promoting its own brands in China did not bring many benefits to the company. Zetas had been losing out in Shenzhen, Guangzhou and Shanghai to smuggled imports and unauthorised Chinese-made phones. As a remedy, S. Megga entered into a joint venture with AT&T and China's Ministry of Posts and Telecommunications to distribute cordless and corded phones from its Chinese plants under the better known AT&T name. In 1994 the company gained 12 per cent of the Chinese market and expects nearly half of its sales to go there within the next five years.

Technological strategy and R&D

The company established a formal R&D department employing 50 engineers and technicians, equipped with sophisticated testing instruments and computer aided design systems. According to Leung, the department did not aim at any technological breakthrough. Instead, the R&D was (1) to ensure that the performance of the company's products was compatible with the standards set by foreign regulatory authorities; (2) to update technological know-how; (3) to improve the quality of existing products. The company sent its engineers to various manufacturers worldwide including AT&T in the USA and JVC in Japan, to obtain the latest technological skills. Substantial research effort was devoted to improve product design, shorten development time and minimise development cost.

While the world moved towards second generation cordless telephones, Leung chose to improve on the first generation model, finding that the company benefited more from this strategy. He refused to manufacture the second generation model because in his view a brand new product at its early stage of life cycle had a limited market and was very risky. He therefore preferred to wait until new models became popular and then enjoyed the advantage of a latecomer.

Spatial arbitrage

Despite spending the equivalent of 6 per cent of total sales on research and development in 1992, almost as much as its Japanese rivals, Leung admitted that S. Megga was unable to make telephones and other electronics products significantly cheaper. Instead the company's competitive edge was derived from relocating production to other countries.

Production in China

The company's facilities in China, which accounted for most of S. Megga's production, were located in Dongguan and had a total gross floor area of approximately 218,000 sq. ft. These factories were equipped with radio frequency testing equipment and auto-insertion, surface mount, automatic soldering and in-circuit testing machines to manufacture cordless and feature telephones as well as satellite receivers. Apart from taking advantage of lower production costs, exports of cordless and feature telephones from China to the USA benefited from most favoured nation status.

Production in Malaysia

S. Megga also produced in Malaysia. S. Meggatel was formed as a result of joint venture agreement in August 1991. The company owned a piece of land in Klang, Malaysia, of approximately 177,000 sq. ft. A factory was constructed on this site with a total gross floor area of approximately 66,000 sq. ft. The plant produced cordless telephones for AT&T.

S. Meggatel was granted Pioneer Status by the Malaysian Industrial Development Authority, under which the firm was entitled to various incentives that were designed to grant tax relief in various forms. One of the incentives was taxation relief for a five-year period with a further five-year period to be granted at the discretion of the relevant authorities upon meeting certain criteria. In addition, Malaysia was one of the countries eligible for the US Generalised System of Preferences.

Conclusion

S. Megga has been an OEM supplier for the US markets. Always acting as a latecomer, the company specialised in one niche product, namely cordless and feature telephones. Although the company engaged in R&D, the money spent was intended to catch up with the technology of the advanced nations. It did not intend to supply radical new products. In other words, the technological strategy of the company was defensive. Its competitive edge derived largely from production in China and Malaysia. Promoting its own brands in China might not be worthwhile for there is no comprehensive intellectual property law protection.

CASE 8   DRAGON PRECISION LTD

Founder: Sze Chak-Tong

Address: Unit 16, 2/F Block A, Po Lung Centre, 11 Wang Chiu Road, Kowloon Bay, Hong Kong

This case reports how Sze Chak-Tong, founder of Dragon Precision Ltd, reverted from innovative to imitative strategies. Sze concluded that innovative strategies were not practical in the environment of Hong Kong.

Sze Chak-Tong and Dragon Precision Ltd

After completing his high school education, Sze Chak-Tong worked as a salesman in electronics components. The job enabled him to build up business connections in the computer industry. In 1984, he and his brother Sze Chun-Kuen established Dragon Precision Ltd Their first factory, located at Cheung Sha Wan, an old industrial district, had a total gross floor area of 700 sq. ft. and employed six workers to produce computer main boards for Apple and IBM compatible computers, XT, Turbo XT, 260 and 460 models. With long working hours, which are quite normal for small firms in Hong Kong, Sze's job ranged from looking for new orders, supervision, day-to-day operations and delivery. Unlike other manufacturing firms in Hong Kong, the factory at that time produced solely for local markets where Sze's business connections were located.

During 1989 91 he expanded his business and rented a larger plant in Kowloon Bay, with a total gross floor area of 1,300 sq. ft, employing 30 people. However, this aggressive move caused him problems. Specifically, his firm adopted innovative strategies and strove to be an early adopter in technology. These strategies were later found to be inappropriate.

Failure of an offensive technological strategy

Sze admitted that he was very ambitious at that time. Right at the beginning, obsessed with sophisticated technology, he established a formal R&D section, employing three electronic engineers to develop some unique design products. However, Sze found that this policy did not work. In fact, large electronics firms in Hong Kong invested in R&D for transferring technology from their overseas parent companies or improving new products of other firms.

Sze explained the cost and benefit of his R&D expenditure as follows. The company employed three graduate electronics engineers, each costing about HK$12,000 per month, with a total for one year approximately HK$400,000. Since the first year was largely a training period, actual results could only be observed at the end of the second so the total cost of employing three engineers for two years were approximately HK$800,000 to HK$1 million. "Despite a large sum of money has been put in R&D, it has not brought the company any net benefits", said Sze. "The technological know-how in Hong Kong is normally half a year behind Taiwan."

Taiwan's manufacturers, with the help of the government, could obtain new technology from their US parent companies much sooner than Hong Kong's small local businesses that had no affiliation with foreign firms. Sze's company had no foreign technological back-up. The so-called new models developed by his R&D team were actually at the mature stage of the product life cycle and lagged approximately half a year behind international markets. For this reason, his products could not compete with those made in Taiwan.

Sze remarked that he spent approximately HK$1 million on R&D, not to mention other equipment and human effort, but did not receive any benefit from it. Therefore in his view, R&D was entirely worthless and even counter-productive.

Remedy: return to imitative strategies

R&D may be useful for those well-established firms which are affiliated with foreign companies. R&D in those firms focused on technology transfer, not on breakthroughs in product designs. Indeed most Hong Kong firms are market driven, depending less on advanced technology and more on predefined product market guidelines to direct their business activities.

Sze soon found where the problems lay. Unable to compete with firms from South Korea or Taiwan, he redirected his production into markets with slim profit margins but high turnovers.

First he closed the R&D department and the company operated on a very low R&D budget. In the management of technology, the firm behaved as a follower and focused on OEM business. Second, he found that his previous production was vertically integrated to a high degree. Sze realised that if a firm expanded excessively through vertical integration it lacked flexibility. For instance, if the market signals a reduction of output, it will be difficult for the firm to retrench workers. In order to maintain flexibility, Sze subcontracted some production processes to China, with the office in Hong Kong serving as a consultancy.

Processing in China

All of the company's output in 1994 was manufactured in Xixiang, Shenzhen Special Economic Zone in China. It operated under a processing agreement by which Shenzhen Arts and Crafts Corporation provided factory premises and workers for the printed circuit board and PC assembly in return for a processing fee. The agreement was signed in March 1993 for a term of six years expiring on 20 March 1999. The company supplied all necessary machinery, equipment, raw materials, supplementary and packaging materials, managed the production and was responsible for the training of workers. Most of the machines supplied by Dragon Precision were outdated in Hong Kong. There were 400 workers engaged in the production of printed circuit board assemblies such as 386/486 main boards and 100K VGA cards. For the complete PC assembly, there were 15 workers with a daily capacity of 100 sets (*Dragon Precision Ltd: A Company Profile*).

Conclusion

One of the entrepreneurial functions is to discover errors under the guidance of profit signals. Once these are discovered, entrepreneurs will revise their plans and make adjustment accordingly. Those who fail to do so will be driven out of markets.

Dragon Precision Ltd failed on several counts. First, it produced only for local markets which had limited sales. Second, it placed too much emphasis on innovation. Third, it did not take advantage of lower cost production in China. However, after the company had identified its errors, it made revisions. Like many other surviving manufacturers in Hong Kong, Dragon Precision aimed at exporting, adopted imitative strategies, and relocated its production to China through subcontracting. As Sze concluded, "The company will steadily grow for it follows what mainstream players are doing. Otherwise, the risk is too high."

CASE 9   VICTORY GARMENT FACTORY LTD

Founder: Ng Mo-Tack

Address: Unit 2 3, 8/F Henley Industrial Centre, 9–15 Bute St., Mongkok

---

This case demonstrates that it is not practical for garment firms in Hong Kong to adopt innovative strategies. Ng Mo-Tack's aggressive attempts at fabric development, fashion design and own label garment promotion resulted in severe financial loss. By contrast, imitative strategies such as subcontracting and concentration on customer label garment business were safeguards against unanticipated business fluctuation.

Ng Mo-Tack and Victory Garment Factory Ltd

The early industrialisation of Hong Kong was led by the textile industry which was developed by a group of immigrant Shanghainese industrialists in the 1950s. Ng Mo-Tack's parents belonged to this group.

Victory Garment Factory Ltd was established 40 years ago by Ng's parents. The factory, located in Shum Shui Po, an old industrial district, produced shirts and underwear to export to the USA and European countries via Hong Kong import/export houses. Later Ng Mo-Tack and other family members, Ng Keng-Po and Ng Mo-Yin, continued their parents' business.

During the 1970s, the company expanded. The new factory premises occupied a total gross floor area of 4000 sq. ft and employed 70 to 80 people to manufacture casual wear such as shirts, T-shirts, jackets and underwear. During the 1980s, production reached maximum capacity. Three production plants, each occupying more than 10,000 sq. ft, designed and manufactured a wide range of casual wear for women between the ages of 25 to 55, including blouses, pants, jackets, shirts and lingerie. In 1992, the total paid up capital was HK$51 million with an annual turnover of HK$15 million (*Directory of Hong Kong Manufacturing Industries 1993*, p. 255). The products were sold mainly to department stores in the USA such as Walmart, K Mart, Target, J.C. Penney, Sears and Montgomery Ward.

Fabric development, fashion design and own label garment promotion

Innovation in garment manufacturing means fabric development, fashion design and label promotion. Fabric development and fashion design require local manufacturers to be familiar with the tastes and preferences of foreign consumers. Redding (1994, p. 81) noted that, for Hong Kong, geographical distance from main markets in Europe and North America is capped by a cultural distance of factories making goods their workers would never use, such as a silk blouse designed for Madison Avenue or the Champs-Elysées. One way to solve this problem is to establish a marketing office overseas and employ foreign professionals to deal with fabric development and fashion design, but this method involves high costs and high risks. Therefore, Hong Kong's manufacturers seldom involve themselves in fabric development, fashion design and own label promotion, though they may have the capability to do so. Ng did not follow the strategies of the majority of garment manufacturers and unfortunately ended up with a severe financial loss.

In 1985 an American garment factory ran into financial problems and persuaded Victory Garment Factory to form a joint venture with them to promote Victory's private label garments in the USA. Since Victory possessed the kind of garment quota for exporting to the USA, Ng decided to give it a trial.

The fabric development and the fashion design activities were principally performed by its US partner. An office with a 20,000 sq. ft warehouse in San Francisco was set up for promotion and distribution of its own label garment,

Victory. Aggressive marketing programmes which included an enlarged sales force and incentive schemes were launched. Initial success was recorded and sales increased from HK$5 million to HK$9 million.

Later, due to personal reasons, the foreign partner withdrew and Ng decided to proceed independently. Having previously relied on the foreign partner, he was unfamiliar with the marketing and promotion strategies necessary for the USA, especially those involving American culture and tastes. To make up the deficiency, the company employed some foreign senior designers and marketing professionals for the US office. However, employing marketing personnel in the USA was very costly. Though the marketing programmes achieved success in generating sales, the strategy later proved to be financially burdensome for the company. Sales continued to increase but the costs required to support such growth escalated out of proportion, therefore contributing to substantial losses. Soon the company ran up a debt of approximately US$2 million.

After reviewing the production and marketing strategies, Ng decided to return to a more conservative approach. The company reduced its reliance on own label and concentrated on customer label garments. In other words, the company was involved mainly in garment manufacturing with foreign buyers selling the products under their own labels. Ng Mo-Tack admitted that producing customer label garments involved much simpler activities and decided to stick to this policy in future. In short, the company reverted from innovative back to imitative strategies.

Spatial arbitrage via subcontracting

High land costs and labour shortages in Hong Kong have made the Territory no longer suitable as a manufacturing centre. Ng, like other manufacturers in Hong Kong, relocated his production activities to China. A garment factory with total gross floor area of 5,000 sq. ft was established in Panyu county, Guangdong, mainly producing shirts, dresses and T-shirts.

One major drawback to establishing a factory in China was that a relatively high degree of supervision would be required to achieve the quality and production timeliness required. This implied a need for experienced production managers. Although China had an abundant supply of unskilled labour, professional staff were few and had to be recruited from Hong Kong where wage rates were very high.

To cope with the monitoring problem, Ng's company utilised a number of subcontractors to supplement its production in China. Subcontractors were selected depending on their past performance. In 1992 the company subcontracted the production of shirts and dresses to ten factories in China, with four major plants supplying 60 per cent of the company's total output. Although there were no exclusive arrangements between the company and its subcontractors, Ng maintained good relationships with them. Many had worked with the company for over four years. According to Ng, though the profit margin from each subcontracting venture was small, the company could avoid heavy capital investment and therefore enjoy flexibility.

From a manufacturing factory to a trading firm

The company began as a manufacturing factory. Within 40 years, the company moved from one strategy to another (from own label garment to customer label garment), from one region to another (from Hong Kong to Guangdong), from one product to another (underwear, shirts, dresses). The development path fully illustrates the adaptability and flexibility of Hong Kong's manufacturers. In 1994 the company's office in Hong Kong had no actual manufacturing activities. It merely performed the functions of a headquarters, involved in sourcing, receiving orders, merchandising, etc. In the future the company planned to expand its business by establishing a retailing chain in Hong Kong. This method was successfully developed by another Hong Kong garment manufacturer, Giordano. The company resembled a trading rather than a manufacturing firm. The differentiation between a secondary and tertiary industry is increasingly difficult. The transformation of the firm partly mirrors the structural change of the Hong Kong economy.

CASE 10   LUKS INDUSTRIAL CO. LTD

Founder: Luk King-Tin

Address: 5/F Cheong Wah Factory Building, 39 41 Sheung Heung Road, To Kwa Wan, Kowloon

---

The survival of Luks Industrial Co. hinged on two crucial elements:

- seizure of opportunities;
- exploration of potential markets in the communist and Eastern European countries.

The founder

Luk King-Tin, founder and managing director of Luks Industrial Co. Ltd, was born in 1937 in Shiu Hing county, Guangdong, and emigrated to Hong Kong in 1962. Because his previous teaching qualification was not recognised by the Hong Kong government, he could only work as a stone cutter at a monthly wage of $150. He was soon promoted to the position of site foreman. The riot of 1967 paralysed Hong Kong's property market and construction industry and Luk was laid off. With no better alternative, he invested $30,000 in wig manufacturing. In the 1970s he moved to the electronics industry, producing transistor radios. In 1976 he expanded his business and became involved in the design and manufacture of liquid display calculators for export to the USA and Europe. Thus, Luk earned his first million dollars.

The survival strategy

Rapid response

According to Luk, Japanese producers have been well known for TV manufacturing. Hong Kong's medium and small firms cannot compete with them. However, the flexibility and adaptability of large firms like Hitachi have been restricted by huge capital commitment. In contrast, Hong Kong's medium and small manufacturing firms are highly flexible and able to adapt quickly to changing market conditions. For instance, given the existing plant structure, the local firms can reshuffle their production lines from transistor radios to electronic watches within three months, or from electronic calculators to black and white TVs within six months, or from black and white TVs to colour TVs within nine months (*Economic Reporter* 1981, p. 19). This was exactly the kind of competitive edge Luk's factory possessed during its early stage of development. Luks Industrial Co. switched from the manufacture of transistor radios to calculators and then to TVs according to market signals.

Alertness to opportunities

Virtually without any government support in R&D, the technological level of Hong Kong's industry has lagged behind that in South Korea and Taiwan (Chen and Wong 1989). The survival of Luks Industrial Co. relied on Luk's ability to identify market opportunities. When he perceived that an overseas market possessed profit potential, he formed joint ventures with local firms there to exploit profits. He illustrated his strategies with the following examples.

For Mr Luk, South Korea and Taiwan are Hong Kong's two major rivals. He utilised the insight of *Sun Tsu Bing Fa*, an ancient Chinese military guide, "If you know thy enemies and know yourself then you will win," and avoided direct confrontation with them. In the 1980s the UK restricted black and white TVs made in South Korea and Taiwan but imposed no restriction on those made in Hong Kong. Therefore, Luks industrial Co. continued to produce and export black and white TVs to the UK, though the product became a low value added item which many producers would not consider.

Furthermore, colour TVs in the UK and certain European countries used the Phase Alternation Line (PAL) system, but South Korea and Taiwan at that time aimed at TVs conforming to the National Television System Committee (NTSC) standard, mainly for US markets. Luk bought the this patent from Telefunken and manufactured colour TV and TV kits conforming to this system and exported them to European countries. In this way, he avoided direct confrontation with South Korean and Taiwan producers. In 1986 the export of TVs to the UK represented approximately 31 per cent of the company's total turnover (*Luks Industrial Co. Ltd: A Company Profile* p. 10).

Prior to 1986, the import of TVs into China was subject to high import duty, whereas the import of TV kits, a collection of components for assembly of a TV, was subject to duty at a much lower rate. So Luk manufactured TV kits in Hong Kong and then sold them to Luks Shekou or other manufacturers in China for final assembly, hence enjoying low customs duties. As a result, total turnover in TV kits increased from approximately HK$40.4 million in 1981 to HK$205 million in 1985, a 500 per cent growth rate (*Luks Industrial Co. Ltd: A company Profile* p. 9).

Similarly, in 1986 the European Common Market initiated an anti-dumping accusation against Hong Kong TV manufacturers. In 1989 a special sales tax was imposed on colour TVs made in China. In the face of this, the company shifted its emphasis to the supply of production equipment and essential component kits, supplemented by the sale of complete TV sets. Furthermore, it established an assembly arrangement through the incorporation of a wholly owned subsidiary in the UK in early 1990 to assemble final TV sets for export to Europe (*Luks Industrial Co. Ltd, Annual Report* 1990, p. 9).

The above example suggests that facing keen competition from South Korea and Taiwan and trade restrictions from advanced industrial countries, Hong Kong producers like Luk can still survive due to their ability to identify and exploit profit opportunities.

Spatial arbitrage

In exploring overseas markets, Luk's strategy was unconventional. He focused his business on the communist economies such as China, Vietnam, and the Eastern European countries because their markets were unexploited. "In mature capitalist economies", Luk said, "one has to compete with many well established manufacturers. So if one tries to penetrate in these markets, it is just like growing young trees in a big forest. The young plant can hardly receive enough nutrition. But for the communist countries which have just pursued open door policies recently, the markets remain unexploited and so possess high growth potential." Therefore, Luk actively sought to penetrate these countries.

The China connection

In September 1979, China announced its new economic policy and welcomed foreign investments. Luk, with his Chinese background, immediately took the chance and invested there.

Lower production costs in China, together with lower import duties on TV kits, enabled the company to sell its products more competitively in China than other importers. This was due to the fact that during the early 1980s, Japanese manufacturers were affected by the strength of the yen, and Taiwan and South Korean manufacturers did not yet have direct trade relationships with China. In 1979 the company supplied production facilities and technical support to a factory in China to enable it to produce black and white TVs. In 1981 the company established its TV assembly line in Hong Kong to produce colour TVs and TV kits to sell to Hong Kong and China.

In the same year the company established production facilities in China for the purpose of manufacturing colour TVs designed primarily for sale there. It entered into an agreement with Zhenhua Electric Industrial Corporation of China and Shenzhen Electric Group to form a joint venture company Huafa in which Luks held a one-third stake. Huafa assembled and sold TVs from TV kits designed and supplied by Luks (*Luks Industrial Co. Ltd: A Company Profile*, p. 6).

Furthermore, in 1981 Luks Shekou, a wholly owned subsidiary, was established in Shekou, a special economic zone in Shenzhen, Guangdong. In 1983 it assembled colour TVs from kits supplied by the company for sale in China. Luks Shekou also undertook chassis subassembly work.

In late 1986 the government of China introduced favourable foreign investment regulations (the 22 rules). Under these new rules the company's subsidiary, Luks Shekou, and the joint venture, Huafa, were able to obtain the necessary import licences (*Luks Industrial Co. Ltd Annual Report*, 1987, p. 8). In 1992 sales of TVs to China accounted for approximately 44 per cent of the firm's total sales.

Vietnam, Eastern Europe and Russia

Having succeeded in communist China, Luk invested in Vietnam which has a similar political and economic background. Vietnam has a high population and its government has recently provided incentive measures for industrial development via an import customs tax. Mr Luk perceived that the company's development potential in Vietnam would be enormous.

In 1991 the company formed a joint venture with Donaco Electronics Factory of Vietnam to manufacture colour TVs, hi-fi equipment, electronic calculators, taperecorders, video tapes and related electronic products mainly for the domestic market. During 1992–3 the sale of colour TVs in Vietnam increased by 25 per cent and was profitable (*Luks Industrial Co. Ltd, Annual Report* 1993, p. 6).

With ongoing political reforms and the gradual opening of the Eastern European markets, Luk considered investing in those countries. In 1989 the company succeeded in penetrating into the communist bloc and received orders for colour TVs from Russia (the former USSR) (*Luks Industrial Co. Ltd Annual Report*, 1989, p. 9). In mid-1991, the company entered into cooperation agreements with a German customer, HCM Electronic AKT Tientesellschaft, to establish a final assembly line for colour TVs in Poland for supplying the Eastern European markets (*Luks Industrial Co. Ltd, Annual Report* 1992, p. 8).

Conclusion

Like many other electronics manufacturers in Hong Kong, the survival of Luks Industrial Co. relied on Luk's entrepreneurship and alertness to opportunities. He was able to identify and exploit profit opportunities. This has been illustrated by his strategies in TV production and sales to the UK, China, Vietnam and various Eastern European countries.

BIBLIOGRAPHY

Abbeglen, James (1994) *Sea Change*, New York: Free Press.

Abramovitz, Moses (1986) "Catching up, forging ahead and falling behind", *Journal of Economic History*, XLVI(2): 385–406.

—— (1988) "Following and leading", in Horst Hannsch ed., *Evolutionary Economics: Applications of Schumpeter's Ideas*, Cambridge: Cambridge University Press, pp. 323–41.

Akamatsu, Kaname (1961) "A theory of unbalanced growth in the world economy", *Weltwirtschaftliches Archiv*, 86(2): 196–217.

Alam, Asad (1995) "The new trade theory and its relevance to the trade policies of developing countries", *World Economy*, 18(3): 367–86.

Alchian, A.A. (1965) "Some economics of property right" in A.A. Alchian (1977) *Economic Forces at Work*, Indianapolis: Liberty Press, pp. 127–50.

Alchian, A.A. and W.R. Allen (1983) *Exchange and Production*, 3rd edn, Belmont, California: Wadsworth Publishing Co.

Ames, Edward and Nathan Rosenberg (1963) "Changing technological leadership and industrial growth", *Economic Journal*, 73(289): 13–31.

Amsden, Alice H. (1989) *Asia's Next Giant: South Korea and Late Industrialisation*, New York: Oxford University Press.

Appelbaum, Richard P. and Jeffrey Henderson (1992) *States and Development in the Asian Pacific Rim*, London: Sage Publications.

Argyris, Chris (1976) "Leadership, learning and changing the status quo", *Organisational Dynamics*, 4 (Winter): 29–43.

Ariff, M. and H. Hill (1985) *Export-oriented Industrialisation: The ASEAN Experience*, Sydney: Allen and Unwin.

Arrighi, Giovanni, Satoshi Ikeda and Alex Irwan (1993) "The rise of East Asia: one miracle or many?", in Ravi Arvind Palat ed., *Pacific-Asia and the Future of the World-System*, Connecticut : Greenwood Press, pp. 41–66.

Asiaweek (1992) "The game of the name", 11 September, pp. 60–62.

—— (1995) "Bottom line", 10 March, pp. 53–4.

Australian Department of Foreign Affairs and Trade (1992) *Australia and North-East Asia in the 1990s: Accelerating Change*, Canberra: AGPS.

Babbie, Earl R. (1973) *Survey Research Methods*, Belmont, California: Wadsworth Publishing Co.

Backhouse, Roger (1985) *A History of Modern Economic Analysis*, New York: Basil Blackwell.

Balassa, Bela (1981) *The Newly Industrialising Countries in the World Economy*, New York: Pergamon Press.

Barnathan, Joyce (1994) "I want to survive. But I don't want to kowtow", *International Business Week*, 5 December, pp. 38–9.

Baumol, W.J. (1968) "Entrepreneurship in economic theory", *American Economic Review Papers and Proceedings*, 58: 64–71.

—— (1988) "Is entrepreneurship always productive?", in H. Leibenstein and D. Ray, eds, *Entrepreneurship and Economic Development*, New York: United Nations, pp. 85–94

Berger, P. and B. Berger (1976) *Sociology: A Biographical Approach*, revised edn, Middlesex: Penguin.

Berger, P. and T. Luckmann (1966) *The Social Construction of Reality*, New York: Anchor Books.

Berliner, Joseph (1966) "The economics of overtaking and surpassing", in Henry Rosovsky ed., *Industrialisation in Two Systems: Essays in Honour of Alexander Gershenkron*, New York: Wiley, pp. 159–85.

Bhattacharya, Debesh (1989) *Economic Development and Underdevelopment*, Sydney: Australian Professional Publications.

Bolton, Michele K. (1993) "Imitation versus innovation: lessons to be learned from the Japanese", *Organisational Dynamics*, Winter: 30–45.

Bradford, Colin I. Jr (1987) "NICs and the next-tier NICs as transitional economies", in Colin Bradford and William H. Branson eds, *Trade and Structural Change in Pacific Asia*, Chicago: University of Chicago Press, pp. 173–204.

Branson, William H. (1987) "Trade and structural interdependence between the United States and the Newly Industrialising Countries", in Colin Bradford and William H. Branson ed., *Trade and Structural Change in Pacific Asia*, Chicago: University of Chicago Press, pp. 27–57.

Brockhaus, R.H. (1982) "The psychology of the entrepreneur", in C.A. Kent *et al.* eds, *Encyclopedia of Entrepreneurship*, New Jersey: Prentice Hall.

Broehl, Wayne G. (1982) "Entrepreneurship in the less developed world", in C. Kent *et al.* eds, *Encyclopedia of Entrepreneurship*, New Jersey: Prentice Hall, pp. 257–71.

Brown, E.H. Phelps (1971) "The Hong Kong economy: achievements and prospects", in Keith Hopkins ed., *Hong Kong: The Industrial Colony*, Hong Kong: Oxford University Press.

Byrne, John (1993) "Enterprise: how entrepreneurs are shaping the world economy – and what big companies can learn", *International Business Week*, 6 December, p. 53.

Carroll, John (1992) "Conclusion: the role of government", in John Carroll and Robert Manne eds, *Shutdown: The Failure of Economic Rationalism and How to Rescue Australia*, Melbourne: The Text Publishing Company, pp. 184–92.

Carroll, John and Robert Manne (1992) *Shutdown:The Failure of Economic Rationalism and How to Rescue Australia*, Melbourne: The Text Publishing Company.

Casson, Mark (1982) *The Entrepreneur: An Economic Theory*, Oxford: Blackwell.

—— (1990) "Entrepreneurial culture as a competitive advantage", in A.M. Rugman ed., *Research in Global Business Management*, vol. 1, Greenwich: JAI Press, pp. 139–51.

Castells, Manuel (1992) "Four Asian Tigers with a dragon head: a comparative analysis of the state, economy and society in the Asian Pacific Rim", in R. Appelbaum and J. Henderson eds, *States and Development in the Asian Pacific Rim*, London: Sage Publications, pp. 33–70.

Castells, Manuel and Laura D'Andrea Tyson (1989) "High technology and the changing international division of production", in R.P. Purcell ed. (1989) *The Newly Industrialising Countries in the World Economy: Challenges for US Policy*, Colorado: Lynne Rienner, pp. 20–82.

Cauthorn, Robert C. (1989) *Contributions to a Theory of Entrepreneurship*, New York: Garland Publishing Co.

Chan, Wai Kwan (1991) *The Making of Hong Kong Society*, Oxford: Clarendon Press.

Chau, L.L.C. (1993) *Hong Kong: A Unique Case of Development*, Washington DC: World Bank.

Chau, Sik Nin (1974) "Family management in Hong Kong", in Lee Nehrt *et al.* eds, *Managerial Policy, Strategy and Planning for Southeast Asia*, Hong Kong: The Chinese University of Hong Kong, pp. 155–8.

Cheah, H.B. (1989a) "Two modes of entrepreneurship: a synthesis of the controversy between Schumpeter and his Austrian critics", Snider Entrepreneurial Centre Working Paper No. 74, University of Pennsylvania.

Cheah, H.B. (1989b) "The entrepreneurial process in the business cycle, product life cycle and organisational life cycle", Snider Entrepreneurial Centre Working Paper No. 76, University of Pennsylvania.

—— (1992) "Revolution and evolution in the entrepreneurial process", Proceedings of World Conference on Entrepreneurship, 11–4 August 1992, pp. 462–74, Singapore.

—— (1993) "Dual modes of entrepreneurship: revolution and evolution in the entrepreneurial process", *Creativity and Innovation Management*, 2(4): 241–51.

—— (1994) "Creativity in the entrepreneurial process", in S. Dingli ed., *Creative Thinking: A Multifaceted Approach*, Malta: Malta University Press.

—— (1995) "Changes in competitive advantage in East Asia and the Pacific: causes and consequences", discussion paper, Economic Research Centre, School of Economics, Nagoya University, Japan.

Cheah, H.B. and Paul L. Robertson (1992) "The entrepreneurial process and innovation in the product life cycle", paper presented to a meeting of the International Joseph A. Schumpeter Society, Kyota, Japan, 19–22 August, 1992.

Cheah, H.B. and H. Volberda (1989) "Entrepreneurial process, flexibility and organisational form", Snider Entrepreneurial Centre Working Paper No. 75, University of Pennsylvania.

Cheah, H.B. and Tony F. Yu (1995) "Adaptive response: entrepreneurship and competitiveness in the economic development of Hong Kong", paper presented at the Sixth ENDEC World Conference on Entrepreneurship, Shanghai, China.

Chee, Peng Lim (1991) "The changing pattern of foreign direct investment in the Asian Pacific Region: implications for Hong Kong" in Edward Chen *et al.* eds, *Industrial and Trade Development in Hong Kong*, Hong Kong: Centre of Asian Studies, pp. 406–26.

Chen, Edward K.Y. (1979) *Hyper-growth in Asian Economies*, London: Macmillan Press.

—— (1983) "Multinationals from Hong Kong", in S. Lall ed., *The New Multinationals: The Spread of Third World Enterprises*, Chichester: John Wiley and Sons, pp. 89–136.

—— (1984) "The economic setting", in David Lethbridge ed., *The Business Environment in Hong Kong*, 2nd edn, Hong Kong: Oxford University Press.

—— (1985) "Maintaining Hong Kong's prosperity", *The China Business Review*, September–October: 37–41.

—— (1987) "Foreign trade and economic growth in Hong Kong: experience and prospects", in Colin Bradford and W. Branson eds, *Trade and Structural Change in Pacific Asia*, Chicago: University of Chicago Press, pp. 333–78.

—— (1988) "The economic and non-economics of Asia's Four Little Dragons", an inaugural lecture, University of Hong Kong, *Supplement to the Gazette*, 35(l) 21 March.

—— (1989a) "Hong Kong's role in Asian and Pacific economic development", *Asian Development Review*, 7(2): 26–47.

—— (1989b) "The changing role of the Asian NIEs in the Asian-Pacific Region towards the year 2000", in M. Shinohara and Fu-Chen Lo eds, *Global Adjustment and the Future of Asian-Pacific Economy*, Tokyo: Institute of Developing Economies, pp. 207–31.

Chen, Edward K.Y. and K.W. Li (1991) "Industrial development and industrial policy in Hong Kong", in Edward Chen *et al.* eds, *Industrial and Trade Development in Hong Kong*, University of Hong Kong: Centre of Asian Studies, pp. 3–47.

Chen, Edward K.Y., M.K. Nyaw and Y.C. Wong (1991) *Industrial and Trade Development in Hong Kong*, Hong Kong: Centre of Asian Studies.

Chen, Edward K.Y. and Teresa Wong (1989) *The Future Direction of Industrial Development in the Asian Newly Industrialised Economies (NIEs)*, Asian and Pacific Development Centre.

Chenery, Hollis and Alan Strout (1966) "Foreign assistances and economic development", *American Economic Review*, 56(4): 679–733.

Cheng, T.Y. (1982) *The Economy of Hong Kong*, Hong Kong: Far East Publications, rev. edn.

Cheung, Fu Keung (1982) "A study of management practices of small-scale electronics industry in Hong Kong", MBA thesis, University of Hong Kong.

Cheung, S.N.S. (1974) "A theory of price control", *Journal of Law and Economics*, 17 (April): pp. 53–71.

—— (1983) "The contractual nature of the firm", *The Journal of Law and Economics*, 26 (April): 386–405.

—— (1984) *Collected Essays*, Hong Kong: Shun Pao (text in Chinese).

—— (1989) "Transaction cost and economic organisation", in M. Eatwell *et al.* eds, *The New Palgrave Dictionary of Economics*, London: Macmillan.

Chia, Siow Yue (1993) "The dynamics of East Asian growth-reform and government management", paper for the Conference on Sustaining the Development Process, The Australian National University.

Chng, Meng Kng (1991) "A comparative study of the industrialisation experiences of the ASEAN countries", in E. Chen *et al.* eds, *Industrial and Trade Development in Hong Kong*, Hong Kong: Centre of Asian Studies, pp. 223–54.

Clark, C. (1940) *Conditions of Economic Progress*, London: Macmillan.

Clark, Cal and Steve Chan (1992) *The Evolving Pacific Basin in the Global Political Economy*, Boulder: Lynne Rienner.

Clarke, Jeremy and Vincent Cable (1982) "The Asian electronics industry looks to the future", in R. Kaplinsky ed., *Comparative Advantage in an Automating World*, Sussex: Institute of Development Studies Bulletin, 13(2): 24–34.

Coase, Ronald (1937) "The nature of the firm", *Economica*, 4: 386–405.

Cohen, Wesley M. and Daniel A. Levinthal (1990) "Absorptive capacity: a new perspective on learning and innovation", *Administrative Science Quarterly*, 35: 128–52.

Cornwall, John (1977) *Modern Capitalism, Its Growth and Transformation*, London: Martin Robertson.

Crisswell, Colin (1981) *The Taipans: Hong Kong's Merchant Princes*, Hong Kong: Oxford University Press.

Dahlman, Carl J. (1989) "Structural change and trade in the East Asian newly industrial economies and emerging industrial economies", in Randall Purcell ed., *The Newly Industrialising Countries in the World Economy*, London: Lynne Rienner, pp. 51–71.

Davies, Howard, Jenny Ling and Freda Cheung (1993) "Product design and the location of production: strategic choice in Hong Kong manufacturing", *Academy of International Business*, 3: 1–14.

De Bono, Edward (1970) *Lateral Thinking*, New York: Harper Colophon.

—— (1992) *Serious Creativity*, New York: Harper Business.

De Geus, Arie P.(1988) "Planning as learning", *Harvard Business Review*, 66(2): 70–4.

Deyo, Frederic (1987) *The Political Economy of the New Asian Industrialism*, Ithaca: Cornell University Press.

Dore, Ronald (1973) "The late development effect", in H.D. Evers ed., *Modernisation in Southeast Asia*, London: Oxford University Press, pp. 65–80.

—— (1994) "More about late development" in W. Macpherson ed., *The Industrialisation of Japan*, Oxford: Blackwell, pp. 311–25.

Dos Santos, T. (1970) "The structure of dependence", *American Economic Review* (May): 231–36.

Drucker, Peter (1984) "Our entrepreneurial economy", *Harvard Business Review* (January–February): 58–64.

—— (1985) *Innovation and Entrepreneurship*, London: Heinemann.

Ebeling, Richard M. (1991) *Austrian Economics: A Reader*, Hillsdale, Michigan: Hillsdale College Press.

Eckhaus, R.S. (1955) "The factor proportions problem in underdeveloped countries", *American Economic Review*, 45 (September): 539–65.

Economic Reporter (1981) "Hong Kong's electronics industry moves toward high value added production", 16 September, pp. 19–20 (text in Chinese).

Economic Reporter (1988a) "The future of Hong Kong's garment industry", 10 September, p. 5 (text in Chinese).

—— (1988b) "The future of Hong Kong's textile industry", 4 November, p. 15 (text in Chinese).

—— (1989) "A meaningful survey of Hong Kong's manufacturing industry", 18 December, pp. 18–9 (text in Chinese).

—— (1990) "A profile of young industrialist", 5 March, p. 6 (text in Chinese).

—— (1991a) "Softwares", 21 January, p. 20 (text in Chinese).

—— (1991b) "Electronics Industry", 25 March, p. 5 (text in Chinese).

—— (1991c) 16 September, p. 19 (text in Chinese).

—— (1992) "Technological cooperation between Hong Kong and China", 7 September, p. 20 (text in Chinese).

Engardio, Pete and Neil Gross (1992) "Asia's high-tech quest", *International Business Week*, 30 November, pp. 64, 67.

Ernst, Dieter and David O'Connor (1989) *Technology and Global Competition: The Challenge for Newly Industrialising Economies*, Paris: OCED.

Espy, John Lee (1970) "The strategies of Chinese enterprises in Hong Kong", unpublished DBA thesis, Cambridge, Mass: Harvard University.

Fallows, James (1994) *Looking at the Sun: The Rise of the New East Asian Economic and Political System*, New York: Pantheon Books.

Far Eastern Economic Review (1993) "Extra large", 2 December, pp. 72–6.

Federation of Industries (1992) *Hong Kong's Industrial Investment in the Pearl River Delta.*

Feng, Bang-yan (1991) "The role of Hong Kong in China's economic modernisation", in Edward Chen *et al.* eds, *Industrial and Trade Development in Hong Kong*, Hong Kong: Centre of Asian Studies, pp. 497–509.

Finday, C., P. Phillips and R. Tyers (1985) "China's merchandise trade: composition and export growth in the 1980s", *ASEAN-Australia Economic Papers*, No. 19, Canberra: ASEAN-Australia Joint Research Project.

Fisher, A.G.B. (1945) *Economic Progress and Special Security*, London: Macmillan.

Forbes (1993a) "Entrepreneurs", April, p. 149 (text in Chinese).

—— (1993b) "The future of Hong Kong's TV manufacturers", October, pp. 68–70 (text in Chinese).

Fortune (1987) "The overseas Chinese", 12 October, pp. 112–13.

—— (1989) "The billionaires", 11 September, pp. 36–69.

—— (1994) "The world's best cities for business", 14 November, p. 69.

Freeman, Christopher (1982) *The Economics of Industrial Innovation*, London: Frances Pinter, 2nd edn.

Friedman, Milton (1976) *Free to Choose*, Chicago: University of Chicago Press.

Galbraith, J.K. (1968) *The New Industrial State*, New York: Signet Books.

Geiger, Theodore and Frances M. Geiger (1975) *The Development Progress of Hong Kong and Singapore*, London: Macmillan Press.

Gerschenkron, A. (1962) *Economic Backwardness in Historical Perspective*, Cambridge, Mass: Harvard University Press.

Gifford, Sharon (1992) "Allocation of entrepreneurial attention", *Journal of Economic Behaviour and Organisation*, 19: 265–84.

Gilad, B.(1986), "Entrepreneurial decision making: some behavioural considerations", in B. Gilad ed., *Handbook of Behavioural Economics*, Hampton Hill: JAI Press.

Gilad, B., S. Kaish, and J. Ronen (1988) "The entrepreneurial way with information", in Shlomo Maital ed., *Applied Behavioural Economics*, Brighton Wheatsheaf, vol. II, pp. 481–503.

Goode, William and Paul Hatt (1952) *Methods in Social Research*, New York: McGraw Hill.

Grilli, Enzo and James Riedel (1993) "The East Asian growth model: how general is it?" paper presented to the Conference, Sustaining the Development Process, Australian National University.

Guo, Wei-Feng (1990) *Dang Dai Quang Tai Nan Yang Jing Ji Qiang Ren Lei Zhuan* [An annotated bibliography of contemporary business people from Hong Kong, Taiwan and South East Asia] Beijing: Economic Daily Press (text in Chinese).

Hagedoorn, John (1989) *The Dynamic Analysis of Innovation and Diffusion: A Study in Process Control,* London: Pinter Publishers.

Hartland-Thunberg, Penelope (1990) *China, Hong Kong, Taiwan and the World Trading System,* London: Macmillan.

Hayek, F.A. (1967) *Studies in Philosophy, Politics and Economics,* Chicago: University of Chicago Press.

—— (1978a) *New Studies in Philosophy, Politics and Economics,* Chicago: The University of Chicago Press.

—— (1978b) "Competition as a discovery procedure", in *New Studies in Philosophy, Politics, Economics and the History of Ideas,* Chicago: University of Chicago Press.

Hebert, Robert and N. Link (1988) *The Entrepreneur: Mainstream Views and Radical Critiques,* 2nd edn, New York: Praeger Publisher.

Hedberg, Bo (1981), "How organisation learn and unlearn", in Paul C. Nystrom and William Starbuck eds, *Handbook of Organisational Design Volume 1: Adapting Organisations to their Environment,* Oxford: Oxford University Press, pp. 3–27.

Heitger, Bernard (1993) "Comparative economic growth: catching up in East Asia", *ASEAN Economic Bulletin,* July, pp. 68–82.

Henderson, Jeffrey (1991) *The Globalisation of High Technology Production,* London: Routledge.

—— (1993) "The role of the state in the economic transformation of East Asia", in Chris Dixon and David Drakakis-Smith eds, *Economic and Social Development in Pacific Asia,* London: Routledge, pp. 85–114.

Henderson, Jeffrey and Richard P. Appelbaum (1992) "Situating the state in the East Asian development process", in R. Appelbaum and J. Henderson eds, *States and Development in the Asian Pacific Rim,* London: Sage Publications, pp. 1–26.

Hicks, George (1989) "The four little dragons: an enthusiast's reading guide", *Asian-Pacific Economic Literature,* 3(2): 35–49.

Higgins, B. (1956) "The dualistic theory of underdeveloped areas", *Economic Development and Cultural Change,* 4 (January): 99–115.

Hirono, Ryokichi (1988) "Japan: model for East Asian industrialisation?", in H. Hughes ed., *Achieving Industrialisation in East Asia,* Cambridge: Cambridge University Press, pp. 241–59.

Hirschman, Albert O. (1958) *The Strategy of Economic Development,* New Haven: Yale University Press.

Ho, Edric Seng-Liang (1985) "Value and economic development in Hong Kong and China", unpublished Ph.D. dissertation, University of Michigan.

Ho, H.C.Y. (1989) "Views on Hong Kong's past growth and future prospects", in H.C.Y. Ho and L.C. Chau eds, *The Economic System of Hong Kong,* Hong Kong: Asia Research Service, pp. 1–5.

Ho, H.C.Y. and L.C. Chau (1989) *The Economic System of Hong Kong,* Hong Kong: Asia Research Service.

Ho, Yin Ping (1992) *Trade, Industrial Restructuring and Development in Hong Kong,* London: Macmillan.

Ho, Yin Ping and Y.Y. Kuen (1993) "Whither Hong Kong in an open-door, reforming Chinese economy", *Pacific Review,* 6(4): 333–51.

Hobday, Mike (1994) "Technological learning in Singapore: a test case of leapfrogging", *The Journal of Development Studies*, 30 (3): 831–58.

—— (1995) "East Asian latecomer firms: learning the technology of electronics", *World Development*, 23(7): 1171–93.

Hong Kong Economic Journal Monthly (1990) "A case study of an electronics firm", December, pp. 96–9 (text in Chinese).

—— (1991) "Utilising China's technology", October, p. 69 (text in Chinese).

Hong Kong Economic Survey Ltd (1989) *Building Prosperity: A Five Part Economic Strategy for Hong Kong's Future*, Hong Kong: Building Hong Kong's Prosperity Society.

Hong Kong Government Census and Statistics Department, *Hong Kong Annual Digest of Statistics*, various issues, Hong Kong: Hong Kong Government Printer.

Hong Kong Government Industry Department (1991) *Techno-Economic and Market Research Study on Hong Kong's Electronics Industry 1988–89*, Hong Kong: Hong Kong Government Printer.

—— (1992a) *1992 Hong Kong's Manufacturing Industries*, Hong Kong: Hong Kong Government Printer.

—— (1992b) *Techno-Economic and Market Research Study of Hong Kong's Textiles and Clothing Industries 1991–92*, Hong Kong: Hong Kong Government Printer.

—— (1993) *Hong Kong's Manufacturing Industries*, Hong Kong: Hong Kong Government Printer.

Hong Kong Government Industry Department and Census and Statistics Department (1991) *Survey on the Future Development of Industry in Hong Kong: Statistical Survey of Manufacturers, 1984–89*, Hong Kong: Hong Kong Government Printer, pp. 84–9.

Hong Kong Government Secretariat, *Hong Kong Hansard*, Hong Kong: Hong Kong Government Printer, various issues.

Hong, Wontack (1991) "Comparative study of the industrialisation of experience of Korea and Taiwan", in Edward Chen *et al.* eds, *Industrial and Trade Development in Hong Kong*, Hong Kong: Centre of Asian Studies, pp. 147–85.

Howard, K. and J. Sharp (1983) *The Management of a Student Research Project*, Aldershot: Gower.

Hsia, R. (1984) *The Entrepôt Trade of Hong Kong with Special Reference to Taiwan and the Chinese Mainland*, Taiwan: Chung-Hua Institution for Economic Research.

Hsia, R. and L.L. C. Chau (1978) *Industrialisation, Employment and Income Distribution: A Case Study of Hong Kong*, London: Croom Helm.

Hsia, R., H. Ho and E. Lim (1975) *The Structure and Growth of the Hong Kong Economy*, Otto Harrassowitz: Wiesbaden.

Hsueh, Tien-tung (1976) "The transforming economy of Hong Kong 1951–73", *Hong Kong Economic Papers*, 10: 46–65.

Hsueh, Tien-tung and Kam-kun Chow (1981) "A dynamic macroeconomic model of the Hong Kong economy", *Hong Kong Economic Papers*, 14: 14–36.

Hughes, Helen (1989) "Catching up: the Asian Newly Industrialising Economies in the 1990s", *Asian Development Review*, 7(2): 128–44.

Hughes, Richard (1968) *Hong Kong: Borrowed Time, Borrowed Place*, London: Andre Deutsch.

Hung, C.L. (1984) "Foreign investments", in D. Lethbridge ed., *The Business Environment in Hong Kong*, 2nd edn, Hong Kong: Oxford University Press, pp. 180–210.

Ichimura, Shinichi (1988) "The pattern and prospects of Asian economic development", in S. Ichimura ed., *Challenge of Asian Developing Countries: Issues and Analyses*, Tokyo: Asian Productivity Organisation, pp. 7–64.

Industry Commission (1990) *Strategic Trade Theory: The East Asian Experience*, Information Paper, November, Canberra: AGPS.

International Business Asia (1993) "Li Ka-Shing", 1 December, p. 18.

International Business Week (1993) "The Global 1000", 12 July, pp. 76–80.

Jacobson, Robert (1992) "The Austrian school of strategy", *Academy of Management Review*, 17(4): 782–807.

Jao, Y.C. (1983) "Hong Kong's role in financing China's modernisation", in A.J. Youngson ed., *China and Hong Kong: The Economic Nexus*, Hong Kong: Oxford University Press, pp. 12–76.

Johnson, Chalmers (1982) *MITI and the Japanese Miracle*, Stanford: Stanford University Press.

—— (1985) "Political institutions and economic performance: government–business relationship in Japan, South Korea and Taiwan", in R. Scaloppine *et al.* eds, *Asian Economic Development–Present and Future*, Berkeley: Institute of East Asian Studies, pp. 63–89.

—— (1992) "MITI and the rise of Japan", in John Carroll and Robert Manne eds, *Shutdown: The Failure of Economic Rationalism and How to Rescue Australia*, Melbourne: The Text Publishing Company, pp. 65–76.

Jones, Leroy P. and Il Sakong (1980) *Government, Business, and Entrepreneurship in Economic Development: The Korean Case*, Cambridge, Mass.: Harvard University Press.

Kahn, Herman (1979) *World Economic Development: 1979 and Beyond*, London: Croom Helm.

Kakwani, N. and K. Subbarao (1992) "Global development: Is the gap widening or closing", University of New South Wales, School of Economics, discussion paper, no.92/22.

Kane, Eileen (1985) *Doing Your Own Research*, London: Marion Boyars.

Kim, Linsu (1988) "Entrepreneurship and innovation in a rapidly developing countries", in H. Leibenstein and D. Ray eds, *Entrepreneurship and Economic Development*, New York: United Nations.

King, Frank H.H. (1987) *The History of the Hong Kong and Shanghai Banking Corporation*, Cambridge: Cambridge University Press.

—— (1990) "Entrepreneurs of Hong Kong", *Asian-Pacific Economic Literature* (March): 116–18.

King, Yeo-Chi (1987) "The transformation of Confucianism in post-Confucian era: the emergence of rationalistic traditionalism in Hong Kong", *Hong Kong Economic Journal Monthly*, 128 (November): 54–62.

King, Yeo-Chi and Peter Man (1979) "Small factory in economic development: the case of Hong Kong", in Tsong-Biau Lin ed., *Hong Kong: Economic, Social and Political Studies in Development*, New York: M.E. Sharpe, pp. 31–64.

Kingston, William (1977) *Innovation*, London: John Calder.

Kirchhoff, Bruce A. (1994) *Entrepreneurship and Dynamic Capitalism*, London: Praeger.

Kirzner, I. M. (1973) *Competition and Entrepreneurship*, Chicago: University of Chicago Press.

—— (1979) *Perception, Opportunity and Profit: Studies in the Theory of Entrepreneurship*, Chicago: University of Chicago Press.

—— (1982) "Uncertainty, discovery and human action" in I.M. Kirzner ed., *Method, Process and Austrian Economics*, Canada: D.C. Heath.

—— (1985) *Discovery and the Capitalist Process*, Chicago: University of Chicago Press.

—— (1986) *Subjectivism, Intelligibility and Economic Understanding*, New York: New York University Press.

—— (1992) *The Meaning of Market Process*, London: Routledge.

Klein, Burton H. (1977) *Dynamic Economics*, Cambridge, Mass.: Harvard University Press.

Kwok, Peter (1978) "Small manufacturing business in Hong Kong", M.Phil. thesis, University of Hong Kong.

Lachmann, L. M. (1956) *Capital and its Structure*, Kansas City: Sheed Andrews and McMeel Inc.

Lam Danny Kin-Kong and Ian Lee (1992) "Guerrilla capitalism and the limits of statist theory: comparing the Chinese NICs", in C. Clark and S. Chan eds, *The Evolving Pacific Basin in the Global Political Economy*, London: Lynne Rienner, pp. 107–24.

227

Langlois, Richard N. (1988) "Economic change and the boundaries of the firm", *Journal of Institutional and Theoretical Economics*, 144 (4), 635–57, reprinted in Bo. Carlsson ed. (1989) *Industrial Dynamics*, MA: Kluwer Academic Publishers, pp. 85–108.

—— (1991) "Transaction-cost economics in real time", *Industrial and Corporate Change*, pp. 99–127.

Langlois, Richard N. and M.J. Everett (1992) "Complexity, genuine uncertainty and the economics of organisation", *Human Systems Management*, 11: 67–75.

Langlois, Richard N. and Paul Robertson L. (1995) *Firms, Markets and Economic Change: A Dynamic Theory of Business Institutions*, London: Routledge.

Lau, Ho Fuk (1991) "Development process of the Hong Kong manufacturing companies: with special reference to the garment firms", in Edward Chen *et al.* eds, *Industrial and Trade Development in Hong Kong*, Hong Kong: Centre of Asian Studies, pp. 427–46.

Lau, S.K. (1982) *Society and Politics in Hong Kong*, Hong Kong: Chinese University of Hong Kong Press, pp. 68–72.

Lau, S.K. and H.C. Kuan (1988) *The Ethos of the Hong Kong Chinese*, Hong Kong: Chinese University Press.

Lee, Eddy (1981) *Export-led Industrialisation and Development*, Geneva: International Labour Organisation.

Lee, Yuan Tsao and Linda Low (1990) *Local Entrepreneurship in Singapore: Private and State*, Singapore: Institute of Policy Studies.

Leftwich, Adrian (1995) "Bringing politics back in: towards a model of the development state", *The Journal of Development Studies*, 31(3): 400–27.

Leibenstein, Harvey (1966) "Allocative efficiency vs. X-efficiency", *American Economic Review*, 56 (June): 392–415.

—— (1968) "Entrepreneurship and development", *American Economic Review*, 58: 72–83.

—— (1978) *General X-Efficiency Theory and Economic Development*, New York: Oxford University Press.

Lewis, W.A. (1954) "Economic development with unlimited supplies of labour", *Manchester School of Economic and Social Studies*, 22(2): 139–91.

Li, Si Ming and Tony F. Yu (1990) "The redistributive effects of Hong Kong's public housing programme 1976–86", *Urban Studies*, 27(1): 105–18.

Lichauco, Alejandro (1988) *Nationalist Economics*, Quezon City: Institute for Rural Industrialisation, Inc.

Lim, David (1994) "Explaining the growth performances of Asian developing economies", *Economic Development and Cultural Change*, pp. 829–43.

Lin, T.B. and Chyau Tuan (1988) "Industrial evolution and changes in trade environment: a case study of consumer electronics and textile/garment industries in Hong Kong" in M.C. Dutta ed., *Research in Asian Economic Studies, Vol. 1 Part A: Asian Industrialisation: Changing Economic Structures*, London: JAI Press.

Long, Wayne A. and W. Ed. McMullan (1984) "Mapping the new venture opportunity identification process" in J.A. Hornaday *et al.* eds, *Frontiers of Entrepreneurship Research*, pp. 567–91.

Luedde-Neurath, Richard (1988) "State intervention and export-oriented development in South Korea", in Gordon White ed., *Developmental States in East Asia*, New York: St. Martin's Press, pp. 68–112.

Lung, Chun Ki (1986) "On the failure of Hong Kong's enterprises", *Hong Kong Economic Journal Monthly* (June): 130–1 (text in Chinese).

McClelland, David C. (1961) *The Achieving Society*, Toronto: Macmillan.

McCord, William (1991) *The Dawn of the Pacific Century: Implications for Three Worlds of Development*, London: Transaction Publishers.

McCormick, Joel (1991) "Hong Kong in 1997: what if it works?", *Electronics Business Asia*, January, p. 39.

Mackie, J.A.C. (1988) "Economic growth in the ASEAN region: the political underpinnings", in Helen Hughes ed., *Achieving Industrialisation in East Asia*, Cambridge: Cambridge University Press, pp. 283–326.

——(1992) "Overseas Chinese entrepreneurship", *Asian-Pacific Economic Literature* (May): 41–64

Majumdar, Badiul Alan (1982) *Innovations, Product Developments and Technology Transfers: An Empirical Study of Dynamic Competitive Advantage, The Case of Electronic Calculators*, Washington DC: University Press of America Inc.

March, J.G. and H.A. Simon (1958) *Organisation*, New York: Wiley.

Martin, Michael J.C. (1984) *Managing Technological Innovation and Entrepreneurship*, Virginia: Reston Publishing Co.

Menger, Carl (1883[1985]) *Investigations into the Method of the Social Sciences with Special Reference to Economics*, New York: New York University Press.

Meier, G.M. and Baldwin R.E. (1957) *Economic Development: Theory, History, Policy*, New York: John Wiley & Sons.

Merton, Robert K., M. Fiske and Patricia Kendall (1990) *The Focused Interview: A Manual of Problems and Procedures*, New York: Free Press.

Mills, C.W. (1963) "Two styles of social science research", in I.L. Horowitz ed., *Power, Politics and People: the Collected Essays of C.W. Mills*, London: Oxford University Press, pp. 553–67.

Ming Pao, (1993) "Competition", 5 October, p. 23 (text in Chinese).

Mises, Ludwig V.(1949) *Human Action*, 3rd edn, Chicago: Contemporary Books Inc.

Mok, Victor (1990) "Trade and industry", in Y.C. Wong *et al.* eds, *The Other Hong Kong Report 1990*, Hong Kong: Chinese University of Hong Kong.

——(1993) *Hong Kong's Economic Growth and Structural Change*, Hong Kong: Joint Publishing Co. Ltd.

Morawetz, David (1981) *Why the Emperor's Clothes are not Made in Colombia: A Case Study in Latin American and East Asian Manufactured Exports*, Oxford: Oxford University Press.

Mukerjee, Dilip (1986) *Lessons from Korea's Industrial Experience*, Malaysia: Institute of Strategic and International Studies.

Nafziger, E. Wayne (1986), *Entrepreneurship, Equity, and Economic Development*, Connecticut: JAI Press.

Nelson, R.R and S.G. Winter (1977) "In search of useful theory of innovation", *Research Policy*, 6 (1): 37–76.

——(1982) *An Evolutionary Theory of Economic Change*, Cambridge, Mass: Harvard University Press.

Ng, Ying Chun (1988) *Hong Kong on the Turning Point*, Taiwan: Commonwealth Publishing Co. (text in Chinese).

Nishida, Judith (1992) "Technology transfer and East Asian business recipes: the adoption of Japanese cotton spinning techniques in Shanghai and Hong Kong" in Jane Marieau ed., *Reworking the World*, New York: Walter de Gruyter, pp. 181–203.

Nyaw, M.K. (1991) "The experiences of industrial growth in Hong Kong and Singapore: a comparative study", in Edward Chen *et al.* eds, *Industrial and Trade Development in Hong Kong*, Hong Kong: Centre of Asian Studies, pp. 185–222.

O'Driscoll, Gerald P. Jr (1977) *Economics as a Coordination Problem*, Kansas City: Sheed Andrews and McMeel.

O'Driscoll, Gerald P. Jr and M. Rizzo (1985) *The Economics of Time and Ignorance*, Oxford: Blackwell.

Owen, Nicholas (1971) "Competition and structural change in unconcentrated industries", *The Journal of Industrial Economics*, 19: 133.

Pang, Fong Eng (1988) "The distinctive features of two city-states' development: Hong Kong and Singapore", in P. Berger and M. Hsiao eds, *In Search of an East Asian Development Model*, New Jersey: Transaction Books, pp. 220–38.

Parry, Thomas G. (1988) "The role of foreign capital in East Asian industrialisation, growth and development", in Helen Hughes ed., *Achieving Industrialisation in East Asia*, Cambridge: Cambridge University Press, pp. 95–128.

Patrikeeff, Felix (1989) *Mouldering Pearl: Hong Kong at the Crossroads*, London: George Philip.

Pavitt, Keith and Luc L.G. Soete (1982) "International differences in economic growth and the international location of innovation" in Herbert Giersch ed., *Emerging Technologies: Consequences for Economic Growth, Structural Change, and Employment*, Tubingen: J.C.B. Mohr (Paul Siebeck), pp. 105–33.

Peebles, Gavin (1988) *Hong Kong's Economy*, Hong Kong: Oxford University Press.

Perez, Carlota and Luc L.G. Soete (1988) "Catching up in technology: entry barrier and windows of opportunity", in Giovanni Dosi *et al.* eds, *Technical Change and Economic Theory*, London: Pinter Publishers, pp. 458–79.

Phares, E. Jerry (1988) *Introduction to Personality*, 2nd edn, London: Scott, Foresman and Co.

Poon, Teresa (1992) "Western technology in a Chinese context: new technologies and the organisation of work in Hong Kong", in Jane Marieau ed., *Reworking the World*, New York: Walter de Gruyter, pp. 205–35.

Porter Michael E. (1990) *The Competitive Advantage of Nations*, New York: Free Press.

——(1991) "The competitive advantage of nations", in Cynthia A. Montgomery and Michael E. Porter eds, *Strategy: Seeking and Securing Competitive Advantage*, Boston: Harvard Business Review Book, pp. 135–69.

——(1991a) "Towards a dynamic theory of strategy", *Strategic Management Journal*, 12: 95–110.

Pribram, Karl (1983) *A History of Economic Reasoning*, Baltimore: John Hopkins University Press.

Rabushka, A. (1979) *Hong Kong: A Study in Economic Freedom*, Chicago: University of Chicago Press.

Rafferty, Kevin (1991) *City on the Rocks: Hong Kong's Uncertain Future*, London: Penguin Books.

Rasin, Steve (1991) "Off and running", *The China Business Review*, September–October, pp. 34–8.

Ray, Dennis (1988) "The role of entrepreneurship in economic development", in H. Leibenstein and Dennis Ray eds, *Entrepreneurship and Economic Development*, New York: United Nations, pp. 3–17.

Redding, S.G. (1988) "The role of the entrepreneur in the new Asian capitalism", in P. Berger and M. Hsaio eds, *In Search of an East Asian Development Model*, New Brunswick: Transaction Books, pp. 99–111.

——(1990) *The Spirit of Chinese Capitalism*, Berlin: de Gruyter.

——(1991) "Weak organizations and strong linkages: managerial ideology and Chinese family business networks", in Garry Hamilton ed., *Business Networks and Economic Development in East and Southest Asia*, Centre of Asian Studies, pp. 30–47.

——(1994) "Competitive advantage in the context of Hong Kong", *Journal of Far Eastern Business*, 1(1): 71–89.

Redding, S.G. and Y.Y. Wong (1986) "The psychology of Chinese organisational behaviour" in M.H. Bond ed., *The Psychology of the Chinese People*, Hong Kong: Oxford University Press, pp. 267–95.

Reynolds, W.A. (1980) *Factors Which Hinder or Help Productivity Improvement*, Tokyo: Asia Productivity Organisation.

Ricketts, Martin (1987) *The Economics of Business Enterprise*, Brighton: Wheatsheaf Books.

Riedel, James (1974) *The Industrialisation of Hong Kong*, Tubingen: J.C.B. Mohr (Paul Siebeck).

—— (1988) "Economic development in East Asia: doing what comes naturally", in Helen Hughes ed., *Achieving Industrialisation in East Asia*, Cambridge: Cambridge University Press, pp. 1–38.

Robertson, Paul L. (1993) "Innovation, corporate organisation and industry policy: William Lazonick on the firm and economic growth", *Prometheus*, 11(2) December.

Robertson, Paul L. and Richard N. Langlois (1992a) "Modularity, innovation and the firm: the case of audio components" in M. Perlman ed., *Entrepreneurship, Technological Innovation and Economic Growth: International Perspectives*, Ann Arbor: University of Michigan Press.

—— (1992b) "Institutions, inertia and changing industrial leadership", working paper, Department of Economics and Management, University College, University of New South Wales.

Rodan, Garry (1989) *The Political Economy of Singapore's Industrialisation: National State and International Capital*, New York: St. Martin Press.

—— (1992) "Singapore", in John Carroll and Robert Manne eds, *Shutdown: The Failure of Economic Rationalism and How to Rescue Australia*, Melbourne: The Text Publishing, pp. 77–89.

Rogers, Everett M. (1983) *Diffusion of Innovations*, 3rd edn, New York: Free Press.

Rosenberg, Nathan (1976) *Perspectives on Technology*, Cambridge: Cambridge University Press.

—— (1982) *Inside the Black Box: Technology and Economics*, Cambridge: Cambridge University Press

Rosenstein-Rodan, Paul N. (1961) "Notes on the theory of the 'big push' ", in H.S. Ellis ed., *Economic Development for Latin America*, London: Macmillan, pp. 57–66.

Rostow, W.W. (1960) *The Stages of Economic Growth*, Cambridge, Cambridge University Press.

Sako, Mari (1992) *Prices, Quality and Trust*, New York: Cambridge University Press.

Schiffer, Jonathan R. (1991) "State policy and economic growth: a note on the Hong Kong model", *International Journal of Urban and Regional Research*, 15(2): 180–96.

Schumpeter, J. A. (1934[1961]) *The Theory of Economic Development*, New York: Oxford University Press.

—— (1939[1982]) *Business Cycles*, Philadelphia: Porcupine Press.

—— (1947a) "Theoretical problems of economic growth", *Journal of Economic History Supplement*, pp. 1–9, reprinted in R. Clemence ed. (1951) *Essays of J.A. Schumpeter*, Cambridge, Mass.: Addison-Wesley Press, pp. 227–35.

—— (1947b) "The creative response in economic history", in R. Clemence (1951) *Essays of J.A. Schumpeter*, Cambridge, Mass: Addison-Wesley.

—— (1949) "Economic theory and entrepreneurial history", reprinted in R. Clemence ed. (1951) *Essays of J.A. Schumpeter*, Cambridge, Mass.: Addison-Wesley, pp. 248–66.

—— (1954[1966]) *Capitalism, Socialism and Democracy*, London: Unwin University Books.

—— (1955) *Ten Great Economists*, New York: Oxford University Press.

Sexton, Donald (1991) *Entrepreneurship: Creativity and Growth*, New Jersey: Prentice Hall.

Shackle, G.L.S. (1958) *Time in Economics*, Connecticut: Greenwood Press.

Sit, Victor and Siu-Lun Wong (1988) *Changes in the Industrial Structure and the Role of Small and Medium Industries in Asian Countries: the Case of Hong Kong*, Tokyo: Institute of Developing Economies.

—— (1989) *Small and Medium Industries in an Export-Oriented Economy: The Case of Hong Kong*, University of Hong Kong, Centre of Asian Studies.

Sit, Victor, Siu-Lun Wong and Tsin-Sing Kiang (1979) *Small Scale Industry in a Laissez-Faire Economy: A Hong Kong Case Study*, Centre of Asian Studies, University of Hong Kong.

Siu, Wai Sum and Robert G. Martin (1992) "Successful entrepreneurship in Hong Kong", *Long Range Planning*, 25(6): 87–93.

Soesastro, Hadi (1985) "Japan teacher – ASEAN Pupils: can it work?" in R. Scaloppine *et al.* ed., *Asian Economic Development – Present and Future*, California: Institute of East Asian Studies, pp. 114–30.

Solo, Robert (1976) *Economic Organisations and Social Systems*, New York: The Bobbs-Merrill Co. Inc.

Soon, Cho (1994) "Government and market in economic development", *Asian Development Review*, 12(2): 144–65.

Sproull, Lee S. (1981) "Beliefs in organisation", in P. Nystrom and W. Starbuck ed., *Handbook of Organisational Design Volume 2: Remodelling Organisations and their Environments*, Oxford: Oxford University Press, pp. 203–24.

Staley, E. and R. Morse (1965) *Modern Small Industry for Developing Countries*, New York: McGraw Hill.

Sung, Yung-wing (1986) "China's entry into world markets: The role of Hong Kong in China's export drive", *The Australian Journal of Chinese Affairs*, 15: 83–100.

—— (1987) "Flexibility and Hong Kong's competitiveness", *Hong Kong Economic Journal Monthly*, February, No. 119 (text in Chinese).

—— (1991) *The China-Hong Kong Connection: The Key to China's Open-Door Policy*, Cambridge: Cambridge University Press.

Swederg, Richard (1991) *Joseph A. Schumpeter: His Life and Work*, Oxford: Polity Press.

Szczepanik, Edward (1958) *The Economic Growth of Hong Kong*, London: Oxford University Press.

Tam, Simon and S. Gordon Redding (1993) "The impact of colonialisation on the formation of an entrepreneurial society in Hong Kong", in S. Birley and I.C. MacMillan eds, *Entrepreneurship Research: Global Perspectives*, Elsevier Science Publisher, pp. 158–77.

Tan, Gerald (1992) *The Newly Industrialising Countries of Asia*, Singapore: Times Academic Press.

Ting, Wenlee (1985) *Business and Technological Dynamics in Newly Industrialising Asia*, London: Quorum Books.

Tornatzky, Louis *et al.* (1980) *Innovation and Social Process*, New York: Pergamon Press.

Tsiang, S.C. and Rong-I Wu (1985) "Foreign trade and investment as boosters for take-off: the experiences of the four Asian Newly Industrialising Countries", in W. Galenson ed., *Foreign Trade and Investment: Economic Growth in the Newly Industrialising Asian Countries*, Madison: University of Wisconsin Press

Tuan, Chyau, Danny S.N. Wong and Chun-Sheng Ye (1986) *Chinese Entrepreneurship Under Capitalism and Socialism*, Centre of Asian Studies, University of Hong Kong (text in Chinese).

UNCTAD (1985) *Exporting Processing Free Zones in Developing Countries*, New York: UN Publications.

United Nations Industrial Development Organisation (1969) *Small Scale Industry*, Monographs 11, New York: UN Publications.

Vesper, Karl R. (1990) *New Venture Strategies*, 2nd edn, New Jersey: Prentice Hall.

Vogel, Ezra F. (1991) *The Four Little Dragons: The Speed of Industrialisation in East Asia*, Cambridge, Mass.: Harvard University Press.

Wade, Robert (1988a) "The role of government in overcoming market failure: Taiwan, Republic of Korea and Japan", in Helen Hughes ed., *Achieving Industrialisation in East Asia*, Cambridge: Cambridge University Press, pp. 129–63.

—— (1988b) "State intervention in "outward-looking" development: neoclassical theory and Taiwanese practice", in Gordon White ed., *Developmental States in East Asia*, New York: St. Martin's Press, pp. 30–67.

—— (1990) *Governing the Market*, New Jersey: Princeton University Press.

Wakasugi, Ryuhei (1989) "Technological innovation in the Asian-Pacific Region", in M. Shinohara and F. Lo eds, *Global Adjustment and the Future of Asian–Pacific Economy*, Tokyo: Institute of Developing Economies, pp. 328–45.

Wang, Daonan (1991) "The economic relations between China and Hong Kong: prospects and principles", in Edward Chen *et al.* eds, *Industrial and Trade Development in Hong Kong*, Centre of Asian Studies, University of Hong Kong, pp. 447–63.

Warr, Peter G. (1994) "Comparative and competitive advantage", *Asian–Pacific Economic Literature*, 8 (2): 1–14.

Watanabe, T. (1991) *Asia: Its Growth and Agony*, Honolulu: East-West.

Weber, Max (1930) *The Protestant and the Spirit of Capitalism*, New York: Free Press.

White, Gordon (1988) *Developmental States in East Asia*, New York: St. Martin's Press.

White, Gordon and Robert Wade (1988) "Developmental states and markets in East Asia: an introduction" in Gordon White ed., *Developmental States in East Asia*, New York: St. Martin's Press, pp. 1–29.

White, L.H. (1976) "Entrepreneurship, imagination and the question of equilibrium", in S. Littlechild ed. (1990), *Austrian Economics*, vol. III, England: Edward Elgar, pp. 87–104.

—— (1977) "Uncertainty and entrepreneurial expectation in economic theory", unpublished Senior Honours Thesis, Harvard College, 31 March.

Whitley, Richard (1990) "Eastern Asian enterprise structure and the comparative analysis of forms of business organisation", *Organisation Studies*, 11(1): 47–74.

—— (1992)*Business Systems in East Asia: Firms, Markets and Societies*, London: Sage Publications.

Wilken, Paul (1979) *Entrepreneurship: A Comparative and Historical Study*, New Jersey: Ablex Publishing Co.

Williamson, Oliver (1985) *The Economic Institutions of Capitalism*, New York: Free Press.

Wilson, Joel (1991a) "Hong Kong board maker sets ambitious PC goals", *Electronics Business Asia* (April): 37–8.

—— (1991b) "It's do or die for a struggling chip industry", *Electronics Business Asia* (July): 71.

Winter, Sidney G. (1986) "The research program of the behavioural theory of the firm: orthodox critique and evolutionary perspective", in B. Gilad and S. Kaish eds, *Handbook of Behavioural Economics Volume A: Behavioural Microeconomics*, London: JAI Press, pp. 151–88.

—— (1990) "Survival, selection and inheritance in evolutionary theories of organisation", in J.V. Singh ed., *Organisational Evolution New Directions*, London: Sage Publications, pp. 269–97.

Wong, C. Y and Y. S. Cheng (1990) *The Other Hong Kong Report 1990*, Hong Kong: Chinese University of Hong Kong.

Wong, Siu lun (1980) "The Chinese family firm: a model", *British Journal of Sociology*, 36(1): 58–72.

—— (1988a) "The applicability of Asian family values to other sociocultural settings", in P. Berger and M. Hsiao eds, *In Search of an East Asian Development Model*, Oxford: Transaction Books, pp. 134–52.

—— (1988b) *Emigrant Entrepreneurs: Shanghai Industrialists in Hong Kong*, Hong Kong: Oxford University Press.

—— (1989) "Modernisation and Chinese cultural traditions in Hong Kong", in H. Tai ed., *Confucianism and Economic Development: An Oriental Alternative*, Washington DC: Washington Institute for Values in Public Policy, pp. 166–94.

Wong, Teresa Y.C. (1990) "The role of Hong Kong in Sino-Taiwan and Sino-Korea trade, 1981–87", *Asian Economic Journal*, March, pp. 16–45.

Wong, Yiu Chung (1989) "Outward processing in China and its implications to the economy of Hong Kong", M. Soc. Sc. thesis, University of Hong Kong.

World Bank (1978) *Employment and Development of Small Enterprises*, Washington DC: World Bank.

—— (1993) *The East Asian Miracle: Economic Growth and Public Policy*, Oxford: Oxford University Press.

Woronoff, Jon (1980) *Hong Kong: Capitalist Paradise*, Hong Kong: Heinemann Asia.

—— (1986) *Asia's "Miracle" Economies*, New York: M.E. Sharpe.

Wu, Joseph S.K. (1989) "Entrepreneurship", in C.Y. Ho and L.C. Chau eds, *The Economic System of Hong Kong*, Hong Kong: Asia Research Service.

Wu, Yuan-li and Hung-chao Tai (1989) "Economic performance in five East Asian Countries: a comparative analysis", in H. Tai ed., *Confucianism and Economic Development: An Oriental Alternative*, Washington DC: Washington Institute for Values in Public Policy, pp. 38–54.

Yamazawa, Ippei and Toshio Watanabe (1988) "Industrial restructuring and technology transfer", in Shinichi Ichimura ed., *Challenge of Asian Developing Countries*, Tokyo: Asian Productivity Organisation, pp. 203–26.

Yin, Robert K. (1994) *Case Study Research: Design and Methods*, 2nd edn, London: Sage Publications.

Youngson, A. (1982) *Hong Kong: Economic Growth and Policy*, Hong Kong: Oxford University Press.

Yu, Tony F. (1993) "Entrepreneurship and the economic development of Hong Kong: an analytical framework", paper presented at the international conference on Chinese and East Asian Economies in the 1990s organised by the Chinese Economic Association (Australia) held at The Australian National University, Canberra, 30 November–1 December, 1993.

—— (1995a) "Kirznerian entrepreneurship and the economic development of Hong Kong: a case study of the electronics industry", paper presented at the international conference on China's Economy Towards 2000: Challenges and Opportunities for Australia, jointly organised by School of Economics, La Trobe University and The Chinese Economic Studies Association (Australia) held at La Trobe University, Melbourne, Australia, 14–15 February.

—— (1995b) "Bringing entrepreneurship back in: explaining the dynamics of the Asian newly industrialising economies, with special reference to Hong Kong", paper presented at a seminar at the School of Economics and Management, University College, University of New South Wales, 5 June.

—— (1995c) "Bringing entrepreneurship back in: an analytical framework for the economic development of the Asian Newly Industrialising Economies", paper presented at the 24th Conference of Economists organised by the Economic Society of Australia held at the University of Adelaide, South Australia, 24–7 September.

Yu, Tony F. and Si Ming Li (1985) "The welfare cost of Hong Kong's public housing programme", *Urban Studies*, 22: 133–40.

INDEX